Quality Function Deployment

Yoji Akao
Author and Editor-in-Chief
Tamagawa University, Japan

Translated by Glenn H. Mazur
and Japan Business Consultants Ltd.

Introduction by Bob King
President, G.O.A.L., Inc.

Productivity Press
CAMBRIDGE, MASSACHUSETTS
NORWALK, CONNECTICUT

Quality Function Deployment

Integrating Customer Requirements into Product Design

Productivity Press
P.O. Box 3007
Cambridge, Massachusetts 02140
United States of America
(617) 497-5146 (telephone)
(617) 868-3524 (fax)

Cover design: Donna Puleo
Text design and composition: Rudra Press, Cambridge, MA
Printed and bound by: Arcata Graphics/Halliday
Printed in the United States of America
Printed on acid-free paper

Library of Congress Cataloging-in-Publication Data

Akao, Yōji, 1928-
   [Hinshitsu tenkai katsuyō no jissai. English]
   Quality function deployment: integrating customer requirements into product design/author and editor-in-chief, Yoji Akao; translated by Glenn H. Mazur; introduction by Bob King.
      p. cm.
   Translation of: Hinshitsu tenkai katsuyō no jissai.
   Includes index.
   ISBN 0-915299-41-0
   1. Quality control — Case studies. 2. New products — Management — Case studies. I. Title.
TS156.A3713   1990   89-43209
658.5'62 — dc20   CIP

90 91 92 6 5 4 3 2 1

Table of Contents

NOTE: Due to the format requirements of the illustrations, many of which are two-page spreads, you will occasionally find a blank page. Please note that these are intentional, and that there is no material missing from the book.

List of Charts and Figures

Publisher's Foreword

How to shorten cycle time while improving product quality is the challenge facing American manufacturers today. We want to deliver quality to our customers. At the same time, to be competitive, we must reduce lead times. (For instance, it takes Honda Motors 32 months to go from design stage to a finished new car model — it takes General Motors 60 months!) This means quality cannot be confined to the plant floor — it must permeate the entire company.

This particular project, *Quality Function Deployment: Integrating Customer Requirements into Product Design*, is one in a distinguished line of primary source books from Japan published in English by Productivity Press. As a topic, quality function deployment contains information critical to the changes occurring in today's manufacturing and service sectors. And, like Johnny Appleseed, Yoji Akao is responsible for sowing the seeds of QFD throughout the world.

Quality function deployment (QFD) was first systematized in Japan in the mid-1970s at Mitsubishi's Kobe shipyards. QFD refers to the functions responsible for quality in a company's areas of design, manufacturing, service, and so forth. QFD includes the numerous quality deployment charts, tables, and descriptive matrices used to design the quality needed in the products or services. Simply stated, through QFD, quality becomes a function of new product development. It becomes an integral part of technology deployment, reliability deployment, and cost deployment. Beginning with customer demands and feeding all the way back to the design stage, QFD bypasses no area of a company.

In this book Dr. Akao defines quality function deployment, and representatives from Japanese companies describe how QFD was employed in their various workplaces. These workplaces cover manufacturing, the construction industry, software developers, and service industries, including a popular Japanese bookstore and a designer of shopping malls.

There is little doubt that this is a brilliant and critically important book — *brilliant* because in homogenous terms it plants QFD across all levels of a company; *important* because it combines theory with practice to produce undeniable results. The manufacturing world is fortunate to have such a standard bearer as Dr. Akao who does not confine the quest for quality to the factory floor, but plants it squarely in both the design and customer ends of the production spectrum.

In my opinion, there are no shortcuts in life. There is simply hard work. And with hard work and thoughtful application of good practices, we grow daily and lead happy, socially beneficial lives. Our workplaces can produce quality products while simultaneously maintaining a quality work environment for its participants. We are grateful to Dr. Akao and the co-contributors to this volume for providing a guide to further endeavors in this area.

Quality Function Deployment is a product of many people's endeavors. I am deeply grateful to Dr. Akao and the Japan Standards Association for allowing us to publish this work in English. I also personally acknowledge the tremendous efforts of Glenn Mazur and the staff of Japanese Business Consultants for translating this work; Nan White, a Cambridge-based freelance editor who turned a technical translation into a masterfully written book; Gayle Joyce's capable staff at Rudra Press; and Productivity Press' project editor Cheryl Rosen and production manager David Lennon.

Norman Bodek
Publisher

Introduction

In October 1983, Yoji Akao introduced Quality Function Deployment (QFD) to the United States in a short article that appeared in *Quality Progress*, the monthly journal of the American Society for Quality Control (ASQC). Today, less than six and a half years later, Quality Deployment is a major force in the Total Quality effort in the United States.

Dr. Akao is Professor of Industrial Engineering at Tamagawa University in Tokyo and is one of the foremost leaders in the Total Quality Control movement in Japan. He has long led and participated in many of the key research committees of the Union of Japanese Scientists and Engineers (JUSE), the Japanese Standards Association (JSA), and the Japanese Society for Quality Control (JSQC), of which he is currently president. In addition to his pioneering work in Quality Deployment, Dr. Akao made significant contributions to the Japanese planning system, *hoshi kanri*. It was Dr. Akao who developed the target-means matrix to help ensure that Japanese companies would meet their quality, cost, and delivery targets.

Dr. Akao has played a pivotal role in the development of Total Quality through QFD. Based on the insights of W. Edwards Deming, Joseph Juran, Armand Feigenbaum, and others from the United States, as well as Kaoru Ishikawa, Shigeru Mizuno, Masao Kogure, and others from Japan, Total Quality spread like wildfire through Japanese manufacturing departments in the 1950s and 1960s. It became clear by the end of the 1960s that the quality of design also needed to be improved. Initially, fishbone charts were used to identify customer demands and to establish design quality. Around 1966, Dr. Akao began expressing the need for critical points of Quality Assurance to be carried through design and manufacturing. These ideas later would be formalized and brought to fruition in QFD. In 1972, with the help of Drs. Mizuno and Furukawa, Kobe shipyard developed a matrix of customer demands and quality characteristics. Two years later, Dr. Akao founded and chaired the JSQC research committee for Quality Function Deployment. As chairman, he helped foster QFD's development as a technique for improving the transition from design to manufacturing during the late 1970s.

In 1978, Drs. Akao and Mizuno co-edited a text on Quality Function Deployment which led to a major increase in the use of Quality Deployment in Japan. In the early 1980s, Dr. Akao integrated QFD with value engineering and other tools for cost deployment through his research and consulting at Futaba and other corporations. He integrated QFD with new technology, reliability engineering, and bottleneck engineering, a methodology developed by Dr. Furukawa for identifying and obtaining critical breakthroughs.

This translation of Dr. Akao's recent Japanese QFD text represents a major contribution to QFD in the United States. It should help U.S. companies go beyond their successful beginnings to customization and integration of QFD with other management activities. QFD has become a key part of new car design as well as parts design in the automobile industry. In the computer industry, QFD has become both a source of customer responsiveness and of significant reductions in the design cycle. Despite the progress, QFD is still in its infancy in the United States.

Most companies have focused on the benefits of the single matrix (sometimes called the "house of quality" because of its shape) which was first developed in Japan in 1977. Some companies, General Electric and Ford to name a couple, have used QFD to ease transition from design to manufacturing (equivalent to Japan in the late 1970s). Hardly any U.S. corporations have fully integrated QFD with cost reduction, new technology, and bottleneck engineering.

This book will be particularly valuable to the progress of QFD in the United States because it gives so many fine examples of customization of QFD and its integration with other aspects of management. Examples from construction, process, service, and software industries should help others to begin to use QFD.

It must be recognized that many in the United States are indebted to Yoji Akao not only for this book but also for his coaching and wise counsel. Dr. Akao is personally committed to helping U.S. manufacturing companies survive. His contribution includes lecturing and consulting with the leading U.S. companies. On a personal note, he was and is particularly helpful in my learnings about Quality Function Deployment, from sharing class notes, to helping find key articles and texts to translate, and providing insightful questions. He is a wonderful teacher.

Bob King
G.O.A.L./QPC

Preface

The concept of quality deployment goes back to the late 1960s. The first documentation of quality deployment appeared in a 1972 article entitled "Development and Quality Assurance of New Products: A System of Quality Deployment" in the monthly magazine *Standardization and Quality Control*. Soon thereafter, the quality chart was published by Mitsubishi Heavy Industries's Kobe shipyards, which in 1978 wrote and published a paperback book entitled *Quality Function Deployment: An Approach to Total Quality Control* that systemized QFD's basic ideas and issues. This demonstrates that the concept of quality deployment has been implemented in industries since 1972.

Its development in so few years has been remarkable. The idea has been introduced with proven results in every aspect of new product and new technology development. With the recent heavy promotion of TQC, the range of quality deployment application includes manufacturing and construction, and even computer software and the service sector. Quality deployment techniques have been introduced into the United States, mostly in the automotive industry, with encouraging results reported by the engineers and managers studying it.

Quality Function Deployment: Integrating Customer Requirements into Product Design was published originally as a series of magazine articles in *Standardization and Quality Control*. As my intention ultimately was to create a book, efforts were made to include the latest information. Each topic includes two case studies, an introduction focusing on the major issues, and tips for actual use. The series was favorably received by readers. I was especially grateful to one reader who wrote: "After reading this detailed explanation of the process of how it *should* work, I have finally understood quality deployment. It was difficult to comprehend by simply studying completed charts."

The first five chapters of this book explain the basics of quality deployment. Quality deployment tied with technology deployment, reliability deployment, and recent approaches to cost deployment are included as well as examples from industries where quality deployment has been newly introduced. Although the contents remains basically the same as in the original journal articles, some revisions and additions have been made based on readers' comments.

When beginning quality deployment, I recommend organizing quality deployment study meetings to try out the use of familiar themes that are not overly ambitious. Once a quality chart is made, select a key subsystem for deployment and experimentation and try to emphasize the most important points. The next step is to form a team of five or six people to gradually introduce quality deployment into organizational operations.

It is my wish that a company develop its own approach to quality deployment suitable to its needs. This book should be used merely as a reference. Quality deployment should help companies through difficult economic times by encouraging the development of "hot" products and more efficient development activities.

I would like to express my gratitude to the companies that provided case studies and to those individuals who took time from their busy days to write their cases. I thank Mr. Iizumi, publishing general manager, and Mr. Ozaki, publishing manager, of the Japan Standards Association, my Japanese publisher; and Mr. Sawada and Mr. Kobayashi for providing tremendous energy in coordinating the material. I wish to acknowledge Glenn Mazur and the staff of Japan Business Consultants, Ltd. for their invaluable translation efforts. Finally, I am grateful to Norman Bodek, my U.S. publisher, and the capable staff at Productivity Press for producing the English edition of this book.

Yoji Akao

CHAPTER 1

An Introduction to Quality Function Deployment

Yoji Akao, Professor of Management Engineering, Tamagawa University

Quality function deployment as an approach to design is a concept I introduced in Japan in 1966. The power of the approach became clear when Nishimura and Takayanagi introduced quality charts in 1972. Since the 1978 publication in Japan of the book *Quality Function Deployment*, many case studies describing this approach have been published.

Despite its remarkable development in recent years, quality function deployment has only been systematized in the specialized book just mentioned. In this book, I will explain quality function deployment, with the input and cooperation of many experts, using recent cases as examples. This is appropriate because quality function deployment is best learned through practice and experience, not theory. The main purpose of this book is to show actual applications. Each chapter will illustrate and explain two such examples.

In many of the published cases, the use of quality function deployment has cut in half the problems previously encountered at the beginning stages of product development and has reduced development time by one-half to one-third, while also helping to ensure user satisfaction and increasing sales. However, if applied incorrectly, quality function deployment may increase work without producing these benefits. To prevent this from happening, I would like to offer some helpful hints for application. Generally speaking, the best method is not to "play it by the book." Since each company's conditions are unique, it is important to be imaginative in applying the rules and to find a method suitable to your company.

What Is Quality Function Deployment?

New Product Development and Quality Assurance

With such fast-paced change occurring these days, especially in our social and economic environment, many companies are facing rapid changes in industrial structure brought about by technological innovation and changing consumer trends. These companies are finding that the effort to develop new products is crucial for their survival.

Quality function deployment as presented in this book provides specific methods for ensuring quality throughout each stage of the product development process, starting with design. In other words, this is a method for developing a design quality aimed at satisfying the consumer and then translating the consumers' demands into design targets and major quality assurance points to be used throughout the production stage.

Design review (DR) is also very important since it represents an opportunity to inspect the design itself. Quality function deployment is a way to assure the design quality while the product is still in the design stage.

Analytical Approach Versus Design Approach

Although today the quality of Japanese products is appreciated throughout the world today, until just a few decades ago, new products and technology were brought to Japan from Europe and the United States so that we could make similar products. When warranty claims occurred, the factors contributing to problems were indicated in a cause and effect diagram so that they could be thoroughly analyzed and actions could be taken to prevent their recurrence. This exercise was repeated time and time again. As a result of these analyses, technology began to accumulate, better quality than the original was achieved, and finally, our general product quality exceeded that of both Europe and the United States. Now that there are fewer things for us to imitate from abroad, Japan is developing many new products herself.

To assure the quality of new products, we must pay close attention not only to the "negative quality" perceptions expressed in consumer complaints, but also to the unspoken, or latent, "positive quality" ideas expressed in consumer demands. We already know what quality items must be assured for existing products. With new products, however, we have to begin by learning "what to assure." In quality function deployment, we start by attempting to understand both the latent and actual already existing qualities demanded by consumers. By doing this, we ensure that the quality plan and design quality will themselves be easier to understand.

Studying consumer complaints about existing products is an analytical approach in which one starts at the downstream (finished product) point and moves upstream through the production process searching for factors that contribute to problems. This is the basic approach used in quality control (QC), and it is likely to remain so in the future.

With new products, however, the approach must be from the upstream end, looking downstream toward the qualities that consumers demand in the finished product. Those demands must be incorporated into the quality plan and design quality and then systematically deployed from the upstream toward the downstream end of the production process regarding greater manufacturing specifics. This method is called a "design approach," and quality function deployment is one such design approach.

Figure 1.2 shows the progress of quality function deployment in terms of numbers of articles on this topic published in *Quality Control* and *Quality* magazines. Its growth since 1981 has been remarkable. Figure 1.3 shows the frequency with which quality function deployment has been applied in various departments. You can see that it has been moving "upstream" into departments such as planning and research & development. This indicates a trend toward reducing quality problems at the earlier stages.

Definitions of Quality Function Deployment

Dr. A.V. Feigenbaum, an advocate of Total Quality Control (TQC), defines a quality system as the system of administrative and technical procedures required to produce and deliver a product of specified quality standards. Dr. J.M. Juran defines a quality function as a function that forms quality. All of the activities such as planning and design shown at the bottom of Figure 1.1 are functions that form, or contribute to, quality. We understand them to mean "planning as a quality function" or "design as a quality function." Now you can see that the quality system as defined above is really a logical arrangement, or sequence, of quality functions.

Dr. Shigeru Mizuno defines the deployment of quality functions as the step-by-step deployment in greater detail of the functions or operations that form quality systematically and with objective rather than subjective procedures. Thus, Dr. Feigenbaum's quality system can be based on the deployment of quality functions.

Generally speaking, you read a lot about structure in TQC books. This is, of course, important. However, when we are developing a quality system, we must analyze and understand the structure of quality itself — not only the structure of procedures to control quality. In other words, the upper portion of Figure 1.1 is as important as the lower.

A machine-assembled product is itself produced by a system. Product quality can be assured through the quality of the subsystems, the quality of the subsystems through the quality of the parts, and the quality of the parts through the process elements (control items). Although the relationships among these are not always explained in books written outside Japan, our experience demonstrates that they can be understood as aspects of quality function deployment.

Now we can define quality function deployment as converting the consumers' demands into "quality characteristics" and developing a design quality for the finished product by systematically deploying the relationships between the demands and the characteristics, starting with the quality of each functional component and extending the deployment to the quality of each part and process. The overall quality of the product will be formed through this network of relationships.

Quality function deployment, broadly speaking, is a general term that means "deployment of quality through deployment of quality functions." Although the two terms are often used interchangeably, in this book we will clarify the differences and relationships between them, focusing our attention mainly on quality function deployment.

How to Implement Quality Function Deployment

Comprehensive Quality Function Deployment

A comprehensive quality function deployment system must reflect technology, reliability, and cost considerations. Figure 1.4 shows the steps by which each of these can be addressed in such a system. Columns I, II, III, and IV show quality function deployment, technology deployment, cost deployment, and reliability deployment, respectively. Each can be deployed from top to bottom, as indicated in rows 1, 2, 3, and 4.

It is best to work on Column I first, then II, then III, and so forth, rather than attempting to work on the whole thing at once. Generally, new product development takes place in parallel with the manufacture of existing products. So, if quality function deployment is introduced in model A, the results of that experience can be used in model B's technology deployment without having to wait for the completion of the model A. This is the most efficient way.

In the remainder of this chapter, we will (1) learn how to construct quality charts and (2) discuss the steps in quality function deployment, using as an example the radio control system made by Futaba Electronics Industry, which we will refer to as Company F.

The Quality Chart

The Demanded Quality Deployment Chart

Information provided by consumers about the qualities that they want in a product must be systematically analyzed if it is to be useful for product development. Chart 1.1 shows one way to convert raw information provided by product users into information that can be used in a quality chart. In this case, two types of information are available: (1) 95 items of information collected directly from hobbyists using remote control devices at a model airplane flight show and (2) information from 420 cards mailed in by users of Company F's radio control system. We must analyze a customer demand such as "I want more than one snap roll button" to find out why the customer made this kind of demand. To do this, we should sample as many consumer comments about this latent quality demand as possible. Comments about existing qualities, such as "It can do complicated maneuvers," can also be sampled. The specific method by which the user wants to be able to perform the maneuvers should be written down in the remarks column. These customer comments, or "verbatims," should be sorted as shown in Figure 1.5, using the procedure described in Chart 1.2. Finally, we can make a demanded quality function deployment chart by arranging the first-, second-, and third-level items as shown in the left-hand column of Chart 1.3.

The Quality Elements Deployment Chart

Next, use the procedures illustrated in Charts 1.4 and 1.5 to generate the list of "quality elements" that will be used to make a quality elements deployment chart like the one displayed along the top of Chart 1.3. Quality elements are design elements that can be measured when we evaluate quality. Design characteristics are the measurable individual aspects of quality elements. When quality elements have multiple quality characteristics, we use a quality characteristics deployment chart to illustrate these relationships. For example, in service QFD, a "smile" would be a quality element — not a measurable quality characteristic.

The Quality Chart

Chart 1.3 shows how a quality chart can be made by combining a demanded quality deployment chart and a quality elements deployment chart to form a matrix, using the steps outlined in Chart 1.6. The symbols ◎, ○ or Δ are used to indicate the strength of the relationship — that is, the degree of correlation — between demanded qualities and quality elements.

The term "quality chart," introduced by Koichi Nishimura, has been defined by Akira Takayanagi as a chart that illustrates the relationship between true or actual quality (as demanded by the customer) systematized according to function, and the quality characteristics as counterpart characteristics. According to Professor Koichi Aiba, quality design is the entire process of converting the quality demanded by the consumer — the true characteristics — into counterpart characteristics, by means of reasoning, translating, and transferring. The quality chart, therefore, is the basic chart for quality design.

As quality function deployment is understood and practiced today, we can say that the quality chart is a graphic device that enables us (1) to analyze systematically the structures of the true or ultimate qualities demanded by customers in their own words, (2) to indicate the relationship between these demanded qualities and certain quality characteristics, (3) to convert customer demands into counterpart characteristics, and then (4) to develop a design quality.

The procedural steps for implementing quality function deployment are outlined below. More details and specific design examples will be presented in the following chapters, so do not be dismayed if certain terms and steps are not entirely clear at this stage.

An Outline of Quality Function Deployment

Developing the Quality Plan and Quality Design

1. First, survey both the expressed and latent quality demands of consumers in your target marketplace. Then decide what kind of "things" to make.
2. Study the other important characteristics of your target market and make a demanded quality function deployment chart that reflects both the demands and characteristics of that market.
3. Conduct an analysis of competing products on the market, which we call a competitive analysis. Develop a quality plan and determine the selling features (sales points). The right-hand portion of Chart 1-I in Figure 1.4 can be used as a guide.
4. Determine the degree of importance of each demanded quality (see Chart 1-I in Figure 1.4).
5. List the quality elements and make a quality elements deployment chart.
6. Make a quality chart by combining the demanded quality deployment chart and the quality elements deployment chart (see Chart 1.3).
7. Conduct an analysis of competing products to see how other companies perform in relation to each of these quality elements. (See the row at the bottom of Chart 1-I in Figure 1.4.)
8. Analyze customer complaints.

9. Determine the most important quality elements as indicated by customer quality demands and complaints.
10. Determine the specific design quality by studying the quality characteristics and converting them into quality elements.
11. Determine the quality assurance method and the test methods.

Detailed Design and Preproduction (Subsystem Deployment)

1. Convert the final product quality into quality characteristics for the components by deploying them first in a unit deployment chart and then in a component deployment chart, which includes the unit deployment chart. Chart 1.7 (which is an expanded portion of Figure 1.4, Chart 3-I) shows an example using the radio control system. You can see that the upper and lower housings have a strong relationship to portability.
2. Clarify unit and component functions, component quality characteristics, and standards (see Chart 1.7). If there are existing products, information on process capability should also be included. Fill in the numbers if a process capability index is available; if not, indicate the level with an A, B, C, and so on.
3. Identify the quality assurance items, function characteristics F, and safety characteristics S of each unit and its components. What we mean here by a function characteristic is a characteristic that must be produced within specified design tolerances if the product is to operate. Safety characteristics are those without which life might be endangered, and whose tolerances must therefore be met. Identifying and indicating these F and S items on the blueprint helps to communicate the intent of a design to manufacturing people. This is the key to quality assurance.
4. Select the inspection items for the units and their components.

Process Deployment

1. Conduct research and, if necessary, develop the various processing techniques that will be necessary to maximize process capability. Test any new or modified techniques.
2. Determine the optimal process methods — the ones that will generate the least cost and yet meet the required degree of precision. To do this, compute the cost-of-precision factor for each process, draw a cost-of-precision curve, and then determine which process method can attain the required precision with the minimum cost.
3. Evaluate the outcomes of all of the previous steps, as well as the prototype results, in order to assess the pros and cons of going into production.
4. Establish the component quality standards, inspection standards, and purchasing standards. Decide whether to produce each component in-house or to use out-sourcing, and establish appropriate standards.

5. Make a process planning chart to be used for facility deployment. When determining the necessary facility and process conditions, identify the QA check points for each machine by constructing a two-dimensional matrix that arrays the final product quality characteristics against the characteristics and conditions of the facility.

6. Make a QC process planning chart for parts processing. Make separate QC process planning charts for each of the major units and their major components. Chart 1.8 shows a QC planning chart for the upper housing of the radio control system.

   Qualities such as configuration, dimension and durability of in-process products — products in the molding process, for example — are called control items or control points. Identify the factors that affect these control items, such as cooling time or injection speed. The control items for these factors are called check items. That is, control points as part quality characteristics (results) are translated into check points (causes) for the process.

7. Make a QC process chart that specifies who will measure the control items and inspection items identified in Chart 1.8, when it will be done, and who will take what action in case of a problem. Chart 1.9 is a QC process chart for the molding process that forms the upper housing.

8. Make a QC process chart for the final assembly process. Using the procedures outlined above, establish a control system for control items in the assembly process.

9. Write operation standards. The control items of the check points must be included without fail.

10. Proceed by deploying to subcontractors and suppliers (partners, in Japanese manufacturing parlance). Have the subcontractors and suppliers submit QC process charts linked to the quality characteristics of each part. If they cannot make them, teach them how, or make the QC charts yourself and teach them how to use them.

11. Conduct a pro-active analysis of all factors. They should be deployed from upstream, that is, according to the design approach. Analyze the data gained through this process and from trial production and preproduction, and feed any information regarding problems back upstream as quickly as possible.

12. Feed the results of these analyses back to the upstream departments or groups for use during model changeover or development of the next new product.

Conclusion

In this chapter we have defined quality function deployment and outlined steps for implementing it. We have provided more detailed information on some topics — especially on how to make quality charts. I hope that you were able to understand this outline. Examples to be discussed in the following chapters will serve as guides for actual application.

All departments should participate in quality function deployment. It may seem confusing at the beginning of the learning process, so it is important to begin by having one person try it on something familiar. Involve a team the next time, and eventually the entire company or organization.

I want to emphasize that an incomplete quality chart can do more harm than good. The most common mistake is putting quality characteristic numeric values, standards, or specifications in the left (demanded quality) part of the matrix, usually as third-level items. If you make this mistake, the top part of the chart will look like a characteristics value deployment chart and will make no sense. The more production-oriented you are, the more readily you will make mistakes of this kind. It is important to recognize that the conversion from the left to the top is really a conversion from the world of the consumer to the world of the engineer.

Another common mistake is letting the creation of a huge deployment chart become the main objective. Prioritizing is the most important activity in quality function deployment. Excessiveness — for example, in the component deployment chart — can be avoided by referring to the quality chart (see Chart 1.3) to determine the major demanded quality and high-priority items, and then deploying only these items into the more detailed quality charts according to a priority system.

In new product development, the first model is seldom completely satisfactory. Repeated model changes are often necessary. Developing the first model may be difficult, but developing subsequent models is usually easier. Getting beyond the first time should be your objective.

References

Aiba, Koichi (1966). Quality Design Seminar (1st Lecture): "What Is Quality Design." *Quality Control*, Vol. 17, No. 1, pp. 88-89, JUSE.

Akao, Yoji (1972). "New Product Development and Quality Assurance: System of Quality Function Deployment, Standardization, and Quality Control." Vol. 25, No. 4, pp. 9-14, Japan Standards Association (JSA).

Akao, Yoji; Ono, Sadatoshi; Harada, Akira; Tanaka, Hidenobu; Iwazawa, Kazuo (1983). "Quality Function Deployment including Cost, Reliability, and Technology (Parts 1 & 2)." *Quality*, Vol. 13, No. 3, pp. 61-77. The Japanese Society for Quality Control (JSQC).

Hasegawa, Ryo; Maekawa, Yoshitomo; Aizawa, Kenji (1983). "Quality for New Product Development, Cost-Technology Deployment Charts, Quality Plan Based On Quality Function Deployment, BNE Sampling Methods For Achieving Target Cost." *Quality*, Vol. No. 3, pp. 92-97, JSQC.

Mizuno, Shigeru; Akao, Yoji (1978). *Quality Function Deployment: Approach for Total Quality Control*. JUSE.

Nishimura, Koichi (1972). "Designing of Ships and Quality Charts." *Quality Control*, Vol. 23, May special issue, pp. 16-20, Union of Japanese Scientists and Engineers (JUSE).

Takayanagi, Akira (1973). "QC in Order Taking/Production in Our Company (#1) QC Activities for Ordered Products: Concept of the Quality Chart." *Quality Control*, Vol. 24, May special issue, pp. 63-67, JUSE.

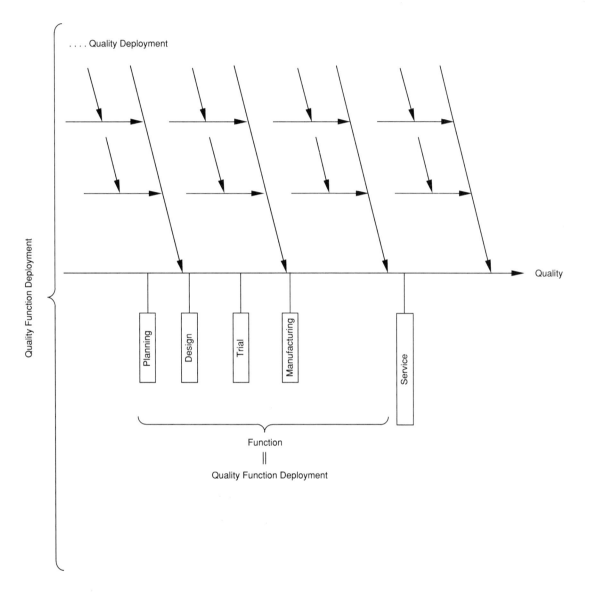

Figure 1-1. Quality Deployment and Quality Function Deployment

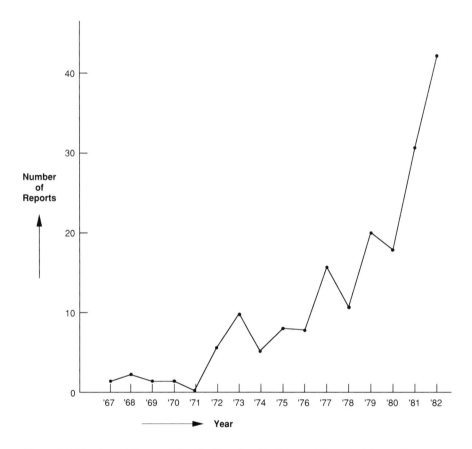

Figure 1-2. Number of Cases of Quality Function Deployment Reported Annually

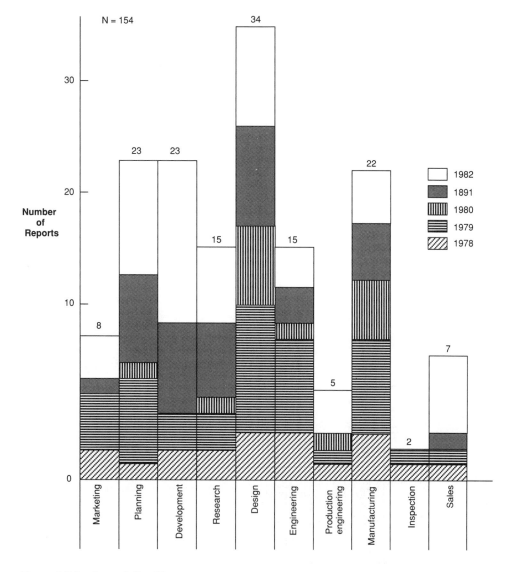

Figure 1-3. Implementation Stage

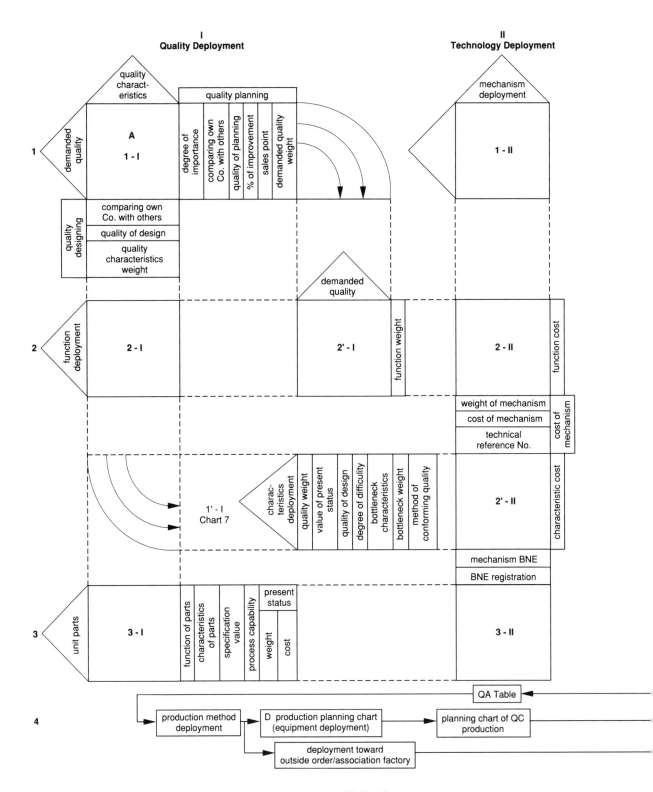

Figure 1-4. Quality Deployment Including Technology, Cost, and Reliability

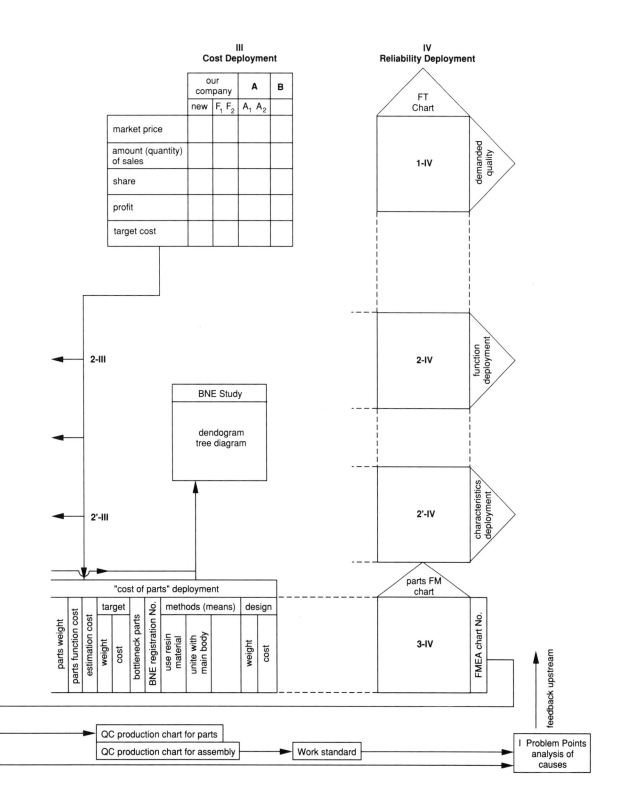

customer verbations	re-worded data	means and remarks
want more than two snap roll buttons	easy to maneuver can handle difficult things	increase snap roll buttons
need a neutral control on the transmitter	movement is stable can do complicated maneuvers	add a neutral control to the transmitter

Chart 1-1. Converting Customer Verbations to Re-worded Data

---

1. Convert customer verbations (the customer's own words) into "re-worded data" using simple expressions limited to a single meaning. (Chart 1.1)

2. Group the re-worded data and assign a heading that more broadly describes the data. Write this on a card.

3. Use these descriptive headings as approximately third-level details. Group these into similar categories assigning descriptive headings into first and second levels, as done in the KJ Method. (Fig. 1-5)

4. Clarify which are first level details of demanded quality. Adjust by adding second and third levels of detail, if necessary, to the demanded quality.

5. Assign classification numbers and organize them into a demanded quality deployment chart.

Chart 1-2. How to Construct a Demanded Quality Deployment Chart

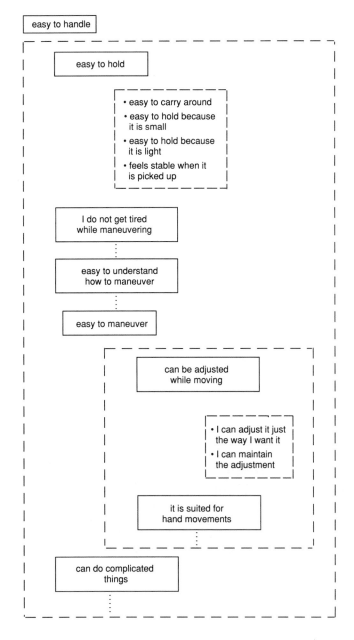

Figure 1-5. KJ Method of Grouping Information Expressed in Words

			quality elements ← 1st level	quality elements ← 2nd level	quality elements ← 3rd level	maneuverability			electrical function				
quality element deployment chart							portability (6)			TRS charact- eristics (7)		IS charact- eristics	
demanded quality deployment chart						measurement	shape	weight	electrical consumption	electric temperature characteristics	operating range voltage	frequency	
1st level	2nd level	3rd level											
1 easy to maneuver	11 easy to hold	111 easy to carry around				◎	◎	◎					
	(1)	112 easy to hold because it is small				○	○						
		113 easy to hold because it is light				◎	◎	◎					
		114 stable when held				◎	◎	◎					
		115 stable when it is put down				○	○	○					
	12 I do not get tired while maneuvering (2)	121 has an appropriate weight											
		122 has an appropriate size											
	13 easy to under- stand how to maneuver (3)	131 easy to understand how to use										○	
		132 easy to maneuver even for beginners										○	
	14 easy to maneuver (4)	141 easy to maneuver even if it is small				○	○	○					
		142 easy to read the indicator										○	

(Diagonal label in upper area: characteristics target values)

Chart 1-3. Quality Chart

How to Construct a Quality Elements Deployment Chart

1. Extract and list the quality elements for each demanded quality (see Chart 1-5).

2. Write each quality on a card.

3. Using these as approximately third-level details, group them into similar categories. Use a KJ-like method to group into first and second levels and assign descriptive headings.

4. Rearrange from the first level to the second and third levels of detail, adding items when necessary.

5. Assign classification numbers and organize into a chart.

6. Use the lower row (third level of detail) as your quality characteristics. Make sure they are measurable quality characteristics.

Chart 1-4. How to Construct a Quality Elements Deployment Chart

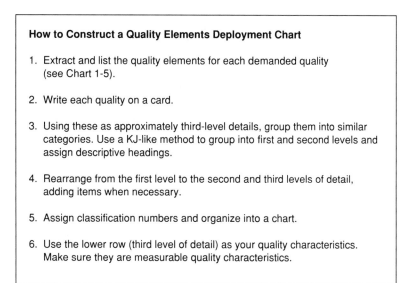

Demanded Items (3rd level items)	Quality Elements
easy to carry around	weight, dimensions, shape, portability
small enough to carry around easily	dimensions, shape, portability
light enough to carry around easily	weight, shape, portability
feels stable when held	weight, center of gravity, angle of inclination
stable when set down	shape, center of gravity, stability
even beginners can operate easily	location of buttons, sensitivity to touch
can be operated easily, even though small in size	weight, shape, effort needed to move stick, stick sensitivity to touch, strength needed to hold lever in position, location of buttons, location of knobs, effort needed to operate knobs, knob sensitivity

Chart 1-5. Extracting Quality Elements

How to Construct a Quality Chart

1. Construct a demanded quality deployment chart.
2. Construct a quality characteristics deployment chart.
3. Combine the above two into a matrix (two-dimensional chart)
4. Mark the corresponding items with symbols such as:

    ◎ : strong correlation

    ○ : average correlation

    △ : some correlation

Chart 1-6. How to Construct a Quality Chart

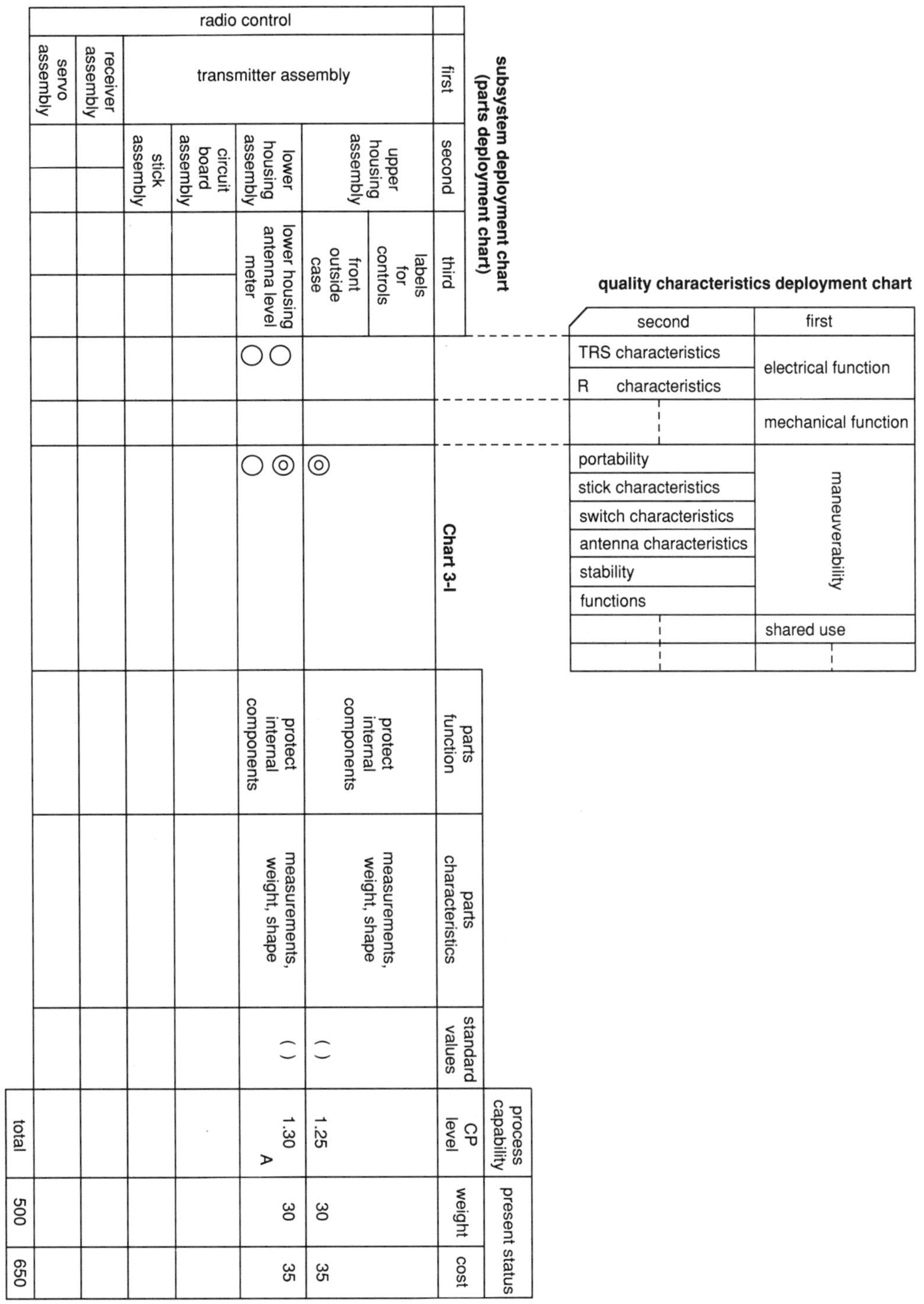

Chart 1-7. Subsystem Deployment

subsystem deployment chart (parts deployment chart)

radio control			
first	second	third	
transmitter assembly	upper housing assembly	labels for controls	
		front outside case	
	lower housing assembly	lower housing antenna level meter	○ ○
	circuit board assembly		○ ◎ ◎
	stick assembly		
receiver assembly			
servo assembly			

Chart 3-I

	parts function	parts characteristics	standard values	process capability	present status
				CP level	weight	cost
protect internal components	measurements, weight, shape	( )	1.25	30	35
protect internal components	measurements, weight, shape	( )	1.30 A	30	35
				total	500	650

quality characteristics deployment chart

	second	first
	TRS characteristics	electrical function
	R characteristics	
		mechanical function
maneuverability	portability	
	stick characteristics	
	switch characteristics	
	antenna characteristics	
	stability	
	functions	
		shared use

Chart 1-I

No.	process	process conditions		part characteristics						process control items
		equipment	conditions	dimensions	shape	weight	durability		○ ○ ○	
1	drying	hopper								temperature inside hopper
2	forming	injection molding machine		◎	◎	◎				primary injection pressure and time
										secondary injection pressure and time
										time, initial charge
										cooling time
				○	○		◎			injection pressure
				○	○					injection speed
										back pressure
									◎	injection temperature

Chart 1-8. QC Process Planning Chart (Upper Housing)

CHAPTER 2

Using the Demanded Quality Deployment Chart: Developing the Quality Plan

Hisakazu Shindo, Department of Engineering, Yamanashi University;
Yasuhiko Kubota, Komatsu MEC; and Yuritsugu Toyoumi,
Electrical Appliance Business Department, Matsushita Electric

Developing the Quality Plan

Competition in new product development is getting tougher and tougher. According to an article in the 10 March 1986 issue of the *Japan Economy Industry Times*, in an average month some 2,768 articles are published on the subject of new products or new technology. This means more than 900 articles are being written per day, or some 40 articles per hour. With continuous innovation in technology and our increasingly diverse lifestyles and values, this trend toward tougher competition in new product development is not likely to subside.

The term "new product development" includes several things:

- *Applying new technology.* For example, making the change from silk to nylon, from vacuum tubes to transistors, or from mechanical watches to electronic digital timepieces.
- *Combining existing and new technology.* For example, producing cameras that incorporate automatic exposure and automatic focusing, or radio-cassette players.
- *Improving quality of performance.* For example, developing HDTV television.

Extending or adding to an existing line of products can also be called new product development. Technology plays a major role in all of these types of new product development. There is a danger, however, that a product may be developed only to exploit a technology. I can think of many product ideas based on epoch-making levels of technology that never developed beyond the idea stage, or that found only a very narrow niche in the marketplace.

These observations indicate that no matter how important the level of technology may be, *quality*, generally speaking, is the extent to which a product responds to the demands of the customer and the marketplace. Thus, it is no exaggeration to say that a thorough and accurate understanding of customer and market demands is the key to successful new product development. From the perspective of quality assurance, we can describe these activities as controlling or monitoring the "source" rather than the "flow".

Quality function deployment is a method for developing a quality plan that begins with source control. In this chapter we will outline the steps in developing a quality plan and present two case studies that show how this approach has been successfully applied to new product development. Although the basic ideas in these cases may be the same, it is important to remember that each of these two companies expended a lot of effort to tailor its quality function deployment methods to its individual situation.

Understanding Demands

Planning is determining *what* to make; designing is deciding *how* to make it. In order to plan, we must gain an accurate understanding of what qualities customers demand in a product. These qualities can then be arranged in a demanded quality deployment chart for quality function deployment, as shown in Chapter 1. When surveying customer demands, the product concept and the product's basic functions should be made clear to the respondents.

Determining the Degree of Importance of a Quality Demand

The relative importance of various quality demands made by consumers must be determined in some way. We can use the remote control system case study from Chapter 1 to show how this can be done. Figure 2.1 shows the questionnaire that was used to investigate the degree of importance of various quality demands for this product. The questions were based on second-level details in the demanded quality deployment chart and were to be answered using a 1-to-5 scale. The questionnaire asked respondents to evaluate competitive products as well. Fifty people were interviewed at an amateur model airplane competition where the model planes were maneuvered by means of hand-held remote control devices. Figure 2.2 shows the results of this survey. Although only mean values are given here, obtaining the variance as well often produces useful information. It is also important to analyze the answers in detail with respect to respondent characteristics, such as age, gender, and socioeconomic factors. When collecting quality demands, the frequency with which a particular demand is mentioned can be a clue to the degree of its importance to consumers.

The Quality Plan

Chart 2.1 shows an example of quality planning using information obtained from questionnaires regarding the degree of importance of various demands and customer product evaluations relative to each demand. In this example, the most practical way to determine the quality plan target level is to use a demanded quality deployment chart that has been expanded to the second level of detail.

The mean values of the responses to questions 1 and 2 in the questionnaires were rounded and entered in Chart 2.1 as "ratings" ranging from 1 to 5, representing the degree of importance. For each demand, the ratings for both our company's product and competitive products were entered in the comparison analysis column. We then put all the analyses together and, to determine the selling features or sales points, added a value representing our company's product strategy. A ○ in the chart indicates a sales point. A ◎ means an especially important item, such as "easy to hold" or "does not make wrong movements."

A thorough study of these values and comparisons will help determine the strategy for the quality plan. In this example, "easy to hold" is a 3 in degree of importance to customers and a 3 in their evaluation of our company's product, while their evaluations of competitive products are represented by a 4. This indicates a potentially important sales point, so in developing our product quality plan we must aim for the highest level, which is a 5. Thus, we can express the improvement we want to achieve in our product plan as:

$$\text{quality plan target level} \div \text{our current product quality equation} = \frac{5}{3} = 1.67$$

The values for "degree of importance" that we entered in Chart 2.1 were obtained just by evaluating the customers' demands. However, in actual practice, the qualities of the product to be developed will also be determined by consideration of company policy. These two types of considerations must somehow be merged.

We did this by computing a number we call the absolute weight, using the equation:

$$\text{Degree of importance} \times \text{percentage of improvement} \times \text{sales point}$$
$$= \text{absolute weight}$$

For sales points, the value 1.5 was assigned to ◎, 1.2 to ○, and 1.0 for anything else. The absolute weight for "easy to hold," for example, was calculated:

$$3 \times 1.67 \times 1.5 = 7.5$$

(This method follows the one described in Chapter 9.) Converting each absolute weight to a percentage of the total value of all the absolute weights gives you the demanded quality weight.

In this case, the total was 88.8 (rounded to 89), so the demanded quality weight for "easy to hold" was:

$$7.5 \div 89 \times 100 = 8.4$$

This figure reflects the influence of company policy on the degree of importance assigned by the customers. When the whole is expressed as 100, the degree of importance is expressed as a percentage. This figure can be used to shape the design quality, because we will want to respond to and deploy those demands with the highest degree of importance.

In the remainder of this chapter, we will present and discuss an outline for developing a quality plan that will serve as a basis for quality function deployment. No theoretical basis has yet been devised for evaluating demanded quality weights. Further studies are needed, but this method seems to have produced good results in practice and its validity is gradually being accepted.

In any case, it is important to study many cases in order to become accomplished at this method. I hope this case will be of some help.

Developing the Quality Plan: The Case of Komatsu MEC

Komatsu MEC was founded in 1965 as a joint venture between Komatsu Manufacturing and International Harvester. It manufactured wheel loaders under this joint venture agreement. In February 1982, the joint venture agreement was terminated. As a result, Komatsu was forced to develop eleven new models of wheel loaders, relying solely on its own technology and that of other members of the Komatsu group. They had a tight deadline of December 1984. The Komatsu group devoted all their efforts to this project, which came to be known as the "WA" series.

Now that this project has been completed and the products have been accepted favorably by the marketplace, it can be said to have succeeded. The details of this project were written up in *Quality Control* magazine, in an article well worth reading. While several factors contributed to the success of this project, the use of QC was the most important.

In this chapter, we will use the WA project to illustrate the process of developing a quality plan.

The Use of Quality Function Deployment in the WA Project

Let's begin by outlining the way quality function deployment was used in this project and then look at the demanded quality deployment part of it. Figure 2.3 illustrates the quality function deployment system used by Komatsu. We call it quality-cost deployment. In this case, new products were really an extension of existing products, so the demanded quality deployment information that we gathered from the sales department already included rather technical terminology.

The first task for the design department was to clarify the relationship between the demanded quality deployment and the quality characteristic items, using a matrix like the one shown in Figure 2.3, chart 1. But merely putting together a matrix did not make it easy to understand the direct connection between the demanded quality and the quality characteristic details. We needed to focus on the items that had the strongest relationship with the demanded quality and select a few of them, using the comparisons shown in Figure 2.3, chart 2. Now, the relationship between the demanded quality and the characteristic items could be seen more directly. This simplification process also enables us to improve and speed up our communication with the sales department on technical matters. Previously, many hours had been spent giving technical instruction to the sales department.

Next, for each of these quality characteristic items, the ratings of our company's current products and those of our competitors were arrayed in a chart, and the target values for the counterpart characteristics of the new products were established. We called this our target control chart (see Figure 2.3, charts 2 and 3).

We established the target values of the counterpart quality characteristics for the new product by comparing the mean values of the ratings assigned by customers to the characteristics of our existing products with those assigned to our competitors' products. We then decided what target value we wanted to assign by relating the product devices to be produced to their characteristic items or characteristic values (see Figure 2.3, chart 4).

The higher the target values for each characteristic, the better. But from the viewpoint of manufacturing, these targets should strike a balance between selling price and cost. We put together two or three ideas for each device, as shown in Figure 2.3, chart 5. We tried to consider the trends our competitors were following and the engineering levels that would be involved in the model changes, and then we made our final decision regarding the target level by combining these considerations. In other words, we established our quality target by analyzing the relationship between quality and cost.

Our target cost was determined by subtracting the target profits from the expected selling price, which was determined by comparing the planned product with competitive models and their selling prices. The target costs for the new devices were determined by means of a cost structure ratio derived from existing products.

Since the degree of importance had been determined for each quality demand by the sales department and indicated in its demanded quality deployment chart, we studied each device in order to obtain two or three ideas for devices that would realize the demanded qualities. It was difficult to estimate the cost of a device at this early planning stage. It was even more difficult when we decided to adopt some new mechanism or new function. What we had to do then was to base our estimates on similar products of our own or our competitor, or do some advance development in order to get some cost information.

Generally speaking, the selling price of a new product is set a little higher than that of an existing product. Planning a new product that incorporated the new requirements indicated by the sales department in addition to the features already found in the existing products would increase our target costs significantly. To avoid this, we had to reduce the cost of some devices. Like many others, we have tried to find a way to quantitatively correlate function and cost, but we have not yet developed a completely satisfactory method. In the case of our WA project, in order to make our final decision, we relied on the engineering department's experience and judgment and on our evaluation of various device concepts in relation to the target cost.

As we studied different device concepts, we clarified certain selling points (Figure 2.3, chart 7) and identified potential engineering bottlenecks (Figure 2.3, chart 8). We applied failure mode effect analysis (FMEA) to the areas needing bottleneck engineering and used fault tree analysis (FTA)) to identify causal factors for the failure modes found in the FMEA. This allowed us to proceed smoothly and crisis-free with our development as we worked through these bottlenecks in the development process. In fact, the problems that did occur involved technology that we thought had already been well established.

We were surprised to find when using FMEA and FTA on parts and devices previously designed with what we thought was sound technology, that, in fact, they had been designed on the basis of no more than experience and perception. While it is physically impossible to use FMEA on all products and parts at the same time. In actual practice, one uses it on the most critical parts or devices first. This allows experience to accumulate into engineering know-how.

Finally, I would like to emphasize the importance of common design in the application of quality function deployment. We were able to study commonality of parts for all models while we were developing the first model, as shown in Figure 2.3, charts 4 and 5. For example, we were able to develop a driver's seat shape that could be used for several models. This gave us a standard design element, and by using this common design, we reduced significantly the number of hours that would otherwise have been required for design.

Using Demanded Quality Deployment

Generally, a demanded quality deployment chart is prepared and submitted to the engineering department by the sales department. In our case, however, where the product concept was already established and the new products were to be extensions of existing ones, a demanded quality deployment chart was not submitted in each case. The reason for this is that the sales department receives regular requests for improvement of some systems, so the demands of the market are already understood to some degree.

Of course, the sales department submits a demanded quality deployment chart at the beginning of the new product development process. Generally, when the new product is an extension of an existing one, the demanded quality deployment charts have been maintained on a regular basis, so there are not many new items to add.

In our company, the engineering department regularly updates demanded quality deployment charts based on information acquired from the marketplace. Figure 2.4 shows part of a demanded quality deployment chart. When we began developing a new product that was an extension of an existing one, a chart like this was partially reviewed by the engineering department in order to compare it more easily with new market information. We deployed demanded qualities to the third level of detail, but the level should be determined for each product. We had about 100 items at the third level of detail.

Unfortunately, market information can be expressed in many different ways, so we have to judge whether some information is really new or whether it is more appropriate as an additional third-level detail for a quality already entered in the chart. In our company, the senior product manager for the model makes this determination and the results are coded into the computer. By regularly compiling and arranging market information in this manner, we are able to keep track of time factors and better understand market trends and customer preferences. This gives us a clearer sense of what items will be required for the next product that we decide to make and guides us in setting our goals.

This, basically, is the system of demanded quality deployment that our company used in the WA project. Some details of the WA project are described in the following pages.

Figure 2.5 is an expanded detail from Figure 2.3, chart 3. One demanded quality we learned from the sales department was expressed as "easy for the operator to drive" or "easy to operate." Although several components are related to ease of operation, the transmission shifting lever is the one operated most frequently — much more frequently than in an automobile. By reducing the effort required to operate the transmission shift lever, we could make the wheel loader much easier for the driver to operate.

Responding to this request from the sales department, the design department set a target value of less than 1 kilogram of force required to operate the transmission shifting lever. As shown in Figure 2.3, chart 5, they studied two or three ideas for achieving this goal, such as improving the mechanical system in the existing model or installing a booster in the transmission linkage. They analyzed each idea in relation to expected cost, performance, and the degree of difficulty in developing the technology necessary to realize them. This analysis helped us make our final decision.

Eventually we decided to use an electrically operated mechanism to shift the transmission instead of a manually operated one. This change reduced the force required to operate the transmission shifting lever to 0.6 kilograms. However, we had very little information about the reliability and durability of the electrically operated mechanism. We conducted a complete bench test, using bottleneck engineering (BNE), to simulate durability under actual use conditions. We tested several dozen electric switches — both prototypes and preproduction products that had been manufactured with the actual production tools and jigs — for durability and reliability.

Next, we used the results of these tests to forecast the failure rate in the field, which we wanted to be somewhat better (lower) than the test failure rate. We wanted to do this because we wanted to build in not just enough technology to achieve our own planned targets, but enough to allow for the perhaps less forgiving judgment of the marketplace.

Figure 2.4 shows the results of this activity. The product evaluation by the marketplace is positive. At the beginning of our WA project, we relied on the judgment of the sales and engineering departments in estimating the degree of importance of each quality demand. In our next development project, however, we will be able to evaluate the degree of importance of these demands ourselves because of our accumulated experience with market demands. Furthermore, now that we have proven that we can clarify product development targets during the planning stage, we know that we also should be able to prevent any problems that we might encounter later on in the development process because our market evaluations have improved the feedback regarding demanded quality.

So far, I have talked about the effects of quality function deployment on the engineering department. I should add that this method has also had positive effects on communication between the engineering department and the sales department, even though there is no paperwork to document this. In the WA project we were able to discuss many of the problems, so that both departments were completely satisfied. Thus, the demanded quality deployment charts played a major role in bridging the communication gap between our department and the sales department.

The previous account covers only a small part of what we accomplished in our WA project, but I hope even this much will be of help to you.

Using Quality Charts for New Product Planning and Development at Matsushita Electric Works, Ltd.

An Outline of the Home Appliance Business Center

"Enjoy life! Electricity for personal needs, electricity for fun!" is the slogan that defines the new business concept for the home appliance division of Matsushita Electric Works, Ltd. Adding "electricity for fun" to the earlier phrase "electricity for personal needs" promotes the "enjoy life" idea to the division's customers and aims to create a new demand for electrical appliances.

In 1986, the home appliance division signalled the importance of its TQC activities by dubbing them "Operation EL 100," and participation by all members is being fostered through human resource development. In this case study we will show how the quality chart was used in the planning and development of an air purifier, which became a new product line among the "enjoy life" products.

The Role of the Quality Chart During the Planning Stage

Some of the most important requirements for creating new demand and new product areas are generally considered to be adding new product functions, ending some dissatisfaction in people's lives, understanding and quantifying latent demands for design, and making the product easy to use — and then creating user anticipation. In this department, we rearrange all user demands for each new product area into demanded quality deployment charts in which we deploy the demanded quality to the third level, assign a weight to each demand, and seek a consensus on whether to continue with the development program.

The decision to develop a new line of business is based on this quality demand analysis activity, which is then correlated with each product's planning activity.

Planning continues until the final output is a product plan that meets all the requirements of an NCP checklist. The acronym NCP stands for identified NEEDS, product CONCEPT, and specifics of the PRODUCT. Chart 2.2 shows the demanded quality deployment chart, and Chart 2.4 shows the NCP checklist.

Creating Product Demand

Expanding Demand

Our air purifiers, called Air-Fresh, have been selling well since 1983, and we have expanded the line to include larger sizes and even models for automotive use. Figure 2.6 shows the sales history of the Air-Fresh products.

Determining Quality Demands

The residential air purifier is designed to clean air in the home, which is a new application for air cleaning. Important points for answering these needs can be understood through technology development and evaluation engineering. The basic quality chart is an important tool that can be used to determine and evaluate specifications for "expected quality", "satisfactory quality", and "quality for safety" — as demanded by the users — and to establish the target values for the design.

The home air purifier has two main functions: (1) removal of cigarette smoke and airborne dust, and (2) deodorizing cigarette smoke and other unpleasant odors. Our company's product, the Air-Fresh air purifier, consists of a prefilter designed to remove large particles, such as fabric lint, a fine-weave fiber filter to remove small particles, such as cigarette smoke and ordinary dust, a deodorizing filter to remove odors, and a fan motor.

Chart 2.4 is a basic quality chart for the air purifier. It conveys information about users' quality demands and comparisons with competitive products to the product planning and development people. We call it a "basic quality chart" because it integrates the demanded quality chart and the corresponding quality items.

Important Activities for Achieving Demanded Quality

To ensure that we would achieve the "expectation, satisfaction, and safety" quality requirements for a new product, we prepared a "new product QA activity plan" like Chart 2.5 as a parallel activity to planning and development. The purpose of doing this was to clarify (1) instructions on how to develop products by organizing them according to quality targets that were related to bottleneck engineering, and arranging them in a basic quality chart; (2) the process of new product development, by identifying and prioritizing the major points to be addressed; and (3) the QA process, by identifying QA problems, describing the organization that will promote QA, identifying the people who will be in charge of QA, and outlining the policy for QA steps to be taken.

Developing Satisfying Products

Establishing Engineering Development Targets by Quantifying Needs

The basic functions of the air purifier are removal of dust and unpleasant odors from the home, but when quantifying needs, research will focus on removing cigarette smoke. There are two types of cigarette smoke — primary smoke, which is inhaled by smokers, and secondary smoke, which comes directly from the natural combustion of the cigarette. Initially, we concerned ourselves only with secondary smoke, but after finding that when people were smoking the concentration of particulate matter in smoke was different, we developed an automatic cigarette-smoking machine that generates both primary and secondary smoke and thus more closely mimics actual smoking conditions. This allows us to measure more accurately the airborne particle removal performance of the air purifier. Figure 2.7 shows the dust removal performance of our product.

The odor of the cigarette can be quantified by (1) the absolute concentration method, based on instrument analysis; and (2) the sensory evaluation method, which relies on the human sense of smell. The effectiveness of sensory evaluation depends on the normality of a person's sense of smell, so candidates for the product evaluation panel had to meet a selection standard before they could evaluate the product's odor removal performance. In this test, predetermined standard odors were applied to pieces of paper, and candidates who scored highest in their ability to identify and distinguish standard odors were considered "normal" and thus eligible to serve on the panel.

Development of New Technology

A W-shaped "magic" filter, which was not being manufactured by any other company, was developed through an accumulation of new technology and new functions. It was designed to improve particulate dust and odor removal performance, which with ease of use are the basic functions of an air purifier.

The particle collection filter is a two-layer filter made of finely woven fabric, with a different fabric density (number of threads per square inch) in each layer, so both small and large particles are filtered out at the same time. The corrugated construction of the filter gives it a larger dust collection area and thereby extends the life of the filter. Figure 2.8 shows an enlarged view of the dust collection filter.

The odor removal filter is also a two-part filter, consisting of both a conventional activated charcoal filter and a new activated charcoal filter treated with an odor-removing agent. This combination filter removes many odors commonly found in homes such as ammonia, hydrogen sulfide, and acetaldehyde. The fabric filter and the activated charcoal filters working together constitute a filtration system that is both chemical and physical.

Figure 2.9 shows the construction of the air purifier. Using a description provided by the engineering department, we built a prototype to be used for evaluation of the product's overall potential, through quantification of quality levels, tests, and third-party evaluations.

Figure 2.10 shows the results of our evaluation of product potential at the completion of planning land development. The results of this evaluation were fed back to the "basic quality chart" and the "new product QA activity plan," which we used to establish quality targets and quality items for the next new product development.

Benefits of Using Demanded Quality Deployment Charts

We obtained the improvements outlined below through the use of demanded quality deployment charts for planning and development of the air purifier.

- New product planning became more specific and made consensus-building within the company easier.
- Extracting the engineering development items for quality characteristics and identifying the test evaluation techniques that would have to be developed helped us to better define and prioritize user needs.
- Planning and development activities were more logically related to the expectations, satisfaction, and safety of users.

As a result of these improvements, our planning and development became more focused, and the air purifier product group was chosen to become a new business group. We believe that using the quality chart as our basic tool for relating consumer quality demands to product planning and development activities has secured the trust of our users through overall improvement quality.

Future Tasks

The benefits of using the demanded quality deployment charts cited in this example are (1) integration of the demanded quality and quality characteristics into a basic quality chart; (2) target-setting based on quantification of users' sensory evaluations (smell tests); and (3) conversion of demanded qualities into measurable design and engineering elements. Many aspects of new product planning and development require further study and practice. Some of the important ones needing further work in the future are:

- Improved methods for quantifying user quality expectations for new functions and product values, and for evaluating the product's ability to meet those expectations.
- Improved methods for processing information about contextual factors, such as changes in our society, into high quality information that can be included in the quality charts.

References

Akao, Yoji et al. (1983). "Quality Function Deployment including Cost, Reliability, and Technology Deployment (Parts 1 & 2): Designing Quality, Cost, and Reliability." *Quality*, Vol. 13, No. 3, JSQC.

Miura, Shin, et al (1985). *Dictionary of TQC Terminology*. Japan Standards Association.

Mizuno, Shigeru; Akao, Yoji (1978). *Quality Function Deployment*. JUSE.

Quality Control editorial staff (1985). "New Product Development and QC in the WA Project at Komatsu MEC." *Quality Control*, Vol. 36, No. 7, pp. 18-27, JUSE.

Two questions will be asked of you. The answer in column 1 indicates how important each item is in influencing your purchase decision. The answer in column 2 asks you to evaluate each manufacturer on each item, after you have tried each one.

Please answer columns 1 and 2 at the same time. Your questionnaire begins on page 2.

Question 1: The items listed here may influence your purchasing decisions for a radio controlled product. In column 1, please rank how much influence these item have on your purchase decision. Please circle the appropriate level.

Question 2: Whose radio control do you currently own. Please fill in the name of the manufacturer.

Company X . . . . . name of manufacturer (   )
Company Y . . . . . name of manufacturer (   )
Company Z . . . . . name of manufacturer (   )

In column 2, please evaluate each manufacturer's product after using it. Please circle the appropriate level.

items to judge the product	Column 1	Column 2
	no influence at all / minor influence / some influence / strong influence / very strong influence	very bad / bad / fair / good / very good
(example) easy to hold	① at 3 (1 2 3 4 5)	X (1 2 3 4 ⑤) Y (1 2 ③ 4 5) Z (1 ② 3 4 5)

Figure 2-1. Questionnaire

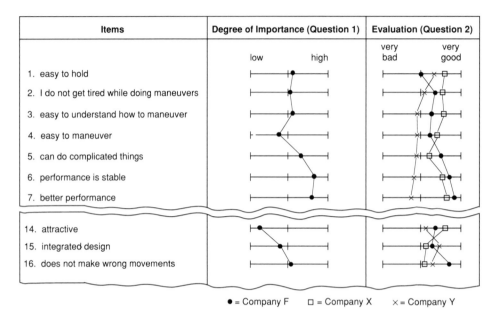

Items	Degree of Importance (Question 1)	Evaluation (Question 2)

Figure 2-2. Consolidated Results of the Questionnaire

● = Company F   □ = Company X   × = Company Y

	demanded quality		quality plan							
			competitive analysis			plan			weight	
		degree of importance	our company	other companies		quality plan	rate of improvement	sales point	absolute weight	demanded quality weight
1st level	2nd level			Company Y	Company Z					
easy to maneuver	11. easy to hold	3	3	4	4	5	1.67	◎	7.5	8.4
	12. I do not get tired while doing maneuvers	3	4	5	4	5	1.25		3.8	4.2
	13. easy to understand how to maneuver	3	4	5	3	5	1.75	◯	4.5	5.1
	14. easy to maneuver	3	3	3	3	4	1.33		4.0	4.5
	15. can do complicated things	3	4	4	3	5	1.75	◯	4.5	5.1
5. safe	51. does not make wrong movements	4	5	4	4	5	10		6.0	6.8
								total	88.8	100

Chart 2-1. Demanded Quality Deployment Chart

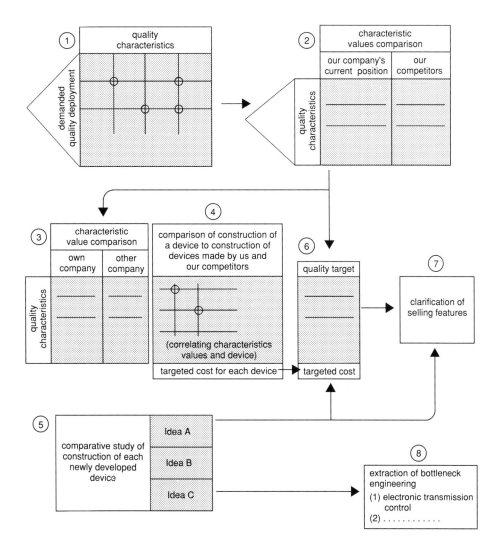

Figure 2-3. Overview of Quality Deployment

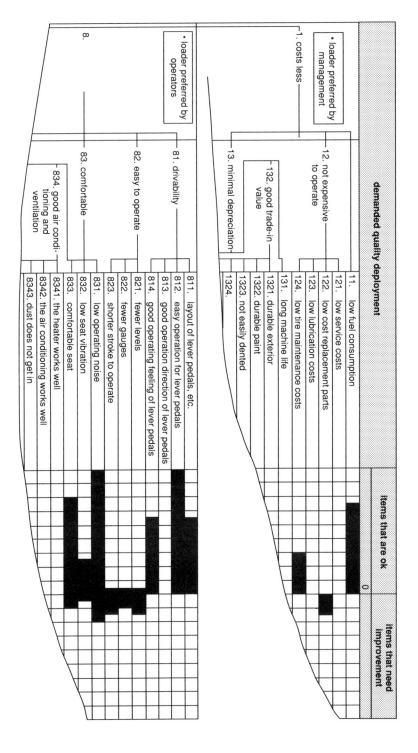

Figure 2-4. Demanded Quality Deployment Chart (Komatsu MEC Case)

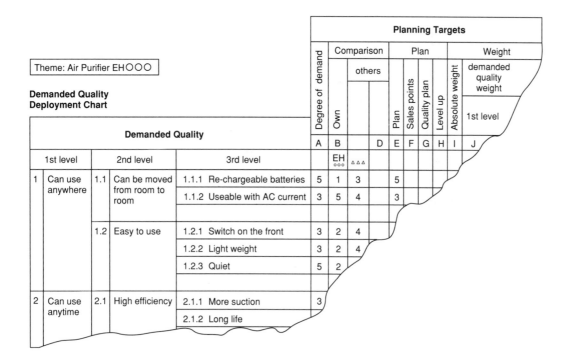

demanded quality deployment			degree of importance		target		competitive comparison model				
1st level	2nd level	3rd level	domestic	foreign	inferior 0 superior		characteristic items	characteristics values			
								WA	A		
work gets done well	good digging and loading ability	can load large amounts at one time	◎	◎		●	bucket capacity (m^3)	2.7	2.7	2.6	
							dumping clearance (mm)	2900	2800	2750	
		smooth starting, forward and backward directions	○	○		●	dumping reach (mm)	1100	980	1000	
easy operation	good operability	light opening touch	◎	◎		●	transmission shift lever (kg X mm)	1.0 x 40	2 x 70		
							operating levers	2.0 x 70	3 x 90		
	good visibility										

Figure 2-5. Demanded Quality Deployment Chart (Komatsu MEC Case)

Theme: Air Purifier EH○○○

Demanded Quality Deployment Chart

				Planning Targets								
Demanded Quality				Degree of demand	Comparison			Plan			Weight	
						others					demanded quality weight	
					Own			Plan	Sales points	Quality plan	Level up	Absolute weight	
												1st level
1st level	2nd level	3rd level		A	B		D	E	F	G	H	I	J
					EH ○○○	▵▵▵							
1 Can use anywhere	1.1 Can be moved from room to room	1.1.1 Re-chargeable batteries	5	1	3		5					
		1.1.2 Useable with AC current	3	5	4		3					
	1.2 Easy to use	1.2.1 Switch on the front	3	2	4							
		1.2.2 Light weight	3	2	4							
		1.2.3 Quiet	5	2								
2 Can use anytime	2.1 High efficiency	2.1.1 More suction	3									
		2.1.2 Long life										

Chart 2-2. Demanded Quality Deployment Chart for the Air Purifier

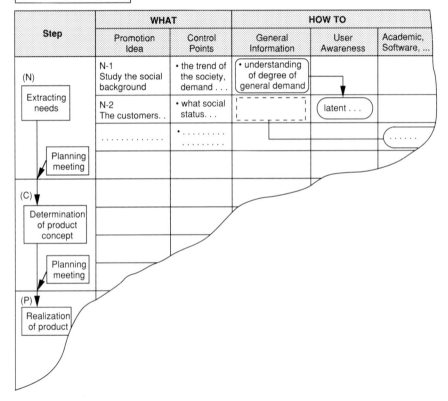

EHOOO (NCP Checklist)

Step	WHAT		HOW TO		
	Promotion Idea	Control Points	General Information	User Awareness	Academic, Software, ...
(N) Extracting needs	N-1 Study the social background	• the trend of the society, demand . . .	• understanding of degree of general demand		
	N-2 The customers. .	• what social status. . .		latent . . .	
	. . . .	•			. . . . . .
Planning meeting					
(C) Determination of product concept					
Planning meeting					
(P) Realization of product					

Chart 2-3. NCP Checklist

Basic Quality Chart for Air Purifier

Demanded Quality			Quality Function System		test/evaluation methods	Specification		Current Quality	Yearly Quality Targets	Examples of Development Improvement		
			Quality Items			general rule of product standard	each standard			Engineering Standard	Engineering Material	Examples of Failures
Good air refresher	Can remove dust	Can remove tobacco smoke	Dust Removal Performance		Dust Removal Performance Test		ΔΔ minutes	xx minutes		HES-000	QEP-00	
			Dust Collecting Performance		Dust Collecting Effect		ΔΔ %	xx %				
		Can remove home dust			Removal Rate 0.01		ΔΔ %	xx %				
					Removal Rate 0.05		ΔΔ %	xx %				
	Can remove odor	Can remove tobacco odor	HC Removal Performance		Removal Performance Test		ΔΔ %	xx %				
			Ammonia Removal Performance		Removal Performance Test		ΔΔ %	xx %		HES-000	QEP-00	
			Nicotine Removal Performance		Removal Performance Test							
		Can remove kitchen odor	Hydrogen Sulfide Removal Performance		Removal Performance Test							

Current Quality columns: grade | inspection stamp | inspection stamp | prepared by

Chart 2-4. Basic Quality Chart for Air Purifier

Sales Volume		'83	'84	'85	'86

Sales Volume: 150, 100

	Large size		EH316		
Home use	Mid-size	EH315		EH318	
	Small size	EH 311	EH312	EH313	
Automotive	Dealer Installed		EH321		
	Built-in Factory Installed		EH329		EH328
	Years	'83	'84	'85	'86

Figure 2-6. Sales History of the Air Purifier

New Product QA Quality Plan	Part No.	(EH 000)	Product Plan-up	S . .	Eng'g Dept. Head	ID	Date of issue	S . .
	Part Name		Date of Sales Start	S . .				
Develop-ment Stage	Aim of QA	Emphasis on progress of activity and work	Tools (information, name of records)		Worker in charge	≈	Follow-up, performance	
Plan	Quantification of pattern of actual use	♦ Research usage mode ♦ Understanding the effect of fragrance	Issue demanded quality deployment chart		○○			
	Assurance of performance target value	♦ Confirmation of performance effect 1. Bench test, establishment of test standards and develop-ment of measurement method 2. Monitor evaluation	Design quality deployment chart Engineering action evaluation chart					

Chart 2-5. New Product QA Activity Plan

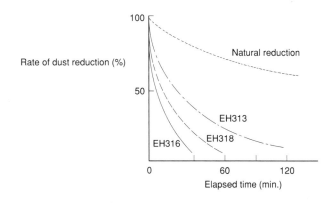

Figure 2-7. Dust Removal Performance of the Air Purifier

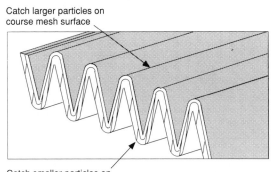

Figure 2-8. Enlarged View of the Dust Collection Filter

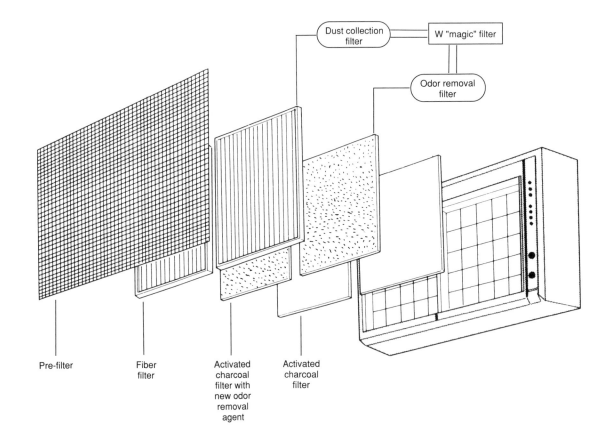

Figure 2-9. Construction of the Air Purifier

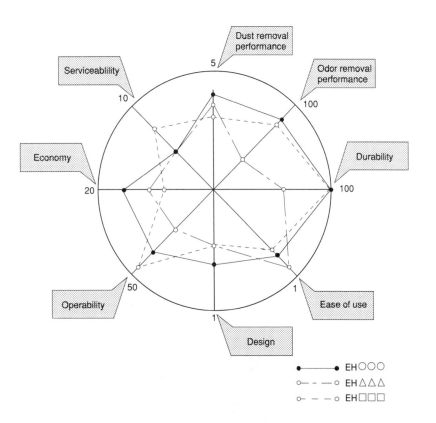

Figure 2-10. Air Purifier Product Potential Evaluation Chart

CHAPTER 3

Using and Promoting Quality Charts

Yoshihiro Mitsufuji, TQC Promotion Department,
Tokyo Juki Kogyo Company;
and Takeharu Uchida et al, Yaskawa Electric Industries

Chapter 1 presented a general discussion of quality charts and included references to illustrate many types of industrial applications. In this chapter, I want to keep generalized discussion to a minimum and try to focus on the quality chart from a different angle. A brief, general discussion that does not repeat material already presented, however, will serve as an introduction to this chapter.

Fundamentals of Quality Charts

What Is a Quality Chart?

The term quality chart can be defined broadly or narrowly. Broadly defined, a quality chart is a matrix or series of matrices used to correlate everything from the product design plan through the quality control process chart, including what we have called the quality function deployment chart. In this chapter we will focus our attention on the narrower definition:

A quality chart is a two-dimensional matrix consisting of a demanded quality chart combined with a quality characteristics deployment chart. Combining the two matrices expresses the relationship between demanded qualities and quality characteristics.

Chapter 2 has described the demanded quality chart, so we will begin this chapter with a brief discussion of the quality characteristics deployment chart and the quality chart.

A quality characteristics deployment chart can be defined as a systematic arrangement, based on tree diagram logic, of the quality characteristics (or counterpart characteristics or quality elements) that make up a subject product or service. By contrast, the quality chart can be defined as a matrix made up of a demanded quality chart and a quality characteristics deployment chart. The matrix is coded with the symbols $\bigcirc$ or $\triangle$ to indicate the strength of relationships between demanded qualities and quality characteristics. Chart 3.1 is a typical example of a quality chart.

Purpose and Objective of the Quality Chart

The fundamental purpose of the quality chart is to convert each quality demanded by customers into quality characteristics expressed in the engineering language used by one's own company. Because the customers' demands are usually expressed in abstract terms that are not specific enough for manufacturing, they must be converted into engineering or design language in order for a company to relate them to design activities and implement them.

Even in the past, of course, companies have converted market demands into engineering language through a process in which a sales group or a product planning group collects the market demands and summarizes them in product planning formats, which are then converted into design plans or design specifications by an engineering or development group. However, in many instances these conversions are subjective mental operations performed entirely within the brains of people in charge. This "black box" conversion process results in biased decisionmaking at development discussion meetings. For example, the stronger or more vocal group often carries more weight, and a correct decision may not be reached.

In other words, although a firm — for the sake of its long-term development — must aim at quality management based on true market orientation, the basic process from product planning to design planning is not often well defined and may even be replaced by less essential matters. The quality chart was developed as a means to solve these problems, and therein lies its objective.

Important Points in Preparing Quality Charts

Quality Characteristics and Quality Elements

The way a company analyzes, describes, and interprets a given set of quality characteristics generally is governed by the amount of engineering capability the company has. Therefore, the more applicable and familiar a subject product is to the company, the better the quality characteristics will be described, both quantitatively and qualitatively. When the subject is a new product requiring technology that is new for the company, describing and deploying a complete set of quality characteristics may be quite difficult. In such cases, I suggest that when you are analyzing the subject product or service, you make the chart for deployment of quality characteristics more practical in terms of their component quality elements, instead of preparing a complete quality characteristics deployment chart at the beginning.

The term quality element is not a familiar term, so you may find it confusing. It may be easier to understand if you realize that designers must always consider these "quality elements" in the process of developing a product, although the results of their consideration are not always visible. Even though this process may be unfamiliar to you and the result of your chart-making efforts may not be perfect, you should be able to come up with some kind of deployment chart if you bring the appropriate people together in discussion groups organized for the purpose of describing quality characteristics. Chart 3.2 is an example of quality element deployment.

Master Charts and Subcharts

Most firms make several different products rather than just one, and this trend is likely to grow stronger in the future. When companies do make multiple products, they must make multiple quality charts. However, since the preparation of even one quality chart takes so much time, preparing charts for every product is, in practice, nearly impossible. How can we solve this problem? One solution is to create product groups by grouping similar products together, and then prepare a master quality chart for each group. Minor modifications of the quality chart can be made to address differences among products.

Once the basic quality chart (master) has been prepared for a product group, quality deployment for individual products within this group will begin with a partially correct quality chart (subchart). The portions needing some modification will be those dealing with features that are specific to an individual product and those that are considered to be items for critical control. The point here is that the logic used for grouping products should be based on the perspectives of both the market and technology, and it demands consideration of market segments by product level and group technology.

Comprehensiveness Versus Prioritizing

As we have said, the first attempt to prepare quality charts requires much effort. Comprehensiveness is not only nearly impossible to achieve at this stage, it is not even a sensible goal. We have already said that both demanded quality and quality characteristics should be deployed to approximately third levels of detail. Although we have also stated that comprehensiveness is a basic concept for quality charts, at this stage it is a good idea to hold detailed deployment in the quality chart to approximately the third level, too. When you deploy to the fifth and sixth levels, specificity increases, but the work required increases geometrically and the quality of your work may decrease with mixed results. Therefore, we consider the use of weighting at the third level a more rational approach, since later deployment can be based on differences in weights.

At any rate, it makes sense to assign different levels of priority to various quality characteristics, basing the priority level on the differences in importance assigned by users, and to deploy only the higher priority demands to the fourth and fifth level. This kind of prioritizing is based on the Pareto concept.

Correlating by Fact Control

The most troublesome work in quality chart preparation is correlating demanded quality with quality characteristics. Often, this correlation is based on experience, intuition, and determination (called the KKD method in Japanese), although it uses symbols such as ◎ to indicate a strong relationship, ○ for an average relationship, and a △ for weak relationship. This correlation should be based, however, on knowing and controlling facts. That is, the relationships and their relative strengths should be based on factual data and statistical analysis. A chart full of symbols based on experience, intuition, and determination may be visually pleasing, but they are unreliable if not confirmed by facts. Furthermore, if the intended users of such a quality chart do not trust it, they will not use it.

Reliance on experience, intuition, and determination may be necessary if some or all of the data needed as a basis for confirming the correlating relationships is not available when the quality chart is being prepared. In such cases, we recommend devising some method to differentiate relationships based solely on experience, intuition, and determination from those based on facts. One method might be to enter correlating symbols based only on experience, intuition, and determination in pencil, and those based on facts in red ink — and to enter the back-up data in the same way. The amount of red ink on the chart will then indicate the reliability of the quality chart at a glance. An increase in red and a decrease in pencil will mean greater reliability in the quality chart, which will permit more accurate control of target levels.

Copy the Spirit, Not the Form

The basic format of the quality chart is a starting point, not a requirement. The types of products, sales method, practices, engineering methods, management systems, and other factors differ from firm to firm. Therefore a wide variety of quality charts is to be expected. One firm's charts might be another firm's poison. A methodology based on objective data, such as the seven QC tools, can be used by almost any firm, but the quality chart is a graphic device that specifies technology based on the characteristics of the individual firm. Put bluntly, quality charts that do not reflect these individual features are like pictures of cake on a menu — pleasant to the eye, but not to the palate.

When preparing a quality chart, one should therefore not pay too much attention to those of other firms but should try instead to understand and copy the meaning or spirit of such charts. Of course, by trying to be independent and unique, one only suffers the first time around. Some copying is necessary. But please heed my words: *Copy the spirit, not the form.*

A Quality Chart Is a Living Thing

Like many standards that are established but never used, quality charts are often prepared but never reviewed. They collect dust. Customers' demands change over time and a firm's technology grows continuously. Likewise a quality chart built on these two elements must also change over time or quickly become obsolete. Accordingly, if you are serious about quality charts, you must revise them constantly so that they will stay alive. To ensure that the revision process is properly and routinely carried out, establish a company rule that clearly defines why the revisions should be made, who should participate, what they should accomplish, and when, where, and how the review of quality charts should be conducted.

The Two-Dimensionality of Quality and the Role of New Technology

As Professor Kano of Science University of Tokyo has pointed out, we are beginning to understand that the relationship between level of quality and degree of satisfaction — which until recently was viewed as being one dimensional — is a two-dimensional relationship. We can distinguish expected quality from attractive quality. Depending on the subject, improvement in expected quality does not lead to a high degree of satisfaction, but a decrease results in dissatisfaction. By contrast, improvement in attractive quality increases satisfaction, but a decrease does not lead to dissatisfaction. Keep this distinction in mind when you are preparing a quality chart. The distinction will be different for each firm, but it will be reflected in the first stage of organizing demanded quality items.

Against a backdrop of intensifying competition among producers of new products, an increase in new products designed to embody attractive qualities or to evoke excitement is predictable. This means that companies frequently will be introducing new technology — which can be a problem, because new technology often becomes an engineering bottleneck. By identifying and analyzing attractive qualities at an early stage in the preparation of quality charts, however, a company usually can predict engineering bottlenecks and the feasibility of solving them. In some cases, however, one may need to go beyond the early stage and deploy the quality elements before such predictions can be made, because some quality characteristics are not easy to pick out, or because a row full of penciled Δ symbols indicates that some ambiguity exists in the relationship. At any rate, when making decisions about the direction deployment should take, one should always consider the two-dimensionality of quality and any associated need for new technology.

Introducing Quality Charts

Up to this point, most of our discussion has focused on preparing quality charts. We now need to talk about promoting and introducing them within the company. First, let's list some of the most common objections to introducing quality charts.

- I can't spend time on such work.
- I'm already working enough overtime each day without making these charts.
- You can't trust quality charts that have been prepared by the sales department.
- What's wrong with the traditional method?
- Someone made the quality charts without asking for our input, so they can't be any good.
- The form is impressive, but the substance is so-so. The charts are probably useless.
- Product design and development should be based on a balance of quality, cost, and delivery factors. Quality considerations shouldn't dominate our planning.

The list could go on and on. Strong opposition to introducing the charts is to be expected. Objections like these often come about, however, when the use of quality charts is rammed through the company without a thorough discussion of the need for them. In other words, it is a case of failing to recognize that change should be presented as a needs-oriented process. Objections similar to these are often raised when a company tries to introduce total quality control (TQC) without first discussing the need for it. This kind of forced introduction only strengthens resistance; it seldom results in meaningful implementation.

A needs-oriented approach is as necessary for introducing quality charts as it is for introducing TQC. Furthermore, when needs are well defined, employees can readily see that the quality charts are not just copies of another company's procedures, but originals correlating product characteristics with the characteristics and needs of their own company. This point is doubly important for readers who are involved in the introduction of quality charts.

Consider the following pointers when promoting and introducing specific quality charts:

- Use the first quality chart on the new product with the highest current priority.
- Choose a few people who are likely to enjoy this type of activity.
- Involve the individual with the greatest responsibility for new products by making that person the group leader.
- To promote better understanding of the quality chart, hold periodic discussions that include people from sales, planning, development, production, and other pertinent groups.
- Use outside consultants when appropriate.
- When problems or questions arise, place them on the agenda for thorough discussion by all participants. Do not remove them from the agenda until they have been resolved or understood. Never leave them unresolved.

These are only a few pointers, but I hope they will be useful.

Using Quality Charts: The Case of Tokyo Juki

We began using quality charts at Tokyo Juki in 1980. By using them to develop many new products since then, we have improved both the format and our manner of applying them. Therefore, the present form and method of application are the results of successive improvements. As such, they may not be very useful to those just beginning to take an interest in quality charts, because, in practice, the process of making them is more meaningful than the final results.

As we have said, the form and method used to prepare quality charts reflect the character of the company, but the underlying spirit is often not evident. However, once you understand the process leading to these results, the reason for so much form and methodology becomes clearer. The points to be addressed in making a quality chart that is to be used in your own company become clearer by comparing your own company needs with those of others.

Unfortunately, due to limited space, much of this important process cannot be introduced here. Accordingly, the examples here represent the results of work done at certain stages — not the entire process. Also, these examples are actual implementations of quality charts at one of our company's departments. We called the quality chart, Chart A.

How to Make Quality Chart A

1. *Gathering demanded quality items.* The most important task in preparing a quality chart is figuring out how to gather and interpret correctly the information obtained from the market and customers. One might use information that has been gathered from within one's own company (including individual employees), or information gathered in the marketplace, or predictions based on stated assumptions. In our company, the usual practice includes a method that involves specialists from various departments, market research conducted by the company's teams with user-customers, and personal know-how gained through analysis of past information.

2. *Making the demanded quality deployment chart.* Demanded qualities are derived from original information collected in the marketplace and arranged according to the KJ method (an affinity diagram system named for its Japanese inventor, Jiro Kawakita) to make a four-level demanded quality deployment chart.

3. *Deploying into quality characteristics.* While there is a method for independently deploying individual quality characteristics, at our company we extract the quality characteristics by a method in which we try to find a number of counterpart characteristics for each individual demanded quality item. The deployment chart is then arranged to take into account the relationship among these characteristics. Figure 3.1 is an example in which deployment is taken to the third level.

4. *Forming a matrix.* The demanded quality deployment chart and the quality characteristics deployment chart are arranged along vertical and horizontal axes, respectively, to form a matrix. The degree of relationship is expressed as ◎ for a strong relationship, ○ for an average relationship, and Δ for weak relationship. Note that factual proof is not that clear at this stage; our assessments of relationship strength are based on experience, intuition, and determination. However, we try to supplement these by checking out complaints (see Figure 3.2).

5. *Making a competitive comparison chart.* Because quality chart A is more a demanded quality chart than a quality chart, we perform a competitive comparison of our own products with other companies' products for each demanded quality item.

6. *Evaluating the importance of a demanded quality item.* We evaluate the importance of a demanded quality item by ranking it A, B, or C, according to the strength of demand expressed by users. While trying many ways of ranking importance, we are still at the trial-and-error stage.

7. *Re-evaluating the importance of demanded quality items using market information.* Customer verbatims are collected from as many users in the marketplace as possible. This information is stratified by commonality of market and, after being evaluated for degree of importance, is entered in the quality matrix. The

same kind of evaluation is applied to past complaint information. The quality chart is then re-evaluated and a final draft is prepared. Figure 3.3 shows an example of a complaint review.

8. *Determining sales points.* Sales points can be determined by further evaluating the relative importance of various demanded quality items on the basis of available information. At this point, the situation of the company, including external factors, should be thoroughly considered.

9. *Evaluating the importance of a counterpart characteristic.* Our company determines which quality characteristic it will explore by converting the importance of demanded quality items into the importance of counterpart characteristics. This conversion of degree of importance into the importance of counterpart quality characteristics can be expressed by the following equation:

$$W_j = \Sigma \times X_i a_{ij}$$

where: x_i = the evaluation score of the demanded quality to be correlated
a_{ij} = the strength of the match

An example of this conversion is given in Figure 3.4. This method is called the independent scoring method.

10. *Investigating the characteristics values of competing products.* Evaluations of the counterpart characteristics of your own company's product should be compared with those of competing products from other companies. This may require actual evaluation tests, although catalogues and other types of product literature usually can provide some valid information. Since data collection is time-consuming, we sometimes decide to rely on this type of information regardless of sources. The data collected is then prioritized according to the degree of importance of the quality characteristics.

11. *Developing the quality design.* We use the information described above as a basis for decisions regarding quality target values and their related specifications. This is the way we establish individual design targets and develop the overall quality design.

Summary

The steps outlined above comprise our company's procedure for making Quality Chart A. This is only one example, however, as I mentioned in the introductory remarks about this case. Each of the three business divisions in our company has its own product development functions, and each division prepares and uses quality charts differently. The example just described comes from one division at a particular time period and may differ from an A chart prepared by another division. Even the chart described in this example may change during the next year.

At any rate, quality charts will be practical only if their preparation is based on an understanding of the characteristics of the company, its products, and its needs — and on the study of an appropriate quality chart.

For reference, Figures 3.5 and 3.6 present, respectively, a brief outline of Quality Chart A and the overall scheme of quality function deployment.

Establishing Quality Targets: The Case of Yaskawa Electric

Our plant and its 1,100 employees specialize in making the manufacturing control devices that are the heart of our automation systems. Using our vast experience in applied electric motor technology and our "quality first" approach, we design, develop, and manufacture new products for systems, as well as independent units, in response to the changing needs of our customers.

Because of the tremendous growth and very stiff competition in their markets, our customers are constantly seeking the best in equipment and systems. The requirement for motorized application systems and related components and variable-speed products has developed into a need for more multifunction, high-performance, high-reliability, and low-priced products.

Since introducing total quality control (TQC) in 1981, we have been deploying quality assurance activities, which we call our ADDS-Y activity. This activity takes advantage of our practice of integrating our component products and system products with each other, so that the products better meet the diverse needs of our more sophisticated customers and are more responsive to the rapid changes encountered. We have established a system that starts building consistent quality into products at the very beginning of development.

In this section we will summarize the way our company has used quality function deployment charts. Basically, our production planning people have used them as a source of guidance for new product development — specifically, to establish appropriate quality targets based on changes in our customers' needs.

Making a Good Quality Chart

Since we introduced TQC, QC activities have been used throughout our entire company. The quality charts used for these activities have improved as their use increases. By improving our ability to combine information on quality as it relates to the sales department, systems engineering department, and technology development department, we have been able to improve the planning of our variable speed products.

Our sales department has deployed a sales plan that is both defensive and offensive — it collects and analyzes in order to foresee changes in market trends and customers' needs. We then reflect these changes in our product planning. The systems engineering department understood the true demands of the customers to be "standardization with greater flexibility." This understanding produced a number of basic quality charts that could be used over and over. The technology development department analyzed the requirements developed by the sales and systems engineering departments which reflected our understanding of both our customers' demands and technological trends to see if they could find any technology "seeds" that could be used in developing the next generation of products. We will look at each step in greater detail.

1. *Quality function deployment in product planning.* In product planning, first we took the original quality demand information collected by the sales department and broke it down into individual demands as shown in Figure 3.7. After translating the individual demands into engineering-oriented language, we then deployed the reworded demanded qualities to the third level and correlated them with the characteristics of the variable-speed products. We used the quality characteristics deployment part of this quality chart to determine which characteristics were most important in responding to changes in demanded quality.

   Next we conducted an applied quality function deployment, which relates the demanded quality to the applications of various items. We also compared our planned product with competitive products. Using these two quality function deployment charts enabled us to:

   • prioritize the quality characteristic details that related to changes in demanded quality;
   • prioritize the demanded quality and the quality characteristic details that related to certain targeted applications;
   • prevent omissions and errors in demanded quality deployment;
   • clarify sales points; and
   • clarify certain basic functions as they related to product diversification.

   Figure 3.8 shows parts of a quality characteristics deployment chart and quality application deployment chart that we did for this product planning.

2. *Quality function deployment in system standardization.* Figure 3.9 is a schematic representation of our conception of the flow of design activities required to realize the quality demanded for a variable-speed drive system. The basic functions and performance, as well as the characteristic target values required for various applications, were clarified and accumulated in a control pattern deployment chart and in control quality charts that were used in our day-to-day design activities for the system.

   The control pattern deployment chart (see Figure 3.10) clarifies the relationships between the machine's possible uses and its various component systems applications. Next, using the control quality chart (Figure 3.11), we deployed the characteristic target values further, as well as the requirements for each machine element. These quality deployment charts enabled us to clarify the quality characteristics relating to the variable-speed products that are the major components in a variable-speed system.

Improving Quality Targets for Use in Product Planning

Product planning is the starting point for new product development. Thus, successful product development depends on the quality targets established at the product planning stage. Variable-speed products are used in both simple and highly sophisticated systems as drive mechanisms for a variety of industrial machines that operate in a variety of ways. Because this is so, we needed to brush up the quality characteristics deployment chart and application deployment charts that we made for product planning. Those charts were based on product planning PT information that had been selected by the systems engineering department, sales engineering department, and the development design department. They were intended to improve our ability to:

- prevent omissions and errors in the deployment of quality characteristic details, thereby allowing us to better accommodate many different kinds of systems applications;
- add more sales points by comparing the characteristics of our own products with those of our competitors'products;
- create attractive and exciting qualities that would satisfy the desires and demands of our customers; and
- define basic functions and optional functions in order to respond to the need for diversification.

In determining the target values for various quality characteristics, we decided to rely on the experience and knowledge of the members of the planning team, and on a comparative study of our own products and competitive products. We emphasized compatibility with every type of application and machine, as well as superiority over our competition, in determining the highest level quality targets.

The following problems occurred in developing product A using this method to establish quality plan targets:

- The quality characteristic levels that we were capable of achieving varied considerably from the targets we had set, resulting in a need to develop new technology "seeds," which in turn caused engineering bottlenecks.
- In the trade-off between quality and cost, the quality target was given greater priority, and as a result, the cost target was not met.
- Solving engineering bottlenecks took a long time.
- The products we developed were compatible only in certain applications that used big systems with highly sophisticated controls — which, of course, became very competitive products (see Figure 3.12).

Later on, when we were planning product B, we used a quality characteristics level deployment chart and the characteristics level distribution chart in order to correct problems encountered with the quality targets that had been set previously for product A — in other words, to set more appropriate quality targets. In the quality characteristics level deployment chart, the third level of the quality target is determined by referring to the column for characteristics values in the quality characteristics deployment chart (see Figure 3.13). The characteristics level distribution chart enables us to evaluate the compatibility of various systems applications so we can set up third-level quality targets (see Figure 3.14).

Using the experience and knowledge of the product planning team and the results of a competitive comparison study, we established third-level quality targets as a first step toward determining quality targets for the major quality characteristics.

The second step was checking the quality levels that we had determined in the first step for their compatibility with systems applications. We did this with the aid of the control pattern deployment chart and the control quality charts used by the systems engineering departments. We also used records and the specification quotations provided by the sales department to make a characteristics level distribution chart for this integration. The third step, the integrated characteristics level distribution, was based on accumulated technology and the seed technology that we had been developing. We compared and used them to determine the final quality targets for the product.

Using this system, we were able to achieve the following results in establishing the quality targets for product B:

- We realized each of the major quality characteristic details without having to aim for the highest level of quality.
- We reduced the number of engineering bottlenecks that had hindered our ability to achieve quality targets.
- By differentiating between the quality targets for the base product and those for optional products, we established quality targets that allowed the base products to meet the requirements for compatibility with small- and medium-sized systems, a large number of which are present units in the marketplace, and allowed the optional products to meet the compatibility requirements for large-scale systems (see Figure 3.15).

More specifically, in developing product A we had to use high-cost components to solve the engineering bottlenecks that had been created in the effort to achieve the demanded quality targets for speed control precision (characteristics B in Figure 3.14). Characteristic b_3 has a high specification value, 0.01 percent. By using the characteristics level distribution charts in developing product B, we were able to demonstrate quantitatively that a 0.01-percent speed control precision level was required only in specific applications for systems S_1 and S_2, and that the B_2 level value was adequate for most general industrial applications. As a result, we set the target level at the B_2 value for the basic product and at the B_3 value for optional products. This enabled us to achieve a balance between quality and cost.

Future Goals

In product planning for product B, we introduced the quality characteristics level deployment chart and the characteristics level distribution chart. Using them enabled us to establish quality targets that were very compatible with the drive systems of various machines, ranging from small scale to large scale. However, there is still room for more study to develop a method for establishing a quality target level that would allow us to develop a product that would be more competitive and would have an even better quality-to-cost ratio. Furthermore, some problems arose as a consequence of not having enough data for the major quality characteristics and having to depend on the experience and knowledge of the product planning group members.

We would like to see more data become available for study in the future, as well as a statistical method that could be used to determine more accurate quality targets.

References

Akao, Yoji, et al (1983). "Quality Deployment including Cost, Reliability, and Engineering (Part 1): Design of Quality Cost and Reliability." *Quality*, Vol. 13, No. 3, JSQC.

Akao, Yoji; Shiino, Jun (1985). "Current Status of Quality Deployment in the Construction Industry." *Quality*, Vol. 15, No. 4, JSQC.

Aoyama, Noritoshi (1983). "Setup of Development Design and QC-Wise Approach at Tokyo Juki Kogyo." *Quality Control*, Vol. 34, No. 6, JUSE.

Ikezawa, Tatsuo (1982). "Rational Quality." *Quality Control*, Vol. 33, No. 8, JUSE.

Kano, Noraiki; Seraku, Nobuhiko; Takahashi, Fumio; Tsuji, Shinichi (1984). "Attractive Quality and Must-Be Quality." *Quality*, Vol. 14, No. 2, JSQC.

Kawano, Tetsuo (1984). "New Product Development by ADDS-Y Activity." *Quality Control*, Vol. 35, November special issue, JUSE.

Mizuno, Shigeru; Akao, Yoji (eds.) (1978). *Quality Function Deployment*. JUSE.

Oho, H. (1985). "The Trend of Variable Speed Application System." *Yaskawa Electric*, Vol. 49, No. 188, pp. 200-210.

Tsunoda, Katsuhiko; Yokoyama, Kiyoshi; Nishihara, Ryoji; and Tomizawa, Ichiro (1985). "TQC and Information Collection, Transmission, and Utilization." *Quality Control*, Vol. 36, No. 9, p. 85, JUSE.

Characteristics Value	No change in angle of light even when car is empty	Works when bouncing	Linked movement with steering wheel	Works in bad weather	Correct direction of light	Wide illumination	Bright even in down position	No scatter of light	Correct direction of light	Wide illumination	Bright lamp	Quality Characteristics (Counterpart Characteristics) 3rd	2nd	1st
	Demanded Quality 1st: Bright and Visible													
	2nd: Works in special environment				Works up close			Works in Distance						
JIS Specification				○	◎	◎	○	◎		◎	○	Distribution	Distribution	Light Distribution
160 ø						○	○			○	○	Size of lens	Distribution	Light Distribution
1°				▷		▷	◎		▷	▷	▷	Switch angle	Distribution	Light Distribution
± 4° (up/down left/right)							▷		◎		▷	Elevation angle	Distribution	Light Distribution
7.5cd/mm²						▷	▷			▷	○	Brightness	Light Flux	Light Distribution
> 0.9						▷	◎			▷	◎	Transmission factor	Light Flux	Light Distribution
> 0.9						▷	◎			▷	◎	Reflectivity	Light Flux	Light Distribution
3000° k							○				○	Chromaticity	Light Flux	Light Distribution
37.5/50w						▷	◎			▷	◎	Electric current	Light Flux	Light Distribution
12.8v							○				○	Voltage	Light Flux	Light Distribution
0.2 atm												Sealing	Efficiency	Life
SAE % Impact 95%												Filament strength	Efficiency	Life
Ar 80% N 20%												Property of sealed gas	Efficiency	Life
⋮												⋮		
⋮												Redundancy	⋮	Safety
5°	◎	◎	◎			◎			◎			Tracking angle	⋮	Safety

Chart 3-1. Example of a Quality Chart (For a Head Lamp)

Chart 3-2. Example of a Quality Chart Deployed for Quality Elements (Pre-fabricated Housing)

Quality Element \ Demanded Quality	Ease of living — Good for family life			Good Environment — Good area environment				Good Environment — Bright indoor		Good Environment — Quiet environment			Good Environment — Good indoor environment		
	Easy bathing (c)	Good for entertainment (c)	Comfortable dining (b)	Good natural environment (c)	Good transportation (c)	Good for studying (b)	Good for living (c)	Ease of lighting (b)	Good natural light (b)	No vibration from outside (b)	No noise from outside (a)	No leak of indoor sound (a)	Proper room temperature (a)	Proper humidity (a)	Fresh air (b)
Indoor Environment															
Openness	△1	△1	△3	△1				○9	◎15	△3	◎25		○15	◎25	◎15
Indoor lighting	○3	○3	○9					◎15	△3						
Cross ventilation	○3	△1	△3	△1				○9	○9	△3	○15	○5	○15	◎25	◎15
Draftiness	○3	△1	△3	△1				△1	△3	△3	○5	○15	◎25	◎25	○15
Heat insulation	○3	△1	△3								△5	○15	◎25	○5	
Heat retention	○3	△1	△3					△9			△5	○15	◎25	○15	
Condensation prevention	○3	△1	△3								△5	○15	○5		
Noise insulation	○3	○3	○3	△1				△1		◎15	◎25	◎25			
Floor impact insulation	△1	○3	○3							○15	○9	△5			
Quietness of appliances	○3	○3	○9									◎25			
Outdoor Environment															
Period of sunlight		△1	△3	○3			○3	○9	○9				△5	△3	○15
Atmosphere pollution			○3	○3	△1				△5						○9
Noise level		△1		○3	○3					○5	◎25	◎15	○15		
Residential Facility															
Transportation				○3	◎5	○9	○3				○3	○9	○15		
Shopping				○3	○3	△3	◎5				△3	○5			
Administrative services				○3	○3	○9	◎5								
Medical facilities				○3	○3	△3	◎5								
Educational facilities				○3	○3	◎15	○3								
Leisure facilities		△1		○3	○3	△3	◎5				△3		○15		

Symbols: ◎ = strong relationship, ○ = medium relationship, △ = weak relationship; accompanying figures indicate degree of importance.

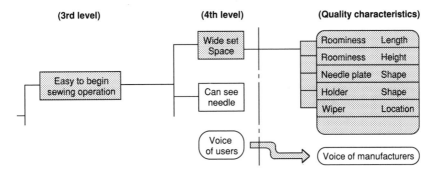

Figure 3-1. Quality Characteristics Deployment

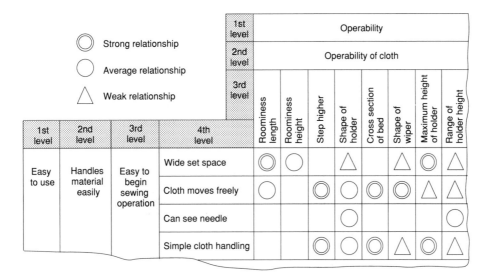

Figure 3-2. Two-dimensional Chart

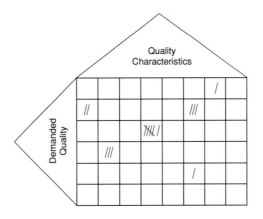

Figure 3-3. Example of a Complaint Check

Overall Evaluation of Quality Characteristics

		Roominess length	Roominess height	Step height	Cylindrical cross-section	Wiper shade	Max. height of holder	Range of holder height
Overall Score		210	54	48	170	53	245	46

Evaluation Points — Quality Characteristics
Quality Deployment 4th level

		Roominess length	Roominess height	Step height	Cylindrical cross-section	Wiper shade	Max. height of holder	Range of holder height
Wide set space	15	75 ◎	45 ○			15 △	75 ◎	15 △
Cloth moves freely	6	18 ◎		30 ◎	30 ◎	18 ○	18 ○	6 △
Can see needle	2							6 ○
Simple handling of cloth	18			18 △	90 ◎	18 △	90 ◎	18 △

Characteristics Value		Roominess length	Roominess height	Step height	Cylindrical cross-section	Wiper shade	Max. height of holder	Range of holder height
	Specification							±2
	Design target	400	210	2	45x45	A Ranking	20	2 step type
	Our current product	315	210	4.5	60x50	A Ranking	15	N/A
	Co. B	300	240	1.8	55x50	B Ranking	16	N/A
	Co. A	350	210	3	60x45	A Ranking	15	N/A

Notes: Conversion from demanded quality evaluation (degree of importance) to quality characteristics overall evaluation (degree of importance): ◎= 5, ○ = 3, △ = 1. Description of first column: the 1st column is 15 x 5 = 75, the 2nd column is 15 x 3 = 45 and the 5th column is 15 x 1 =15. The other columns are evaluated in similar manner. The vertical sum of these points is the overall score.

Figure 3-4. Quality Characteristics Evaluation

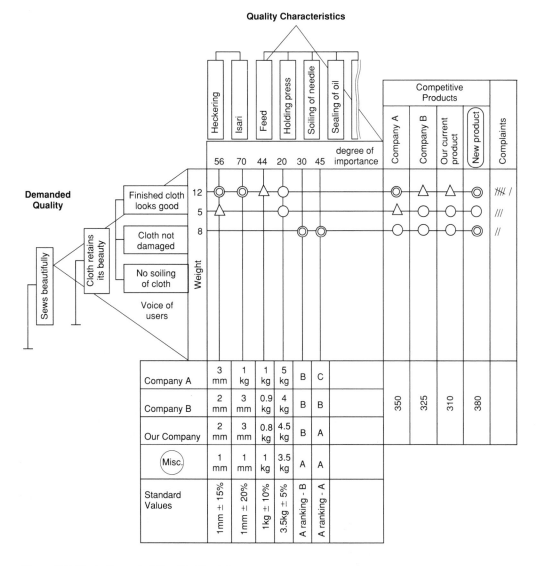

Figure 3-5. Basic Format of Quality Chart A

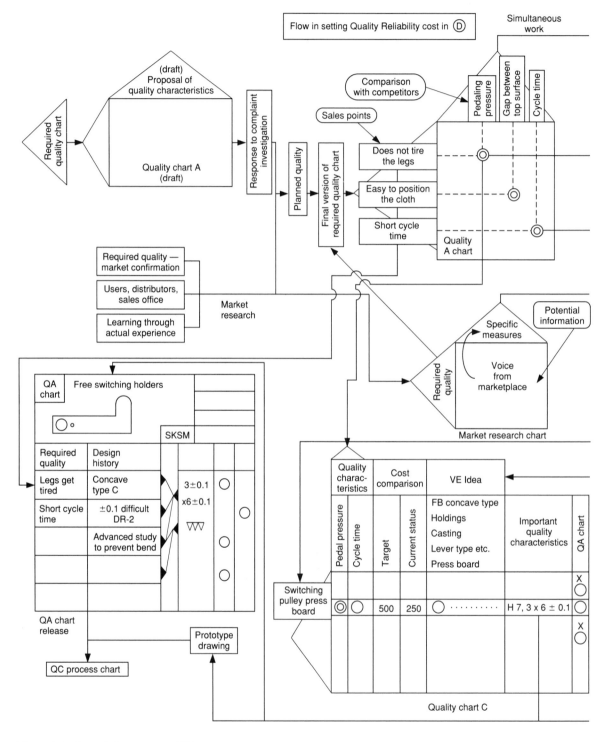

Figure 3-6. Overall Summary of QFD

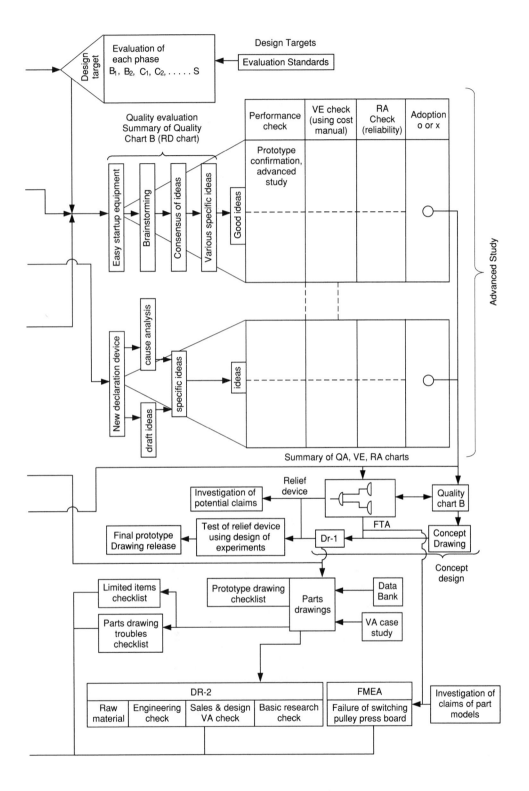

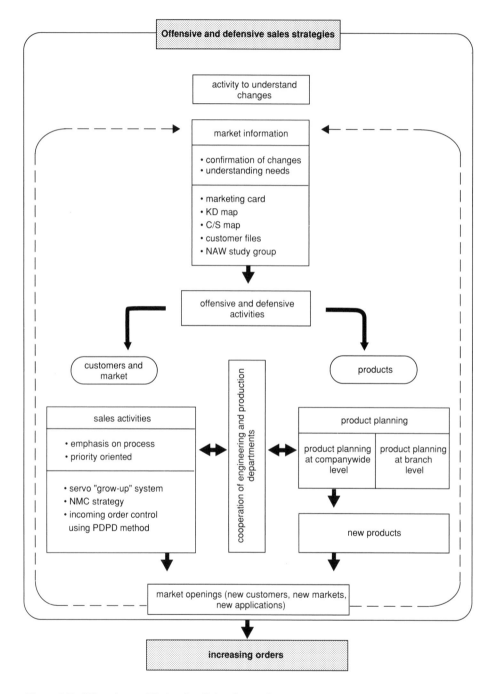

Figure 3-7. Offensive and Defensive Sales Strategies

			quality characteristics deployment	quality application deployment

counterpart quality characteristics/ application			1st level	01	electrical characteristics								01	application							
demanded quality			2nd level	011	power source		012	rating		013			011	simple variable speed system							
			3rd level	0111	0112	•	•	0121	0122	•	•	•	•	0111	0112	•	•	•	•	•
1st level	2nd level	3rd level		voltage	frequency (Hz)	•	•	•	•	•	•	•	fan blower	pump	•	•	•	•	•	•

01	011	0111	motor appropriate to increased capacities		○		○	○				○	○	○	◎	◎	◎	○
	a lot of functions	0112	wide capacity range for 200V class		○			○				○	○					
		•						○					○		○			
		•		○	○		○		○					○				
		•		○	△						○	○	△	○		△		
012 variety of operating modes	0121										○	○	◎	◎	◎	◎		
	0122																	
	•																	
	•																	

		•									○		○		○			
		•									○	○	○	○	○	○		
		•									○	○		○	○			
11	111	1111									○	△						
		•									△	○	○					

	planning characteristics	200/220V	50/60Hz	•	•	•
our company	product X					
	product Y					
competitors' products	Company A					
	Company B					
	Company C					
	Company D					

Figure 3-8. Quality Characteristics and Application Deployment Charts

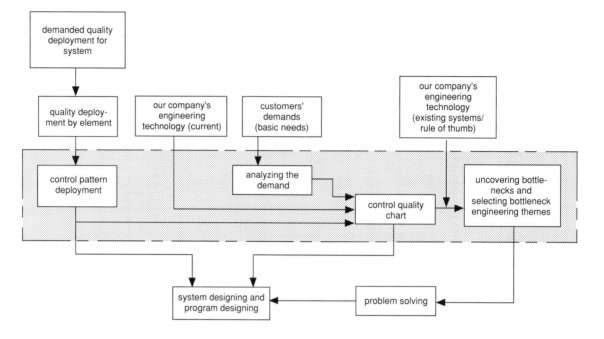

* This lists the demanded functions and performance in patterns and characteristic values to be used for performance analysis.

Figure 3-9. Variable-speed Drive System Design Flow Chart (Partial)

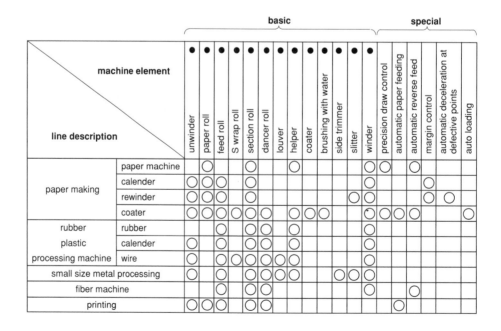

Figure 3-10. Control Pattern Deployment Chart (Application Deployment)

machine element / control item	speed						tension				
	set	**set**	**control**	**control**	**control**	**control**	**set**	**set**	**control**	**control**	
	range [m/mm]	slow movement/inching [m/mm]	resolution [%]	precision [%]	response [rad/sec]	sagging characteristics	range [kg]	resolution [%]	precision [%]	response [rad/sec]	looper position accuracy ±100mm
center	10-80	25	0.1	±1	30						
intake side	10-120	25	0.1	±1	30						
outlet side	10-130	25	0.1	±1	30						
bay off reel	10-120	25	0.1				60-650	0.1	±3	130	
No. 1 bridle	10-120	25	0.1	±1	30						
intake accumulator	0-105	25	0.1				200-1000	0.1	±3	5	±100[mm]
No. 2 bridle	10-80	25	0.1			10					
brush scotch	10-80	25	0.1			5					
No. 3 bridle	10-80	25	0.1	±1	30						
No. 4 bridle	10-80	25	0.1								
laminator	10-80	25	0.1			5					
chlorinated vinyl boss	10-80	25	0.1			5					
No. 7 bridle	10-80	25	0.1			10					
No. 6 bridle (leveler)	10-80	25	0.1	±1	30						
No. 7 bridle	10-80	25	0.1			10					

Figure 3-11. Control Quality Chart

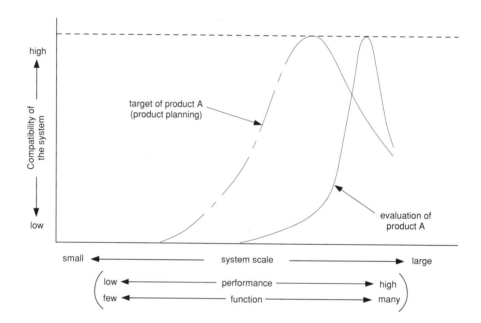

Figure 3-12. Product A Compatibility Evaluation

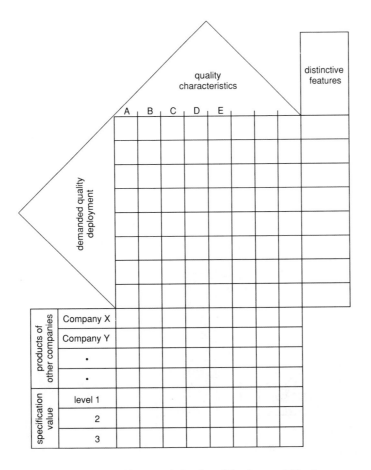

Figure 3-13. Quality Characteristics Level Deployment Chart

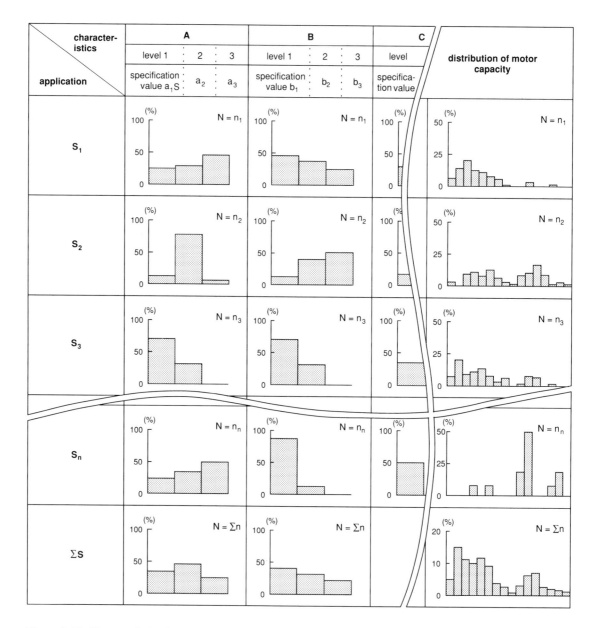

Figure 3-14. Characteristics Level Distribution Chart

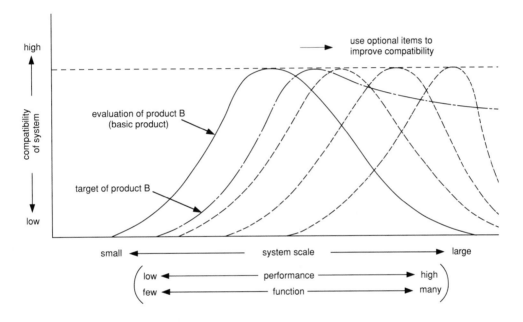

Figure 3-15. Evaluation of Compatibility for Product B System

Using Quality Deployment Charts: Subsystems, Parts Deployment, Quality Assurance Charts

Hideaki Aoki, Assistant Chief of No. 2 Engineering Department, and Yukio Kawasaki, Department Head, Toyoda Gosei Company; and Takao Taniguchi, Engineering Head, Aishin-Warner

In previous chapters, we defined quality deployment as converting the user's demand into quality characteristics, identifying the related product design quality elements, and systematically deploying the relationships among these into the quality of each functional part, the quality of individual parts, and even the essentials of the manufacturing processes. This chapter will describe the deployment of quality to subsystems, parts, and processes — focusing mainly on the procedure for making a quality deployment chart. This procedure can involve many departments and engineers when we are deploying quality to subsystems, parts, and processes.

Since industries and the products they make may differ enormously, you should develop and use quality deployment charts in a way that seems appropriate for your own company and invites participation by everyone. Figure 4.1 shows the overall flow of quality function deployment.

Detailed Design and Preproduction Steps for Deploying Quality to Parts and Subsystems

Quality function deployment begins with the quality plan and quality design. Charts 1, 2 and 3 of Figure 4.1 show the basic relationship between demanded quality and quality characteristics. Machined-assembled products usually consist of many elements, including subsystems, component units, and parts. At the detailed design stage, it is important to clarify the relationships between the quality demanded for the final product and the quality characteristics necessary for each part. This process is called subsystem deployment, but you could also call it target or goal deployment — that is, deploying the demanded quality into the *means* such as subsystems to achieve the objective — and then linking each of them with the required engineering.

Chart 1.7 in Chapter 1 shows an example of first-level, second-level, and third-level deployment of quality into subsystems, units, and parts for Company F's radio control system. This deployment consists of the following steps:

1. Deploy quality characteristics into the subsystem, unit, and parts, in that order, and express the relationships between the results and the final product quality characteristics with symbols such as ◎ (strong relationship), ○ (moderately strong relationship), and Δ (weak relationship).

2. Clarify the functions of the unit parts, the part quality characteristics, the specifications, and so on. At this stage, you should also review complaints that have been collected regarding each unit and part (of current and similar products), as well as related product liability (P/L) matters. Doing this will enable you to designate parts that have been the subject of P/L-related complaints as critical safety parts and critical functional parts. Special attention should be given to process controls for these parts.

Unfortunately, quality deployment to subsystem levels can be quite voluminous, so it is best limited to approximately third-level parts. The deployment from critical component units to individual parts deployment charts can help prevent too much complexity.

Chart 4.1 shows the parts deployment for an electric light bulb, which is the component unit subsystem deployed in Figure 4.1, chart 3. You can see, for example, that materials, wire diameter, and wire length have been identified as the elements governing the quality of the filament, which in turn influences such final product characteristics as brightness and color temperature. In other words, the final product quality has been related to part quality.

Process Deployment

Quality assurance (QA) charts identify the control items that must be incorporated in the process design to implement the quality characteristics being deployed. In other words, the QA chart communicates design objectives and QA points to the production team.

Quality function deployment starts with the customers' demands and deploys them into the unit components, which are then moved into the production process. Charts 4, 5, and 6 of Figure 4.1 depict this flow — which includes two major steps:

1. *Selection of part quality standards, inspection items, and inspection standards.* Based on the deployment described above, a thorough prototype evaluation should be conducted as an assurance audit of the designed quality in order to set up production criteria. Next, inspection standards must be established, including the characteristics to be inspected, the part quality standards (which indicate the quality characteristics levels to be assured for each part), and the inspection methods to be used.

2. *Facility and process deployment.* The process flow from raw material to final product, as well as the necessary facility and process conditions, are summarized in a process plan chart. The quality characteristics and the quality standards for parts, interim products, and semiproducts — as determined by the quality function deployment — must be deployed into process control items (check points). These deployments are summarized in the QA charts or the QC process plan charts.

Chart 4.2 shows a QC process plan chart for the electric light bulb that was used as an example in Figure 4.1. For example, when control points are being established for assurance of quality characteristics in the degassing process, "vacuum level" and "gas pressure" are identified as the control points because the outcome of the vacuum process affects the "life" and "anti-vibration property" of electric light bulbs. In other words, the characteristics of an electric light bulb (part) are converted, or related, to process control points. These control points are transferred to the QC process chart, as shown in Figure 4.1, chart 6.

Normally, the production engineering department develops the process design, but the QA chart or QC process plan chart is an important connection and device for information transmission between the design and production departments. Therefore, thorough communication prior to the preparation of these charts is essential.

The QC process plan chart for critical units or critical parts should be prioritized according to the magnitude of the process or its degree of newness. Either the QA chart or QC process plan chart specifies who is involved, and when. This information can be transferred to the QC process chart, which becomes the basis for quality assurance on the production floor.

Summary

Competition in new product development — which is the basis for almost any industry's survival — is ever intensifying, and the time available for developing new products is, in general, being shortened. Under these conditions, quality function deployment is the best short-cut, no matter how time-consuming it may seem. The quality function deployment chart incorporates control engineering and engineering technology, and once prepared it can be applied to similar products, which will then also benefit from a shorter development period.

Finally, product development is not always an orderly process, and often the development of several products overlaps. Under these circumstances, the parties involved need to communicate effectively with each other. The quality function deployment chart is a device that enhances communication among all participants.

The Role of Quality Function Deployment Charts in the Network of Assurance: The Case of Toyoda Gosei

In the automotive industry, Toyoda Gosei is an exclusive manufacturer of rubber and plastic parts. Our quality assurance activity is based on the concept of supplying high-reliability products that anticipate the needs of the market and consumers, under management's "Quality First" motto.

Our company works with polymer products that are susceptible to various stresses encountered in automotive use and its environment. Many of our products are also governed by safety and a variety of other laws and regulations. Given these company characteristics and some reflection upon our past development failures, our main emphases in this quality assurance activity are:

- engineering development that anticipates the needs of the market and the consumer, and
- thorough study of the product concept before design and development begins, guaranteed communication of information to the downstream process, and deployment of various QC methods. Quality deployment and the use of various quality charts throughout product planning and production are key elements in these quality assurance activities.

The Structure of Quality Assurance and Quality Function Deployment

Our quality function deployment is based on the use of the quality charts numbered I through V in Figure 4.2, on a network of assurance, and on the QC process chart. Figure 4.2 shows the orientation of all of these within the structure of quality assurance. Quality charts I and II, quality charts III and IV, quality chart V, and the "network of assurance" are used at the stages of product planning, product design, and production preparation, respectively, and all are connected to the QC process chart.

Using the Quality Function Deployment Chart

Overview

Figure 4.3 is a schematic representation of the roles played by various kinds of quality charts in quality function deployment and in the "network of assurance." The quality charts used are: I (demanded quality versus quality characteristics deployment), II (demanded quality characteristics and means of implementing them), III (deployment of demanded quality characteristics versus part characteristics), and IV and V (deployment of part characteristics versus process characteristics at the prototype and preproduction stage). Here, quality charts IV and V are similar except that quality chart IV specifies the methods and conditions of prototype production, whereas quality chart V specifies the process deployment for mass production. Chart V is based on quality charts IV and I and III, which themselves are based on the "network of assurance." There is also a pre-problem study using failure mode and effects analysis (FMEA) and fault tree analysis (FTA). Therefore, quality charts I, III, and IV play an important role in transmitting information from the design stage to the preproduction stage.

At the production stage, we apply quality assurance intensively in the effort to achieve "no defects made or passed on" status. One important part of these activities is preventing avoidable human errors. (From now on, we will call these mistakes "defects.") We emphasize mistake-proofing at the preproduction stage by predicting what defects will occur and what impact they will have on critical control items. Figure 4.4 outlines this activity, in which the "network of assurance" plays an important role. The network of assurance consists of a matrix of defects to be prevented and the related processes, as well as checks for defect occurrence, defect flow prevention, and the status of the assurance.

Examples

Figure 4.5 shows quality charts III, IV, and V for product A. In this case, we are not deploying subsystem elements; we are deploying various design elements at the parts level, called parts characteristics, into details on quality chart III.

For new products or parts, we often cannot set the target levels at the product planning or initial design stages so that they will be built-in as part characteristics. In these cases, targets have to be established by identifying engineering bottlenecks and studying them at the predesign stage or on the results of FTA studies conducted at the design stage. In other words, quality chart III is revised as development progresses.

Figures 4.5-1 and 4.5-2 are examples of establishing tolerances on the basis of a new engineering study, which is reflected in quality charts III and IV. The tolerance study data — along with quality charts III and IV — are transmitted to the preproduction department to serve as base information for establishing tolerances.

As shown in Figure 4.5, in quality chart V, we evaluate process characteristics (items to be controlled within a process) by rating them , using what we call evaluation points. These evaluation points are derived according to the following formula:

Evaluation points = Σ (degree of importance of part characteristics)
$\times$ degree of importance of process characteristics
$\times$ degree of interrelationship

Process characteristics with a high score are identified as critical control items.

Figure 4.6 shows an example of an activity — based on FTA and a network of assurance — that is intended to prevent defects from being either generated or passed on. In general, this network of assurance works somewhat like a QA chart. FTA is performed on a new process where defects have been singled out for improvement, with a goal of achieving less than 6 RPN.

While checking for defects that might be generated and passed along throughout the production process, and using the network of assurance to involve plant personnel, we try to improve control items that appear to be inadequate for preventing defects (as indicated by $\bigcirc$ or Δ symbols). Then we revise the network of assurance where necessary.

The results of all this work are transmitted to the appropriate plant departments for deployment into QC process charts, work standards, and operating manuals for the production floor.

Results

The benefits of introducing the concept of quality function deployment, the use of the quality chart, and related procedures into new product development and QA activities are:

• the development of a new product that meets customers' demands, leads the market, can be developed in a timely manner, and wins the trust of our customers; and

• improvement of interdepartmental cooperation and communication of development-related information, identification of problems at the initial stage of product development, and predesign studies, resulting in large-scale reductions in development time and process time (see Figure 4.7).

Summary

A trend toward product diversification, multifunctioning, and cost reduction is becoming more and more evident these days. To ensure survival, we must stay ahead of this trend by creating new engineering and new products. Improvement in control engineering and technology is, therefore, essential. Quality function deployment can play an important role in meeting these challenges because the emphasis is on:

- information control connected to medium- and long-term development plans that are oriented to anticipating needs;
- reliability control in response to the demands for polymer substances; and
- enhanced design engineering using simulation.

Although we could not introduce them here because of limited space, in addition to the activities described above, we are conducting materials quality function deployment as a step in parts deployment, and quality function deployment for equipment and facilities. For further information on these subjects, we direct the reader to the Okumoto and Kurashige references at the end of this chapter.

We hope this case study will be useful to those who are interested in this subject.

Developing Automatic Transmissions for Automobiles: The Case of Aishin-Warner

Our company is an exclusive manufacturer of automobile automatic transmissions (A/T), involved with development, production, and sales. The automatic transmission is an important functional part of a vehicle, assuring efficient transmission of engine output. It is also strongly related to various aspects of vehicle reliability and quality, including fuel consumption, driveability, and noise. Accordingly, since our company was founded, it has pursued a management strategy based on the concept of "quality supremacy". Our new product development activity is based on the philosophy that the product must always be conceived from the viewpoint of the user and that the company's long-term progress must be planned in relation to that viewpoint. Our company's new product development organization is shown in Figure 4.8, where the activities of quality function deployment, design, and test evaluation are stratified and correlated in parallel for each step of quality assurance. Our deployment of new product development is based on the application of quality charts for each step of quality assurance. These will be described next, with an example of design optimization for a damper disc, which is used as our new product C.

Product Concept Stage

Smaller size and higher rotational speeds are the demands for improved function we had to meet for new product C. In addition, development time had to be short if we were to match our customer's vehicle production schedule. Using the quality charts shown in Figure 4.9, we established a target plan. By eliminating various concept plans, we finally came up with one basic concept drawing. Once we had produced the drawing, we recognized an engineering problem that could cause damage to the damper disc. Figure 4.10 shows how we used the quality chart at this stage.

Product Planning Stage

We used the finite element method (FEM) analysis to build in quality during the product planning stage. As shown in Figure 4.9 (1), the result of the test plan analysis differed from the FEM engineering model analysis. Therefore, we had to study the applicability of FEM modeling — first, by making an engineering model, and then by measuring stresses and comparing them to the stress values generated by the FEM analysis. Further, as indicated in Figure 4.9 (2), we used FTA to identify the factors related to strength, and then, using the test plan method, we applied FEM analysis to those factors. In the course of doing this, we realized that we could use FEM to predict the stress value. Thereby, we decided to perform an experiment using design of experiments. We constructed an orthogonal array (see Figure 4.9) using dimensions A, B, ... as the factors. Then, by analyzing the data from the FEM, we were able to express quantitatively the degree of contribution of stress reduction and to develop a formula for predicting stress.

Product Design Stage

During the product design stage, we developed two plans for deploying factors A, B, and E in such a way as to minimize stress under prevailing constraints, such as space and availability of material. Then we developed a stress prediction formula, which is shown in Figure 4.11 (1). Next we compared and evaluated these plans with respect to product engineering to establish a final plan.

Once we had a final plan, we repeated the stress evaluation by FEM analysis. We started work on the detailed design. After confirming the safety factor, using an ultra-small telemeter, we measured the actual stresses on the prototype at high rpm. As Figure 4.11 (2) indicates, test evaluations for the final plan confirmed a correspondence between the measurement and the FEM analysis results. At the same time, test evaluations showed that we were achieving our targeted performance and durability levels. The evaluation results on safety strength and deformation at high rpm were also good.

Conclusion

The pursuit of new products and quality are the ever-present goals in our new product development activities. Introducing quality charts and applying the concept of quality function deployment in the development of product C produced the following benefits:

- Identifying, clarifying, and solving engineering problems related to demanded quality at the upstream end of the development process enabled us to develop a new product in a more timely manner than would otherwise have been possible.
- Quality-related information was communicated among departments more smoothly, and more development activity was deployed throughout the company at the upstream stages.
- From planning to preproduction, we were able to see more clearly the relationships between systems, which provided us with a structure that enabled us to cope with more diversified development projects.

References

Akao, Yoji (1983). "On the Recent Trend of Quality Deployment." *Quality*, Vol. 13, No. 3, pp. 9-19, JSQC.

Akao, Yoji (1986). "The Practice of Application of Quality Deployment for New Product Development, General Theory of Quality Deployment." *Standardization and Quality Control*, Vol. 39, No.4, pp. 63-72, Japan Standards Association.

Akao, Yoji; Ono, Sadatoshi; Harada, Akira; Tanaka, H.; Iwasawa, Kazuo (1983). "Quality Deployment including Cost, Reliability, and Technology (Part 2)." *Quality*, Vol. 13, No. 3, pp. 71-77, JSQC.

Ishikawa, Kaoru (1983). "Quality and Reliability." *Quality*, Vol. 13, No. 1, pp. 5-10, JSQC.

Kawai, Maso; Hayabuchi, Masahiro (1983). "Design of A/T Parts by using FEM." *Quality Control*, Vol. 34, No. 5, pp. 47-50, JUSE.

Kurashige, M.; Kamobe, Masatoshi (1985). "Quality Deployment for Equipment Design." *Quality Control*, Vol. 36, Nov. special issue, pp. 228-231, JUSE.

Mizuno, Shigeru; Akao, Yoji, eds. (1978). *Quality Function Deployment*. JUSE.

Moroto, Shuzo (1983). "Future TQC Viewed from New Products." *Quality Control*, Vol. 34, No. 4, pp. 15-19, JUSE.

Okumoto, T. (1983). "Application of Quality Chart for Material Development for Rubber Products." *Quality Control*, Vol. 34, Nov. special issue, pp. 276-281, JUSE.

Shindo, Hisakazu; Kubota, Yasuhiko; Uchida, Takeharu (1986). "The Practice of Application of Quality Deployment for New Product Development, Application of Demanded Quality Deployment Chart: Determining Planned Quality." *Standardization and Quality Control*, Vol. 39, No. 5, pp. 72-84, Japan Standards Association.

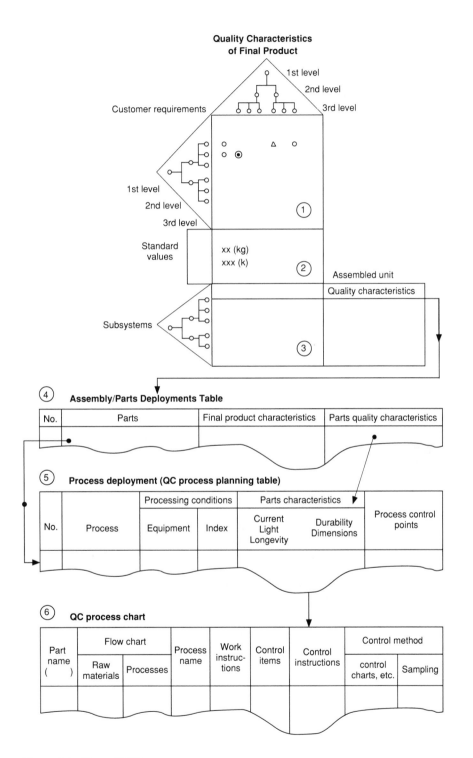

Figure 4-1. Flow of QFD

No.	Parts	Final product characteristics	Part quality characteristics
1	Bulb	% of light transmitted	Glass thickness
		Volume of bulb	Dimensions, shape
2	Filament	High-/low-beam switching angle	High-/low-beam filament positions
		Luminous intensity	Diameter, length, composition
		Color/temperature	"
3	Shade	Light distribution	Position, shape, dimensions
5	Terminal	Tightness of connection	Dimensions
		Dimensions	"
		Material	"

Chart 4-1. Parts Deployment Table of Assembled Unit (Electric Light Bulb)

No.	Process	Processing conditions		Parts characteristics							Process control points
		Equipment	Index	Current	Beam	Longevity	Vibration-resistance	Dimensions	Others		
1	Flaring process	Flaring machine	2-3 seconds					○	○		Inner/outer diameters, thickness, dimensions, cracks and scratches
2	Stem processing	Stem former machine	2-3 seconds					◎	○		Dimensions, internal strain, temperature
3	Mounting process	Mounting machine	5 seconds	◎	◎	◎	◎	◎	○		L.C.L. filament gap
4	Sealing	Sealing machine	3-5 seconds					○	○		External appearance, dimensions, strain
5	Exhausting air	Air exhausting machine	3-5 seconds	Δ	○	◎	○		○		Vacuum level, gas pressure
8	Final inspection	Photometer		±10%							(± 10% 850 6251m)
		Longevity tester				600/700					
		Vibration tester					JIS D 1601				(JIS D 1601 4G level; 8 hr)

Chart 4-2. Process Deployment (QC Process Planning Chart)

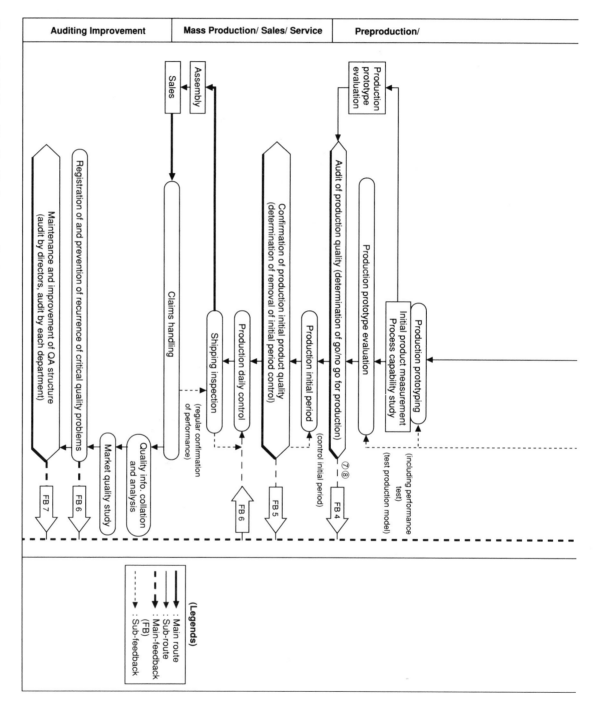

Figure 4-2. Outline of the Quality Assurance System

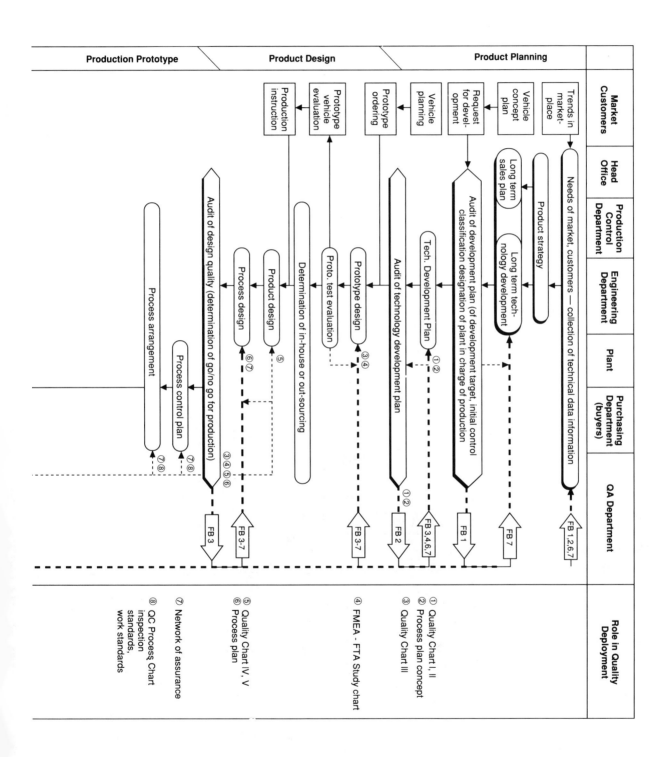

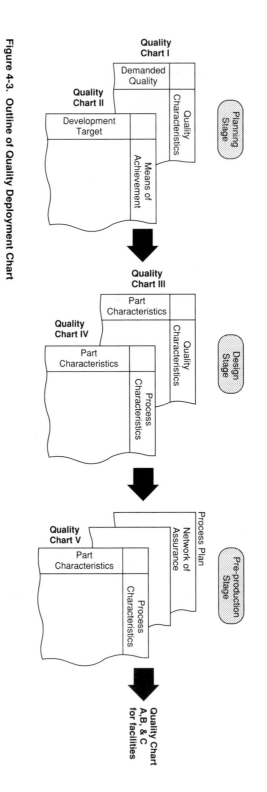

Figure 4-3. Outline of Quality Deployment Chart

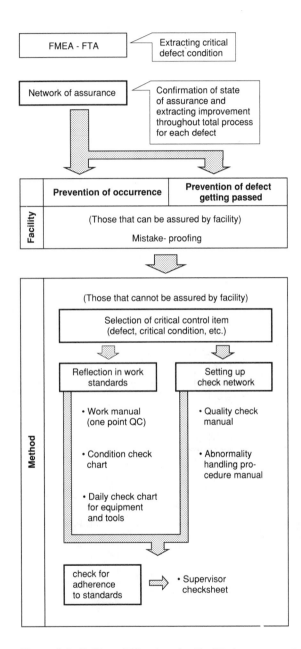

**Figure 4-4. Outline of Structure for Facility Improvement
and Standards of the "Network of Assurance"**

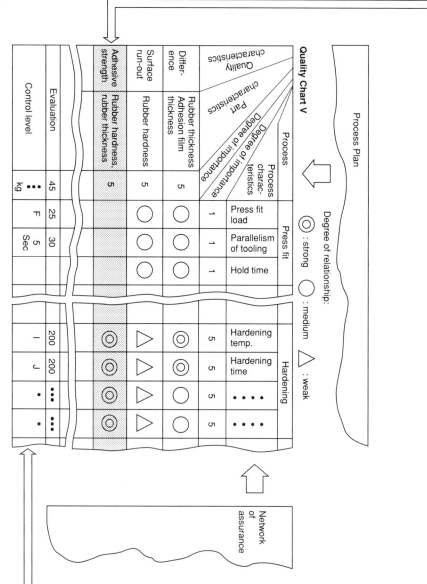

Figure 4-5. Example of Quality Charts III, IV, and V (Product A)

Note: Demanded quality characteristics are deployed into part characteristics in Quality Chart III. The extracting of part characteristics is performed by accumulating technology on similar products or pre-studying engineering bottlenecks (see Figure 4-1). Part characteristics tolerances are established as a level of target for part characteristics (ex. rubber thickness tolerance, t+δt). Quality Chart IV is the deployment of the relationship between critical part characteristics at the prototype stage and the conditions for production; no. ⑯ of the figure indicates Figure 4-2. That is, it clarifies the production conditions necessary to build-in part characteristics. Quality Chart V deploys part characteristics and process characteristics for production processes. Process characteristics are singled out based on Quality Chart IV and the network of assurance. Upon confirmation of assurance of quality characteristics and process capability of part characteristics, the level of controlling end process characteristics is established.

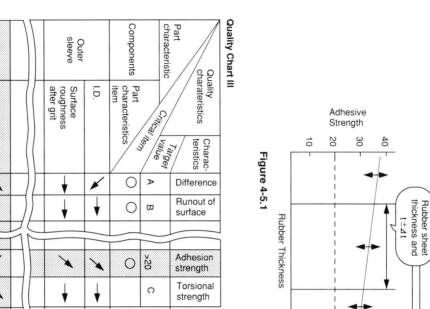

Figure 4-5.1

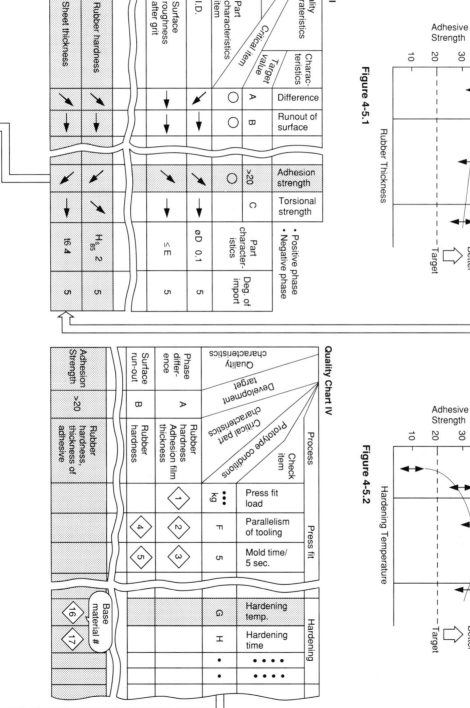

Figure 4-5.2

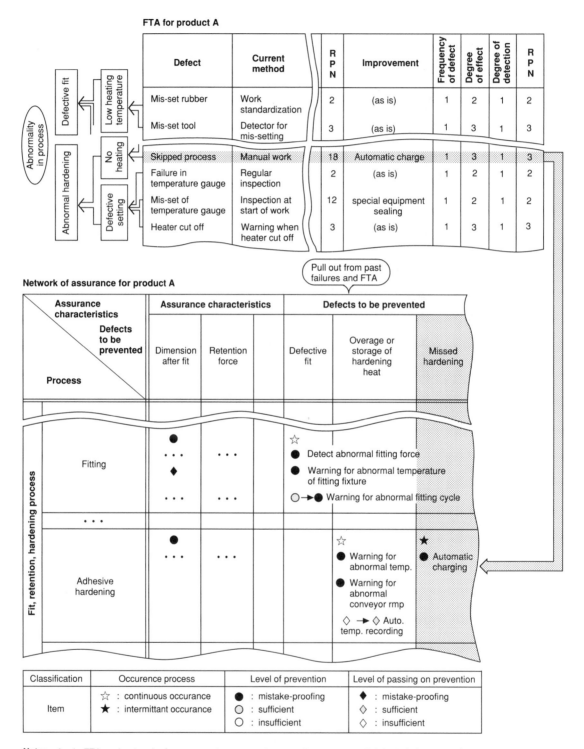

Figure 4-6. Preventing the Generation and Passing on of Defects by the Network of Assurance and FTA

Notes: Apply FTA and network of assurance to process to prevent occurrence of defects being passed on. Defect is predicted for new process by FTA of process and check (RPN evaluation) of current status for process planning. Improvement is made to high RPN (above 6) to make it below RPN 6. (ex: manual work [RPN:18] ◊ Automatic charging [RPN:3]). Meanwhile, the network of assurance is used to check the status of the prevention of occurrence and passing on throughout the total process the defects to be prevented or pulled out through cooperation between engineering and the plant. Automatic charging (mistake-proofing) for "missed hardening" by FTA brought the prevention level to: ●.

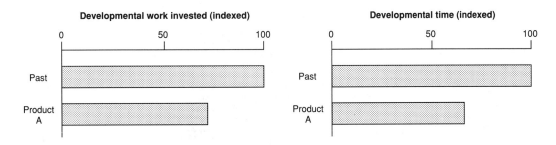

Figure 4-7. The Effect of Quality Deployment Activity on Product A

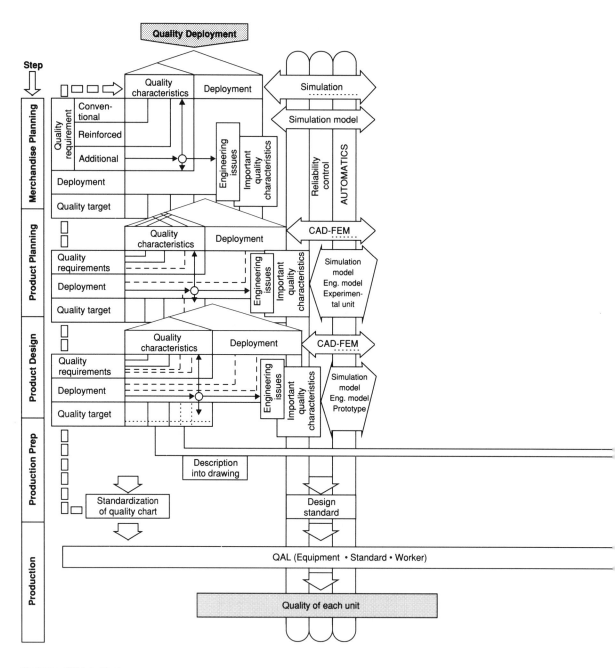

Features of the system:

1. Quality requirement, function mechanism, and quality characteristics are deployed in detail according to quality assurance step. Each engineering issue is defined and deployed as well as establishment of each target from development target to quality target and design quality.

2. For early solution of engineering issues reliability control, our management information system AUTOMATICS and PM are utilized.

Figure 4-8. New Product Development System

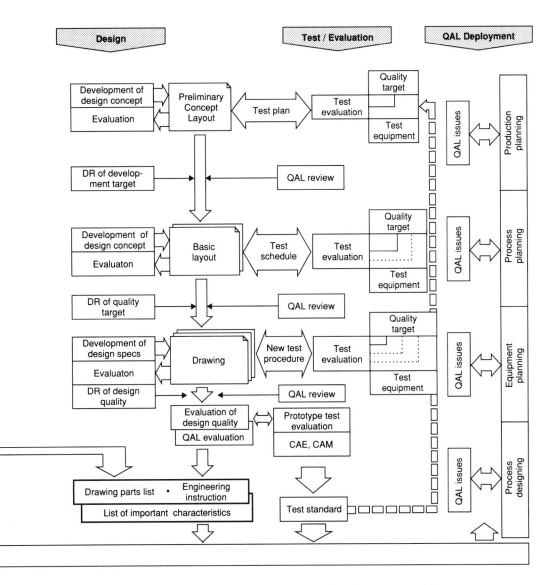

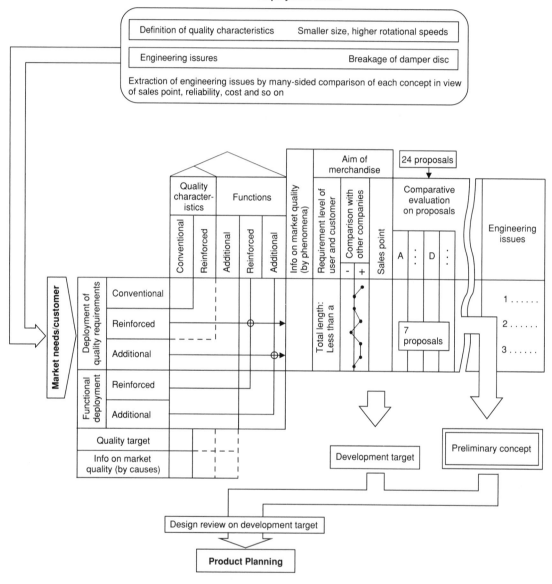

(1) Reinforced additional items are focused as object of quality deployment by stratification of quality requirement from market intoconventional, reinforced and additional items.

(2) Preliminary concept and engineering issues are defined by functional deployment and mechanical deployment in parallel with deployment of quality requirements.

Figure 4-9. Establishing a Development Target and Preliminary Concept (Merchandise Planning Step)

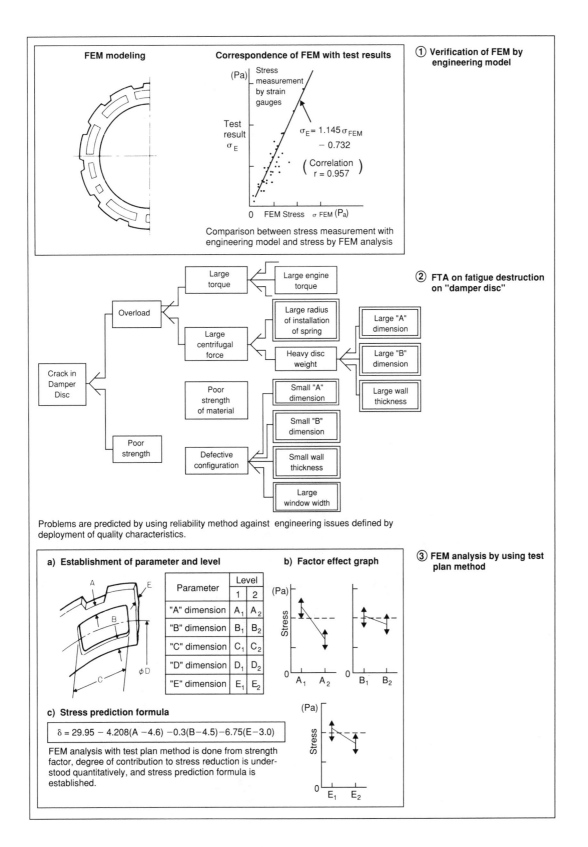

FEM modeling

Correspondence of FEM with test results

(Pa)

Stress measurement by strain gauges

Test result σ_E

$\sigma_E = 1.145\,\sigma_{FEM} - 0.732$

$\left(\begin{array}{c} \text{Correlation} \\ r = 0.957 \end{array} \right)$

0   FEM Stress σ_{FEM} (Pa)

Comparison between stress measurement with engineering model and stress by FEM analysis

① **Verification of FEM by engineering model**

② **FTA on fatigue destruction on "damper disc"**

Crack in Damper Disc
- Overload
  - Large torque — Large engine torque
  - Large centrifugal force
    - Large radius of installation of spring
    - Heavy disc weight
      - Large "A" dimension
      - Large "B" dimension
      - Large wall thickness
- Poor strength
  - Poor strength of material — Small "A" dimension
  - Defective configuration
    - Small "B" dimension
    - Small wall thickness
    - Large window width

Problems are predicted by using reliability method against engineering issues defined by deployment of quality characteristics.

③ **FEM analysis by using test plan method**

a) Establishment of parameter and level

Parameter	Level	
	1	2
"A" dimension	A_1	A_2
"B" dimension	B_1	B_2
"C" dimension	C_1	C_2
"D" dimension	D_1	D_2
"E" dimension	E_1	E_2

b) Factor effect graph

(Pa) Stress — A_1 A_2

Stress — B_1 B_2

(Pa) Stress — E_1 E_2

c) Stress prediction formula

$\delta = 29.95 - 4.208(A - 4.6) - 0.3(B - 4.5) - 6.75(E - 3.0)$

FEM analysis with test plan method is done from strength factor, degree of contribution to stress reduction is understood quantitatively, and stress prediction formula is established.

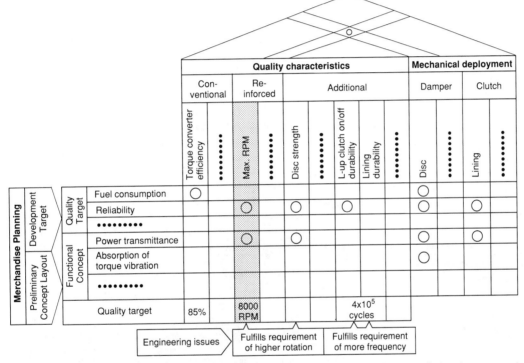

Quality requirement is deployed into function and mechanism based on preliminary concept layout, quality target is established and new engineering issues are defined.

Figure 4-10. Setting Quality Targets (Product Planning Stage)

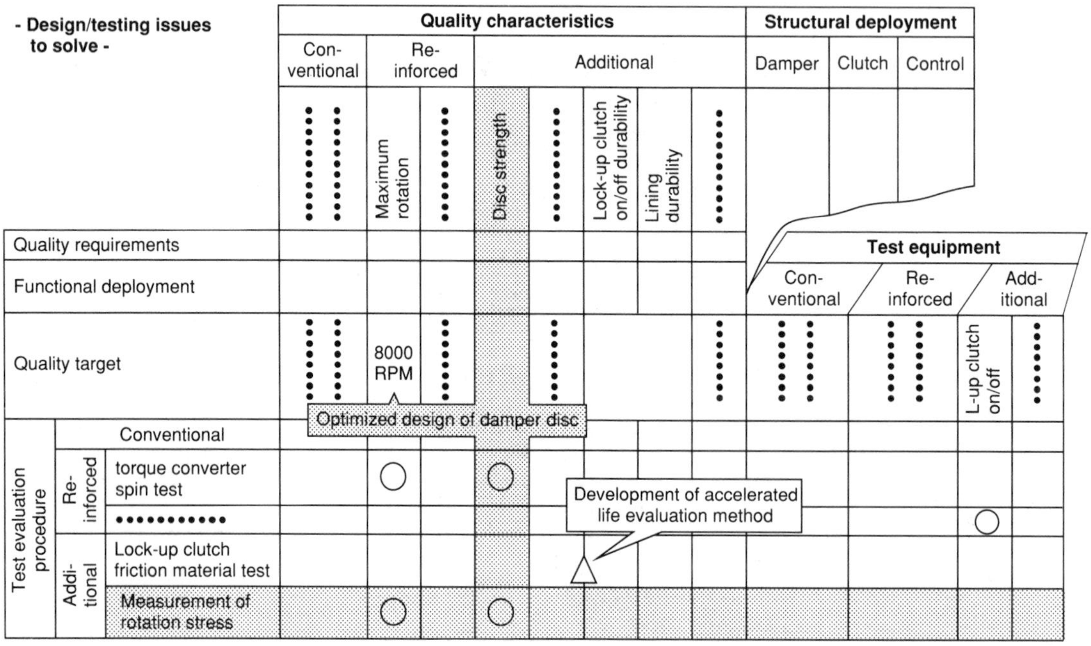

- Design/testing issues to solve -		Quality characteristics							Structural deployment		
		Con- ventional	Re- inforced	Additional					Damper	Clutch	Control
		••••	Maximum rotation ••••	Disc strength	••••	Lock-up clutch on/off durability	Lining durability	••••			
Quality requirements									Test equipment		
Functional deployment									Con- ventional	Re- inforced	Add- itional
Quality target		••••	8000 RPM ••••	••••	••••			••••	••••	••••	L-up clutch on/off	••••
		Optimized design of damper disc									
Test evaluation procedure	Re-inforced	Conventional torque converter spin test	○	○							
		••••••••••								○	
	Addi-tional	Lock-up clutch friction material test			△	Development of accelerated life evaluation method					
		Measurement of rotation stress	○	○							

Make a matrix of quality characteristics, test evaluation procedure and test equipment, development of new test procedure, and early procurement of test equipment.

Figure 4-11. Quality Target Development (Product Design Stage)

Deployment Status

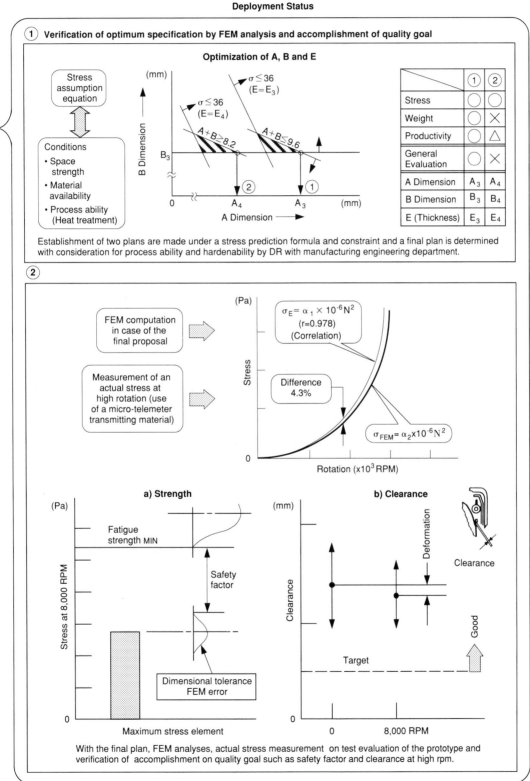

① **Verification of optimum specification by FEM analysis and accomplishment of quality goal**

Optimization of A, B and E

Stress assumption equation

Conditions
• Space strength
• Material availability
• Process ability (Heat treatment)

	①	②
Stress	○	○
Weight	○	✕
Productivity	○	△
General Evaluation	○	✕
A Dimension	A_3	A_4
B Dimension	B_3	B_4
E (Thickness)	E_3	E_4

Establishment of two plans are made under a stress prediction formula and constraint and a final plan is determined with consideration for process ability and hardenability by DR with manufacturing engineering department.

②

FEM computation in case of the final proposal

Measurement of an actual stress at high rotation (use of a micro-telemeter transmitting material)

$\sigma_E = \alpha_1 \times 10^{-6} N^2$
(r=0.978)
(Correlation)

Difference 4.3%

$\sigma_{FEM} = \alpha_2 \times 10^{-6} N^2$

Rotation (×10³ RPM)

a) Strength

Fatigue strength MIN

Safety factor

Dimensional tolerance FEM error

Maximum stress element

b) Clearance

Deformation

Clearance

Good

Target

0   8,000 RPM

With the final plan, FEM analyses, actual stress measurement on test evaluation of the prototype and verification of accomplishment on quality goal such as safety factor and clearance at high rpm.

CHAPTER 5

Using Quality Control Process Charts: Quality Function Deployment at the Preproduction Stage

Hiroshi Takamura, Engineering Department Head,
Komatsu Cast Engineering Company
(former QA Head, Komatsu Zenoah Company);
and Tadayoshi Ohoka, QC Head, Production Engineering Center,
Matsushita Electronic Components Company

The aim of quality function deployment at the preproduction stage is to achieve mass production of a product with assured quality, with ease of manufacturing, and at minimum cost. To accomplish this, we must build in quality all the way through to the mass production stage. This requires the participation of the production department at the new product development planning stage, so that their ideas can shape development. This allows the greatest efficiency.

Recent progress in materials science, machinery technology, automation, flexible manufacturing systems (FMS), production technology, and QC technology has been remarkable. We must therefore always be alert lest we lose out to the competition in quality or cost. Furthermore, overseas procurement of materials or components and offshore manufacturing have become important issues because of trade friction and the strong yen. In view of these factors, quality function deployment at the preproduction stage requires more prioritizing, a broader scope, and more efficient implementation than ever before.

In this chapter, we will discuss quality function deployment as it relates to the preproduction stage of new product development. The first half of the chapter will deal with general concepts; the second half will discuss case studies from the Komatsu Zenoah Company and the Matsushita Electronic Components Company

Production Department Participation at the Development and Planning Stages

Quality assurance cannot be expected to produce much in the way of large scale cost reduction unless the production department conducts advanced test research and participates in new product development from the concept evaluation stage. The main activities at this stage are design considerations for:

- efficient use of new materials,
- application of new processing technology,
- introduction of large-scale flexible production lines and process equipment that can be used with various types of machinery,
- production efficiency of process robots, and
- large-scale improvements in product quality.

Communicating Quality Assurance Items from the Design Department

Figure 5.1 shows a generalized version of the flow of quality function deployment as it relates to the preproduction stage. A brief description of principal activities in each step will follow.

Quality Assurance Charts

The design department performs various quality function deployments, FMEAs and FTAs, and establishes its development goals. It then looks for ways to implement them by blending the requirements of the marketplace, the sales department, and the production department. These activities establish the direction of the development process.

The QA chart is used to communicate the design department's ideas and requirements to the production department. It also transmits important quality assurance points from the design department to the production department. We see, therefore, the following items covered in a QA chart:

- development aims and related changes,
- points where caution must be exercised in production, as a result of changes in material and construction,
- major changes in specifications due to changes in design constraints,
- points related to quality improvement and caution,
- safety and other critical factors, and
- effects to be expected on upper level systems or products if design tolerances are not met.

Many product development failures have occurred because tighter control should have been applied to prevent variance in wall thickness or surface roughness, both of which are important, because of trends toward lighter-weight and smaller-size products. A quality assurance chart should not be just a chart full of symbols and numbers; notes and comments on items such as the ones just listed are very valuable.

Process Deployment

Large-scale line layouts or outlines for large-scale equipment are deployed when development concepts are being formed; smaller-scale details and general facility requirements are investigated at this stage. Process deployment deals with the selection of appropriate process methods and equipment based on a balance between quality and cost by:

- comparing with processes and process capabilities using existing machinery,
- reviewing production problems and identifying points needing improvement, and
- comparing the costs of various process methods.

Critical Process Analysis

Critical process analysis consists of determining the control features of the production process and discussing various ways to assure the required accuracy. The production department conducts this analysis after receiving the design department's requirements for critical features, changes, and improvements. Process analysis should include the following activities:

- converting the requirements transmitted by the design department into production process control items,
- determining whether the required process capability is obtainable,
- evaluating the relationships between equipment capacity and assurance of process capability, and determining how changes in equipment capacity would affect labor requirements,

- identifying engineering bottlenecks that could limit your ability to satisfy quality, delivery, and cost requirements, and
- determining whether you can mistake-proof the production process.

You should also conduct a design review (DR) at this stage, focusing especially on the quality assurance of products and productivity, predicted quality problems at the mass production stage, and potential difficulties in production. The results should be fed back to the design group to capture in the drawings. You should also make a prototype to confirm the quality of the design. The production department should use it to review predicted production quality problems during mass production. After all of the results of this critical process analysis have been obtained, specific process designs can be made.

Solving Production Engineering Bottlenecks at an Early Stage

The production engineering problems that have been identified by critical process analysis must be solved before mass production begins. When a chronic shortage of process capability exists, the cause of the shortage must be eliminated and optimum production conditions determined by repeating the cause analysis or conducting other experiments.

When a new process is being introduced, you must be sure that equipment and line process capability will be adequate, that no ripple effects will arise from quality problems, and that stable production can be achieved. Going into mass production without addressing and solving such problems can result in high losses in quality, cost, delivery, and other factors.

Because human error is a reality, past failures should be reviewed in order to mistake-proof the production process. You may decide to launch an "error-free operation" system, employ mistake-proof equipment, or use automation.

Quality Control Process Chart for In-house Processes

As we have said previously, building in quality at each stage is very important, so every effort should be made to do this. Solving all production-related quality problems prior to mass production is desirable, but in practice this is often not done. Building in quality during the production process means considering various conditions in controlling production processes, and the core tool for such control is the QC process chart.

I regard the QC process chart as a record of the promises made between production and inspection departments regarding the way in which quality features will be controlled and the quality of the final product assured. The following items are usually specified in a QC process chart:

- the quality features to be assured and the degree of importance for each production process,

- the sampling frequency, methods of measurement, and the production department person responsible for confirming quality characteristic values,
- the methods to be used in controlling factors that can cause variance in the quality characteristic target values, and
- the inspection frequency, inspection methods, and sampling size to be used by the inspection department.

The most important steps in preparing QC process charts are determining the control methods and selecting control items to be monitored. Selection of control items for the quality characteristics must be based on consideration of the quality assurance items transmitted from the design department, and on the degree to which they can be deployed into production engineering.

The choice of a control method is usually determined by:

- the relative importance of the quality characteristic to be controlled,
- the process capability and the nature of its variance, and
- the possibility of discovering any variance in the subject characteristic during a later in-house process.

When in-house processing is to be used, plenty of production engineering information of the types listed below should be available, and efficient control methods can be based on it.

- Process methods, procedures, and process standards.
- Equipment and facility capability.
- Preventive maintenance information for equipment and tools.
- Recommended frequency of tool change.
- Human factors.

Quality Control Process Chart for Out-Sourced or Purchased Parts

When parts are out-sourced or purchased, the response of and guidance provided to the supplier by the manufacturer will vary according to the level of process quality control being applied by the source side. The following important points are based on our experience.

A considerable amount of information can be obtained and exchanged in the process of offering guidance to an outside supplier. In this respect, outside suppliers can become an extension of in-house activity. High-priority items and critical points for production and inspection can be communicated to outside suppliers at engineering meetings, and QC process charts and inspection standards can be prepared by the outside supplier for approval by the manufacturer. If any problems are discovered, the appropriate information can be fed back to the supplier for problem-solving. Usually purchased parts are purchased for the firm's own product, and the parts are designed and produced to the purchaser's specifications. The suppliers are usually exclusive manufacturers with special expertise or a high level of control.

Generally speaking, suppliers submit QC process charts and inspection standards to the manufacturer for approval. The following points are crucial and should always be indicated in the charts:

- specifications,
- the way the performance, function, and durability tests are performed by the supplier,
- the way performance, function, and durability will be tested after installation of parts on the firm's own product, and
- the way in which problems are solved.

It is important to cover these points adequately at the prototype test stage so that problems can be worked out by both firms. The results of these problem-identification and problem-solving activities can then be built into the specifications or reflected in the QC process charts. The effectiveness of the changes made should be confirmed on the first mass production run following the changes.

When trouble occurs after mass production begins, it is important not only to obtain a corrective action plan from the supplier, but also to confirm that the corrective measures are implemented in the supplier's production process and reflected in their operation standards. This is standard practice in our domestic Japanese market. When purchasing parts or materials from overseas or from overseas local production, however, other factors must be considered in relation to quality assurance — factors such as social customs, the way of life, and education level. We will discuss these considerations in greater detail in some of the following chapters.

Having provided this general description, I'd like to turn now to examples from the Komatsu Zenoah and Matsushita Electronic Components companies.

Communicating Quality Assurance Items for Quality Function Deployment: The Komatsu Zenoah Case

Komatsu Zenoah has 900 employees and annual sales of $200 million. The firm makes small 2-cycle engines for agricultural equipment and "mini" power shovels and iron-moles for construction machinery, as well as hydraulic equipment. The company is also in the business of overhauling aircraft engines.

We have deployed the KZ 83 and CAP 10 projects and have been building a base that we hope will enable us to become a first class company. Improvements in new technology and new product development are part of this effort.

Quality function deployment is an important technique for building in quality at the development stage. Fundamentally, it consists of:

- placing emphasis on building in quality during the planning, design, and preproduction stages — in other words, at the source;
- giving priority to quality, even when the company is constantly scrutinizing the balance between quality and cost and looking for ways to achieve large-scale cost reduction; and
- focusing on the most critical quality targets and prioritizing thoroughly.

Our example in this case is the development of a small 2-cycle engine — the G002 — for agricultural equipment. We will focus mainly on the production department's use of quality function deployment in crankcase production (see Figure 5.2). A flexible manufacturing system (FMS) concept has already been applied to crankcase production, so a few different types of products are being machined in one transfer machine. Production engineers and design engineers have collaborated in building the project since the concept development stage, placing emphasis on the factors listed below:

- commonality of parts and a serialized design
- unification of process standards and processing
- implementation of a single setup

The first product was a K-series engine; the G002 was developed in order to expand the product line.

Communication of Quality Assurance Items from the Design Department

The design department establishes design direction, builds in quality, and transmits its requirements to the production department. These requirements are based on a review of the quality demands voiced by users and the problems occurring in similar products.

Figure 5.3 shows one review method used by the design department, called the MAC (Matrix Analysis of Claims). It enables us to study the relationships among various parts, their use conditions, and the frequency of problem occurrence as indicated by all claims and complaints involving similar models.

The problem to be solved in this case is lack of engine output. The crankcase is not the object of the complaints, but it is related to the problem. The design department maintains that the lack of engine output relates to the user's demanded quality, so the design group has specified the bore diameter of the crankshaft insert, depth of the hole, and the run-out of the shaft center — all of which must be confirmed in the prototype engine's performance test for assurance of product quality.

Figure 5.4 shows the format we use for communicating important points from the design department to the production department. It is the same as a QA chart. Our company also marks important QA characteristics with a special symbol right on the drawings.

Quality Function Deployment at the Production Development Stage

Process Deployment

The process methods and facilities are first determined by process deployment. Process deployment chart I, shown in Figure 5.5, provides a format for comparing the process method and process capability required to produce each quality characteristic of an individual part that can be used in similar pieces of equipment. The chart also enables us to analyze production problems relating to parts that may be used in similar pieces of equipment so that we can review the process and make improvements. Process deployment chart II, shown in Figure 5.6, enables us to compare quality and cost factors related to the process being considered.

Critical Process Analysis

Figure 5.7 is an example of a critical process analysis chart, in which demanded quality characteristics have been deployed into characteristics that the design department has designated as the quality characteristics for production. The chart allows us to study relationships between these characteristics and the processes that produce them — and to identify processes or parts of processes that are critically important in achieving process capability. We can then undertake one or more of the following steps to prevent or eliminate problems.

1. Process factors that have been assigned a high rating in an evaluation of the degree of importance to production are selected as process capability control items.
2. Where process capability appears to be insufficient, we prepare a plan for improvement.
3. We study processes that might be particularly vulnerable to problems caused by human factors, or subject to other unexpected failures, to see if we can find ways to mistake-proof them.

Because we had received complaints about a shortage of output power, as we mentioned earlier, we created a machining datum plane on which we indicated such items as the location of holes and the center of the shaft, as shown in Figure 5.7. Once we had made this chart, we were in a better position to try various ways of solving the engine output problem and improving process capability. First, we tested methods of clamping with minimum strain, and then we found a way to improve the simultaneous machining of the hole diameter and end surface. These modifications enabled us to achieve a process capability (Cp) greater than 1.33.

Quality Function Deployment at the Mass Production Stage

We have already described the process by which the design and production engineering departments build in quality at the development stage. Now we will move on to the next stage, in which the production and inspection departments will determine ways of controlling mass production.

Before preparing a QC process chart, the inspection department must review once again — from their own point of view — the claims and in-house production problems. This review relates to the cause and effect deployment chart depicted in Figure 5.8.

Quality Characteristic Factor Deployment Chart

The following items can be studied with the aid of the cause-and-effect deployment chart:

- claims and in-house production problems
- the process associated with each problem and the method of assurance use
- the control method applied by the production and inspection department to the production process

QC Process Chart

All of the building-in of quality at the development stage was summarized in the QC process chart. The control methods to be used by the production and inspection departments are determined by considering the degree of importance of each quality characteristic, the associated process, the process capability and its variance, and other related factors. The methodology was described in the section "Solving Production Engineering Bottlenecks at an Early Stage" in this chapter. Figure 5.9 shows a QC process chart that includes the following items related to process control:

- items or features to be assured, and the degree of importance assigned to each related process
- self-inspection methods for production workers
- factor control methods for use in the production process
- confirmation methods for use by the inspection department

The assurance items, or features, relating to the lack of output power need to be checked only briefly at the time of process start-up, setup change, and tool change, because sufficient process capability will be available under these normal conditions. For factor control in the production process, the play in the tool bench and the parallelism of the workpiece with the shaft in the direction of tool bench movement are controlled. Even QC process charts for mass production are prepared at the preproduction stage.

Work Standards and Inspection Standards

Work standards, inspection standards, and checksheets are prepared in accordance with the QC process chart, which serves as the basic guide for work on the production floor.

Summary

We have described the concept of quality function deployment for the production department at the preproduction stage and provided examples. As we mentioned at the beginning of this chapter, progress in technology and the globalization of production can be expected to continue at an even faster pace in the future. In view of this, quality function deployment is an important tool for the rational handling of problems and related tasks. We hope to foster even wider use of this technique in order to enhance our ability to keep pace with changing circumstances.

Using QC Process Charts: The Case of Matsushita Electronic Component Company

We are an integrated electronic components manufacturer selling semiconductors and various other electronic parts, with the exception of large-scale integrated circuits (LSIs). We sell some 50,000 different components to electronic equipment manufacturers and to foreign and domestic automobile manufacturers. We have been promoting QC throughout the company for some 30 years now, because we believe that QC is a control technique that should involve the entire management team in emphasizing quality. Our commitment to this belief has allowed us to develop, manufacture, sell, and support the highest quality and most reliable products in order to satisfy our customers.

Concept of the QC Process Chart

The QC process chart — which our firm calls a control process chart — is an effective tool for quality assurance and thorough control of production processes for electronic components. We have been using this chart for the past twenty years or more, mainly in the production department, but we are now using it as a tool for process quality design at the design stage. This means that it is much more than just a control tool for the production process. We began using the process control chart this way as a result of the mechanization of production lines, labor reduction, and elevation of quality assurance levels that have occurred in recent years.

Quality function deployment is a design approach, and QC process charts are to be transmitted from upstream downward. However, the transmission to all related departments is sometimes difficult because prioritization may differ from department to department. In such cases, QC process charts should be prepared by the production floor group. The method for preparing the QC process chart under these circumstances is described next.

A control process chart depicts a process from material supply and parts to the shipment of completed products. A separate chart is prepared for each product, defining the point and method of control for each unit process, specifying which checksheets or control charts should be used to control which feature in what process, and showing the sequence of the various unit processes. Figure 5.10 is an example.

Making the Control Process Chart

As Figure 5.10 shows, preparation of the control process chart should be based on the *Manual for Preparation of Control Process Charts*. The manual was developed to provide guidance for complete implementation of control process charts. It explains how to write correct descriptions, how to prepare and read control items, how to use process charting symbols, and how to draw process flow charts — all according to Japanese Industrial Standards (JIS) rules published in booklet Z 8206.

Production Process Control Points

At Matsushita Electronic Components Company, we define control points as yardsticks for assessing our achievement of a given task. They are also essential for performance of the control cycle P-D-C-A (Plan-Do-Check-Action). Control items are factors or features related to quality, cost, delivery, morale, and safety (Q,C,D,M,S), and they must be checked. Check items are process elements or conditions that have a causal relationship to the control items. The causes may be related to man (operators), machine, material, methods, or measurement (the 5M's). Figure 5.11 shows the relationship between control points and process control activity.

Making the Control Process Chart

- *Selecting a process for charting.* As the processes to be used are determined, the production department summarizes them in a process flow chart, as shown in Figure 5.12. This chart consists of unit processes and block processes that include some unit processes. These processes are based on the production specifications established in cooperation with the engineering, quality control, and industrial engineering departments.
- *Determining control items.* In accordance with the methodology of function analysis used for value engineering (VE), the function of a given process is defined by using both nouns and verbs (X is Yed), and the process characteristics are extracted from the verbs in order to establish the control items.

The steps in this procedure are:

1. *Defining the unit process.* Using the example of one unit process, the "flux coating" process included in Figure 5.12, the definition is "to coat flux on circuit board."
2. *Defining the higher level function of the unit process.* Further questioning is applied to the unit process defined as "to coat flux to circuit board" in order to clarify the higher level function of the process — its purpose or role. For example, we extracted the higher level function "preparing an oxidation-preventing film" by asking such additional questions as, "Why is the flux coated on the circuit board?"
3. *Determining control items.* As the higher level functions are extracted, we match their relationship to final quality assurance characteristics with product specifications in order to establish a control item, such as "to improve adhesion of solder." This series of procedures is shown in Figure 5.13.

4. *Investigating the control method.* Using the worksheet shown in Figure 5.14, we determine the control method for the selected control items.

- *Determining check items.* Using work analysis methods developed for industrial engineering, we conduct motion studies on the work of each unit process in order to clarify the work elements and establish check items. This procedure consists of identifying the required manpower, materials, tools, work methods, and related conditions. Figure 5.15 shows an example of a unit process motion study.

  To determine the check method, we use the worksheet shown in Figure 5.16 to further clarify the contents of the 4M's (man, material, machine, and method) involved in each work element.

- *Making the control process chart.* The control items, check items, and control methods for each unit process are entered on the control process chart worksheet, shown in Figure 5.10. This enables us to conduct an overall review of the total process or to study the relationships among block processes so that we can prepare a control structure. Problems that surface from an investigation or day-to-day control activities are solved mainly by the production department, in cooperation with related departments. The control process chart is revised as corrective action is completed. This enhances the process control structure. Figure 5.17 shows a control process chart that was prepared using this process.

Using the Control Process Chart

Design, production, and QC departments use the control process chart as a tool for day-to-day control. They consider the chart one of the indispensable standards for quality control in the production processes.

To summarize our discussion, the two main uses of the control process chart and the associated benefits, are:

- To devise a control structure for the production process.
- Production floor personnel can better understand what must be controlled for quality assurance.
- The search for causes of quality problems occurring in production and their analysis is easier.
- To serve as a tool for new product quality process design.
- The chart helps to clarify cause-and-effect relationships between quality characteristics and their assurance characteristics and to facilitate quality assurance activities for the new product at the preproduction and production start-up stages.

References

Mizuno, Shigeru; Akao, Yoji, eds. (1978). *Quality Function Deployment.* JUSE.

Nakae, Y. (1983). "Study and Implementation of Method of Establishing the Control Points for Production Processes." *Quality Control,* Vol. 24, May special issue, pp. 203-207, JUSE.

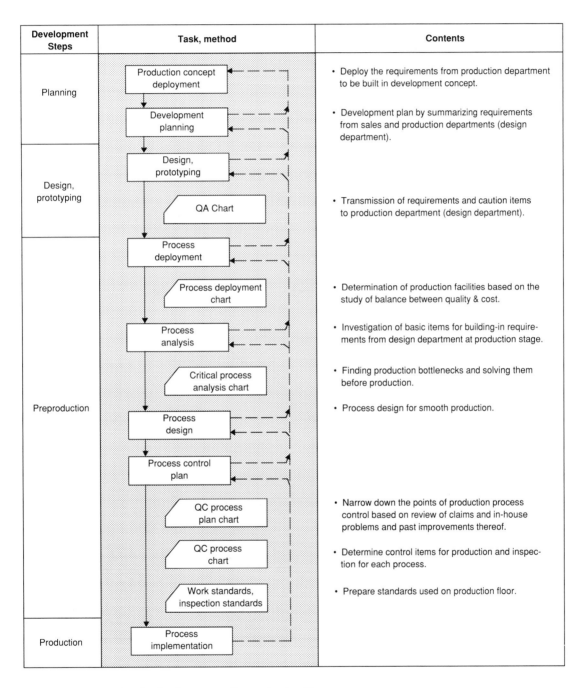

Figure 5-1. Flow of Quality Deployment at Preproduction Stage

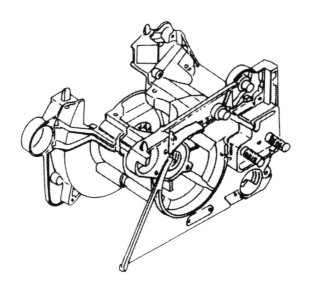

Figure 5-2. Crankcase

Figure 5-3. MAC (Matrix Analysis of Claims)

No.	Part name (Part number)	No.	Location	Item	Specification	Degree of importance	Reason for selection of critical marks					Effect of deviation from specifications	accept reject (inspect dept. head)	Reasons
							Safety Item	User demanded quality	New item	Past quality problem	Test item during prototyping			
1	Crankcase G 002-21100	1	Main bearing	Depth of hole	xx±xx	A		◯			◯	shaft rotation problem		
				Hole diameter	xx±xx	A		◯		◯	◯	inadequate output	◯	center mismatch with cylinder
				Center run-out	xx	A		◯				boss friction (bearing)	◯	bearing creep

Figure 5-4. Critical Mark Communication Form

No.	Model part no. / Construction / Weight of material / Features-Process Capability-Process — Features	Model G001	Part No. 2110		Model G002	Part No. 2110	
		Material ×××	Raw Material ×××	Completed ×××	Material ×××	Raw Material ×××	Completed ×××
		Features	Process Capability	Processes	Features	Process Capability	Processes
1	Flatness of cylinder base surface	×××	××	Milling	×××	××	Milling
2	Surface roughness of cylinder base surface	×××	××	"	×××	××	"
3	Bearing bore diameter	×××	××	Boring	×××	××	Boring (grind)
4	Location of bearing bore	×××	××	"	×××	××	"
5	Concentricity of bearing bore	×××	××	"	×××	××	"
6	Parallelism of base surface to bearing bore	×××	××	"	×××	××	"
7	Location of base surface to bearing bore	×××	××	"	×××	××	"
Past failures		• Lack of detection of missed machining, broken taps • Time consumed for bearing bore machining with one plastic bit and dimensioning of seat location			(Grind) • Improvement in detection of missed machining • Simultaneous machining of bearing bore diameter and wall with separate tools		
Points of process and other cautions							

Figure 5-5. Process Deployment Chart I

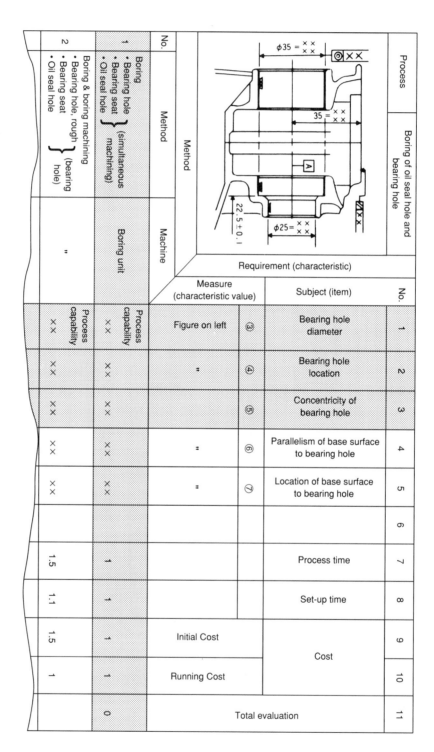

Process: Boring of oil seal hole and bearing hole

No.	Method	Machine	No.	Subject (item)		Measure (characteristic value)	Method No.1 (Process capability)	Method No.2 (Process capability)
1	Boring • Bearing hole • Bearing seat • Oil seal hole } (simultaneous machining)	Boring unit	1	Bearing hole diameter	③	Figure on left	x x	x x
			2	Bearing hole location	④	"	x x	x x
			3	Concentricity of bearing hole	⑤		x x	x x
2	Boring & boring machining • Bearing hole, rough } (bearing hole) • Bearing seat • Oil seal hole	"	4	Parallelism of base surface to bearing hole	⑥	"	x x	x x
			5	Location of base surface to bearing hole	⑦	"	x x	x x
			6					
			7	Process time			1	1.5
			8	Set-up time			1	1.1
			9	Cost — Initial Cost			1	1.5
			10	Cost — Running Cost			1	1
			11	Total evaluation			0	

Figure 5-6. Process Deployment Chart II

Figure 5-7. Critical Process Analysis Chart

Name of line under consideration	Process			Failure mode and degree of importance							Detection		Claim		Evaluation				Element					Process capability					FPing	Remarks
Crankcase G002	Major classification no.	Minor Class.	Minor Class.	Major classification no.	Failure mode	Cause	Item to be quality assured	Method	standard	degree of importance	on-line	off-line	inner company defects	outside claims	1. degree of importance	2. output of investigation	3.	multiply 1. 2. and 3.	i. people	ii. mechanism	iii. people/ mechanism	process in question	Cp	Plan	Actual	Plan	Plan	Control Chart		
	1	ZTR	cylinder base surface	①	inadequate output		die control	die control	xxx	A	×	×	×	×	3	3	1	9		○		◎	xxx		1/84	6/84	6/84			clamp improvement
				②	=	pitch of base surface and shaft of opening	height of base surface	preventive maintenance	xxx	A	×	×	×	×	3	3	1	9		○		◎	xxx							
			crank hole	③	*	parallelism of base surface and shaft opening	parallelism of base surface		xx	A	×	×	×	×	3	3	1	9		○		◎	xxx		1/84	6/84	6/84	○		
			muffler mounting hole		"	degree of center of shaft opening	degree of center of shaft opening			B	×	×	×	×	2	2	2	8												
			unit mounting hole	④	=	gap between shaft opening and crank opening	position of wall surface	adjust when re-tooling	xxx	A	×	×	×	×	3	2	2	12		○		◎	xxx		1/84	3/84	3/84	○		
			cylinder mounting hole	⑤		crank opening position	opening edge surface position			A	×	×	×	×																
			cover mounting hole																											
			Fan cover mounting hole	⑥		bearing journal width	bearing journal width	accuracy of cutting tool (control chart)	xxx	A	×	×	×	×	3	2	1	6		◎		◎	xxx		1/84	2/84	3/84			accuracy improvement in simultaneous machining

Figure 5-8. Cause and Effect Deployment Chart

Item of assurance		Assured feature			Failure	Assurance process			Assurance method for production department							Assurance method for inspection department		Mode of failure	
Part name	Part no. sketch	No.	Feature	Degree of importance	output shortage	Machining	Assembly	Shipping inspection	Control by voluntary inspection			Factor control in process				Method of inspection	Interval	Claim	Drive test
									Measurement method	Interval	Record	Cause	Method of confirmation	Standard	Interval				
Crankcase	G002-2110	1	Crank → shaft, bore diameter → large / small	A / A / A	○ ○ ○	Boring			cylinder gauge / Ring gauge	1/day / 2/day	Control chart	Assumed loose, major shaft base	Regular test, bar	Regular inspection, standard Accuracy inspection std. re-tooling standard	1/4 mo. / 1/yr.	—	—		

Process	Sketch	Record	Features to be assured		degree of importance	confirmation by meeting	inspection	Control by voluntary inspection			
			Feature	Standard				measuring method	interval	in charge	record
Milling ZTR - 2ST (R)	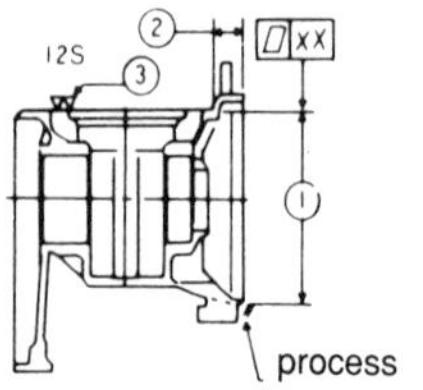 process standard	1	cylinder surface height	×××	A	O		measuring tool	1/a 3/bc	operator	data sheet
		2	width	×××	B	O		calipers	1/a 3/bc	"	
		3	surface roughness	×××	B	O		loose and standardized	"	"	
		•	flatness	×××	A	O	O	measuring tool	1/c	"	
		•	cylinder base surface	×××	C	O		visual	1/a 3/bc 1/day	"	
Boring ZTR - 3ST (R)	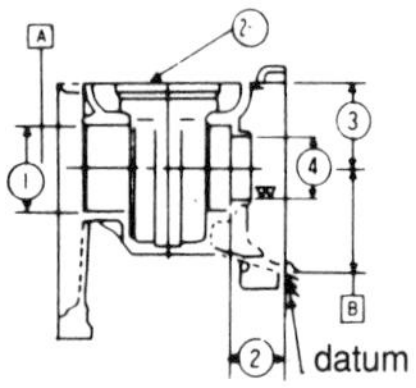 datum plane	1	crank hole diameter	×××	A	O		ring gauge cylinder gauge	1/a 2/bc 2/day	operator	control chart
		•	surface roughness	×××	A	O	O	measuring tool	1/c	"	
		2	accuracy of setting Brg. position	×××	A	O		depth gauge	1/a 3/bc 2/day	"	control chart
		•	concentricity to A	×××	A	O	O	measuring tool	2/day	"	control chart
		2-1	base surface paralell to A	×××	A	O	O	"	"	"	"
		3	cylinder surface height	×××	A	O	O	measuring tool	1/a 2/bc 2/day	"	data sheet
		4	oil seal hole	×××	A	O		ring gauge cylinder gauge	1/a 2/bc	"	data sheet

a: start of work b: set up change c: tool change

Figure 5-9. QC Process Chart

Production department						Inspection dept.		
Factor control in process						inspection method	interval	process
factor	method of confirmation	standard	interval	in charge	record	method of confirmation		
accuracy of measuring device	regular inspection	regular inspection standard	1/yr.	group leader				
accuracy of calipers	"	"	1/4 mo.	"				
						small tester	regular	
play in cutter support	dial gauge	precision inspection standard	1/yr.					
parallelism of workpiece axis and cutter support	"	"	"	"				
cutter precision	counter	inspection standard manual						
link gauge cylinder gauge precision	regular inspection	regular inspection standard	1/4 mo.	operator	check sheet			
						roughness meter	regular	
depth gauge precision	regular inspection	regular inspection standard	1/yr.	group leader	gauge record			
						3-dimensional	regular	
						"	"	
accuracy of measuring device	regular inspection	regular inspection standard	1/yr.	group leader	gauge record	"	"	
	regular inspection	regular inspection standard		group leader	gauge record			

Product Name	Product A	Process	Overcoat	**Overcoat Product A Control Process Chart**
Specification	ESU—245 Type	Issue Date	May 21, 1986	
Part Number	2413	Implementation Date	June 1, 1986	

Process					Control Points					
Main Process					Control Item (check by result)					
Part, material work-station	Raw Mat'l Process	Cost Process	Control Items	(Contents of Process)	Factors (5M)	Degree of Import.	Inspection Items	Constraint	Degree of Import.	Control Item (inspection item)	Abnormality Judgement Standard
Key top already printed with Tanpo			▽	Storage							
			◯	Surface wipe (to remove dirt and foreign matter from surface)	Method	C	Impregnation		B	Thread dust rejection	By control chart
					Method	C	Bencott				
					Method	A	Wiping				
			◯	Air spray (to remove all foreign matter from surface)	Facility	A	Air pressure		A	Thread dust rejection	By control chart
					Facility	C	Alcohol adhesion	2.5±0.5 kg/cm²			
			◯	Masking	Tooling	C	Mask hole diameter	Keytop outer diameter			
UV coating	▽			Storage	Material	B	Paint viscosity	0.6 ± 0.4 poise			
					Material	C	Storage period	< 3 months			
					Material	C	Storage place	< 30°C			
Xylene resin		▽		Storage	Material	B	Viscosity	0.4 ± 0.2 poise			
					Material	C	Storage period	< 3 months			
					Material	C	Storage place	< 30°C			
			◯	Adjustment of paint viscosity (smooth coating)	Method	AA	mix ratio 4:1 weight ratio 2:1		AA	Viscosity	Drop = 9 ± 0.1 second
					Method	B	Stirring	> 5 minutes			
					Method	C	Supply to container		C	Weight	5 ± 0.1 kg.
			◯	coating key-top surface	Facility	C	main air pressure	6.0 ± 0.2 kg/cm²			

	Code	Rev. Date	Revision Reasons	In Charge	Confir-mation	Code	Rev. Date	Revision
Revisions	△1	• •				△4	• •	
	△2	• •				△5	• •	
	△3	• •				△6	• •	

Figure 5-10. Example of Control Process Chart (QC Process Chart)

Approval	Discussion					Prepared by				Control No. FOC—001	
Plant Super.	QC	Engineer-ing	Production Engineering	Purchas-ing		Production Section Head	Seal	In Charge			
Sasaki	Fumabashi	Nakamura	Tanizaki	Katigiri		Hata	Mizuno				

Control Method											Remarks
Sampling Measurement Method				Control Information		Control (C) Arrangement (A) In Charge				Method of Judging Abnormality	Addition of related sheets (work instruc-tion, work guidance sheet)	
Frequency	Sampling Method	Measurement Method and instrument	In Charge	Control Chart	Check Sheet	Section Head	Group Head	Super-visor	Reserve Group Leader	In Charge		
Per 10 units	Regular sampling	Visual	Worker					A		C		Instruction sheet no. OC-01
2/day	a.m. 9:00 p.m. 1:00	Press meter	Worker		OS-02			A	C			Instruction sheet no. OS-02
Per 20 units	Regular sampling	Visual	Worker		OS-11							
———	By instruc-tion sheet	Calipers	Sub-worker		OS-21				C			Instruction sheet no. OS-02
———	Sampling	Viscosity meter	Sub-group		OS-12			A	C		Disposition of material	Material spec. sheet 433K-ST-1501
"	100%		"		OS-12			A	C			
"	100%		"					A	C			
———	Sampling	Viscosity meter	Sub-group		OS-12			A	C		Disposition of material	Material spec. sheet 433K-ST-1502
"	100%		"		OS-12			A	C			
"	100%		"					A	C			
										C	Disposition of mix solution	Instruction sheet no. OC-04
										C		Viscosity measurement method
										C		
———	Sampling	Stopwatch	Sub-group	X - R		A		C				433K-SU-7400
"	100%	Balance	"		OS-12							OC-01
2/day		pressure gauge			OS-12			A	C			instruction sheet no.

Reasons	In Charge	Confir-mation	Code	Rev. Date	Revision Reasons	In Charge	Confir-mation
			△7	• •			
			△8	• •			
			△9	• •			

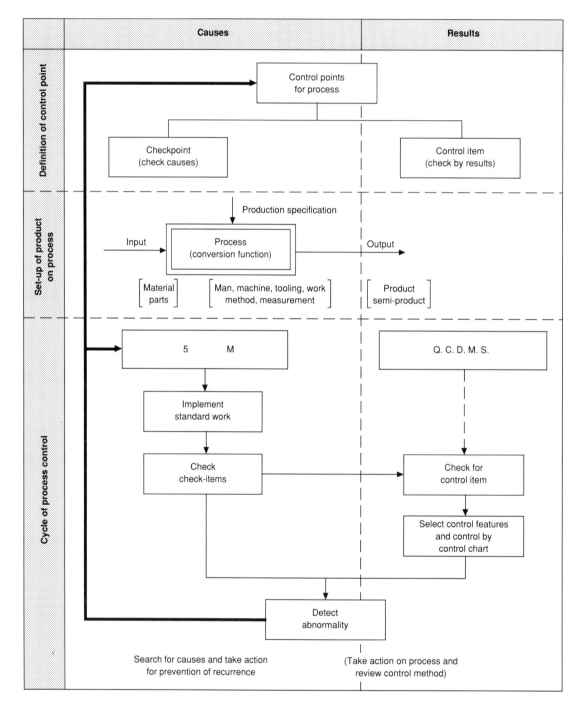

Figure 5-11. Relationship Between Control Points and Process Control Activity

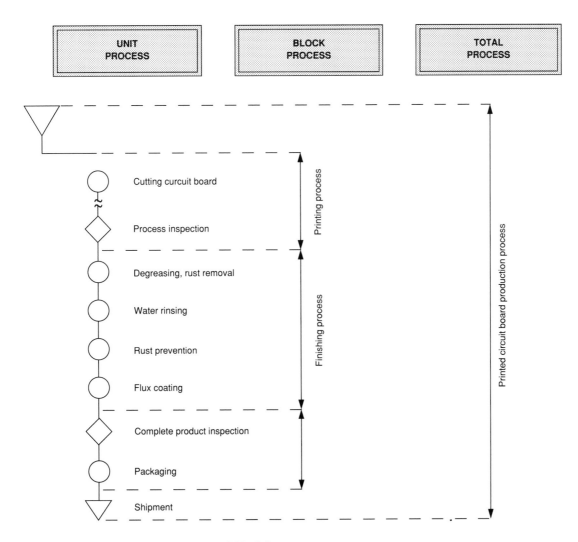

Figure 5-12. Example of Unit Process and Block Process

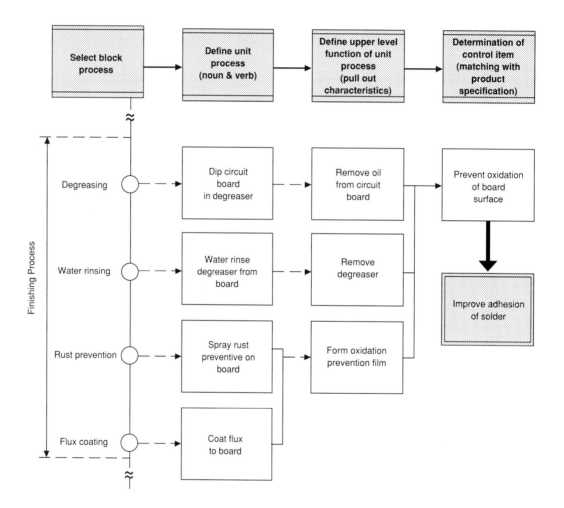

Figure 5-13. Procedure of Determining Control Items

Function (purpose)	Features (characteristic values)		Difficulty	Result				
						Control method		
		A B C		Item	In charge	Frequency	Handling data	Handling method (in charge)
(Upper level function)		A B C						
Improve adhesion	Solder adhesion	A	○	solder	AC section Kitasaka	n = 5/lot	Test data	Study of disposition between QC decision and production section
to solder								
(seek upper level function)				control test				
Prevent oxidation	Degree of oxidation prevention	A	×	adhesion				
(definition of function process)	Adhesion of oxidation	A	×					
Coat flux	prevention film							
(definition of process)								
→								
Coat flux	State of flux coating	A	○	State of flux coating	Kajiya	Twice/day	Check sheet	Report to boss — disposition
State of flux coating	· Uniformity			(limit sample)				
	· Good filling of holes							

Figure 5-14. Control Method Study Worksheet

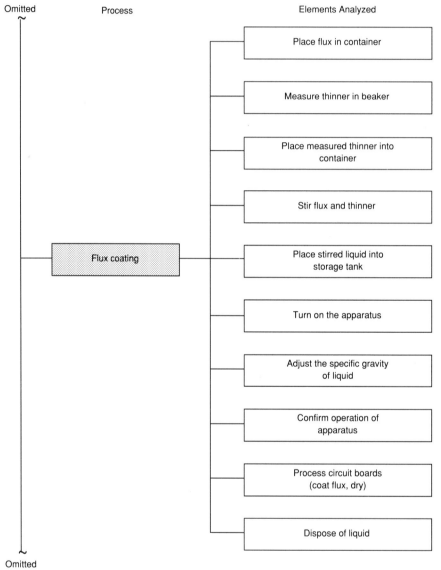

Figure 5-15. Example of Unit Process Motion Study

Process Classification	Finishing	Process	Flux Coating

		A B C		Cause				
	Contents			Check method				
				Item	In charge	Frequency of others		Handling (in-charge)
Man								
Parts, materials	(1) Flux contents							
		A	×	brand specs	Kajiya	check branch	—	report to boss
	(2) Thinner contents							
	•	A	×	brand specs	"	"	—	"
Equipment, toolings	(1) Container							
	• capacity ——→			container specs				
	(2) Beaker							
	• capacity ——→			container specs				
	(3) Flux coater							
	• roller distance	B	○	roller distance	Kajiwa	—	—	worker adjusts
	• flow of flux	B	○	flow of flux	"	"	—	
	(4) Drying oven							
	• temperature	A	○	temp.	"	twice/day	checksheet	report to boss
				regular inspection	—	one/3 month	regular check chart	
	(5) Specific gravity meter							
	(6) Stirrer							
Method	(1) Compounding of liquid							
	• be sure of mix ratio ——————→			mistake-proofing				
	(2) Adjust specific gravity of liquid							
	• specific gravity	A	○	spec. gravity	Kajiwa	once/1/2 hour	graphs	report to boss
	(3) Volume of liquid	B	○	volume of liquid	"	at start of work	checksheet	worker adjusts
	(4) Use period of liquid	A	○	use period	"	once/15 days		record checksheet renewal day

Figure 5-16. Worksheet for Study of Check Method

office #	2	PCB Business Dept.,No. 2 Printing Plant.Production Section		
		Prepared Date	Section Head	Preparer

Parts	Flow Chart (raw mat'l process / prep. process / main process / omitted (finishing process))	Process	Work Instruction Sheet	Control Item	control instruction manual	control chart	in-charge (work)	in-charge (action)	sampling measurement	Inspection Item	Inspection Method	Remarks
De-greaser, rust-removal liquids		degreasing rust prevention	263-BD-32	(check item)	273-BD-22	check sheet	Naka-mura	Kajiwa	concentration check 1/day			
		water rinse	263-BD-33	(liquid concentration) (water rinse nozzle) (water pressure) (ph of board surface)		check sheet " " "	" " " "	" " " "	2/day visual 2/day confirm meter 2/day — 2/day			
Rust-preventive water		rust prevention	263-BD-34	(liquid concentration) (ph of liquid) (vol. of liquid) (flow of liquid) ———	273-BD-23 273-BD-24	check sheet " " "	" " " "	" " " "	2/day color meter 2/day — 2/day n = 5 visual 2/day n = 5 visual			
Flux thinner		flux coating	263-BD-35	(spec. gravity of liquid) (vol. of liquid) (drying temp.)	273-BD-25	graphs check sheet check sheet "	Naka-mura " "	Kajiwa " "	1/hr. measure w/ spec. gravity meter 1/day measure w/ level gauge CFM 2/day temp. reading 2/day n = 5 visual			
		control test	321-BD-12	solder adhesion		test data	"	"	n = 5/lot test adhesion			

Figure 5-17. Control Process Chart for Printed Circuit Board

CHAPTER 6

Quality Function Deployment and Technology Deployment

Yoji Akao, Professor of Management Engineering,
Tamagawa University;
Akira Harada, Electronics Division, Futaba Electronics Industries;
and Kazuo Matsumoto, TQC Promotion Manager,
Taikisha Company, Ltd.

In the previous chapters, we have presented a basic outline of quality function deployment and some practical applications. Quality function deployment is essentially communicating information related to quality, and then assuring quality through a chain-like system. A company's special technology, reliability, and cost considerations must also be reflected in quality function deployment. A number of trial runs relating to these factors have been conducted by various companies, and we will discuss them in Chapters 6 through 8.

Chart 6.1 was introduced in Chapter 1, but we are including it here again as a quality deployment chart that includes technology, reliability, and cost factors as well.

When the product quality plan and quality design are developed from a quality chart, and a quality target value is set at a higher level than the previous standard, and this level is difficult to achieve, we have what we call an engineering bottleneck. Professor Furukawa calls efforts to solve such problems bottleneck engineering (BNE). When bottlenecks are encountered in the latter stages of product development, they can cause considerable delay in the development schedule, as well as other major problems — or even losses. It is not surprising that most of the troubles that occur during product development are of this kind. We can say that early detection of bottlenecks is a high priority activity in source control and is the main point of quality function deployment.

A common misconception is that a company's special technology and control are unrelated. Although there is no doubt that a company's special technology is directly involved in forming product quality, we must add that the systematic detection and elimination of bottlenecks should also be considered essential when using this technology. In this chapter we will discuss technology deployment in relation to quality deployment.

Bottleneck Engineering

Figure 6.1 shows an example of technology deployment as carried out at Kayaba Industries. Let us first explain the terminology that we are using. Narrowly speaking, a quality chart is a chart that converts demanded qualities into quality characteristics. Various charts that we use in the QC process charts are also included in what we call quality deployment charts, or quality charts — the latter term having the broader meaning. When used in this broad sense, the various quality charts are usually designated simply as charts A, B, and C as shown in Figure 6.2, or as charts I, II, and III, or some other general sequential categories.

Among these various charts developed for communicating intention and design information to the manufacturing department is one that comes immediately before the QC process chart. Quality chart A in Figure 6.2 is a quality chart in the narrow sense. This chart is the one we use to determine quality design and to determine whether the targeted quality level can be achieved with existing technology.

If it cannot, that problem is designated a bottleneck in the engineering chart (the production engineering chart in Figure 6.2). Development then continues, with a special focus on these problem areas.

I would like to call attention to the key points in the far right column of Figure 6.2. There is a production engineering chart B that corresponds to quality chart B. In it, mass production quality assurance is confirmed by evaluating each step, from the development of production engineering to mass production. Production engineering charts C1 and C2 are made to correspond to the QA chart. In Figure 6.2 these are called process know-how charts. They clarify the know-how and the know-why of production engineering at the preproduction level and communicate them to mass production. Production engineering chart B spells out the preventive measures for previous quality problems and new process problems.

It is important to note that quality deployment and technology deployment develop in a mutually consistent and parallel way, as we have described, and that a quality to technology trade-off relationship exists. This case study discusses a practical application at Kayaba Industries of Professor Furukawa's idea, about the relationship between quality and technology.

Functional Deployment and Mechanism Deployment

Even when the design quality has been determined by converting each demanded quality into quality characteristics related to each of the quality charts, it is still difficult to immediately create a link with the technology needed to achieve these qualities. First, we need to determine what product functions will express these quality characteristics and what mechanisms will be required to realize them. This process of realizing quality characteristics can be expressed as:

quality deployment → function deployment → mechanism deployment

When all of these steps are taken together, the activity is called technology deployment. Generally speaking, satisfying the demands of the customer is the basis for developing a product that will be accepted and bought. However, this cannot be the basis for every aspect of product planning. We shall explain why, using prefabricated housing as an example.

Figure 3.2 from Chapter 3 shows a quality chart for mass produced houses. In using a chart to deploy the different parts of a house or the process of building one, we would naturally expect to find something in the chart that relates to the characteristic "foundation of the home" or "laying the foundation." When we examine this chart, though, we discover a problem: When the demanded quality priorities were converted according to the method described again in the Futaba Electronics case in this chapter (introduced previously in Chapter 3), neither the foundation nor the laying of the foundation was extracted as an important element. Since they are obviously important elements, as they hold up the house, why didn't they emerge as such? The reason is that the consumer takes it for granted that a "dwelling has a solid foundation" and does not explicitly specify it as a demand. Therefore, it does not show up strongly as a voice of the customer in our survey of demands.

Similarly, there is no doubt that items like "provide shelter from the elements" and "prevent intruders from entering" have been recognized as important basic functions of a house since time immemorial — but these characteristics, too, are taken for granted. Attention is no longer focused on these functions because they have been built into the long history of construction engineering know-how and methods, and they are no longer consciously recognized.

We find the same phenomenon in general manufacturing industries. In order to improve technology, including a company's special technology, we must clarify the functions of products. If the basic function of a product is not fulfilled, even if the product is developed and marketed, it will be worthless. This point has been emphasized in value engineering (VE) all along, and it is the main point in the "function deployment" part of quality function deployment. It must also be considered the starting point for the technology deployment with which function deployment is to be combined.

In value engineering, many practitioners suggest that when defining a function, it is best to use an expression consisting of a verb plus an object. We have already given examples of this in defining the functions of houses. In the demanded quality deployment charts we have looked at already, we can find many demands expressed in a way that makes it difficult to distinguish the user from the function. Clearly separating them in a demanded quality deployment chart and a function deployment chart makes their respective roles much more distinct. With demanded quality deployment, there is no need to limit oneself to verb-plus-object expressions; simple expressions that include adjectives or any other type of word may be used.

Technology Deployment

Figure 6.1 shows how the demanded quality deployment chart and the function deployment chart are combined into a matrix (Chart-I) and customer demands are converted into functions that the product should have. Converting the demanded quality priorities into function priorities is important, but it is also important to determine the priority of the functions themselves from a technical standpoint. The Analytical Hierarchy Process (AHP) should be used for this purpose. Professor Tone has written a good manual on the AHP system, which was developed by Saaty. I recommend this book highly.

Next, the function deployment chart and the mechanical deployment chart are combined in a matrix (Chart 2-II) and the functions of the products are converted into mechanisms that the product should have. Technical standards or technical data are entered on this mechanism deployment chart. Comparisons of these two charts may reveal that the functions and methods needed to achieve the demanded qualities cannot be obtained by an extension of existing technology. In that case, the function should be designated as one that requires bottleneck engineering.

In the effort to resolve a bottleneck, methods such as PDPC or the reviewed dendrogram proposed by Japan Aircraft can be effective. Each time a bottleneck is resolved, one should compile the technical data and references while this is still easy to do and they can be effectively organized into engineering standards.

In using this method, I would like to point out that we don't just call the chart that we initially used for bottleneck engineering a technical chart. Rather, the various charts we have described that are used to extract technology deployment and bottleneck engineering from the process of achieving user demands and relating the product's functions to a company's special technology can all be called "technology deployment charts."

Technology Deployment in Remote Control Products: The Case of Futaba Electronics Industries

In Chapter 1 we used a case involving the development of remote control hobby products to show (1) how to extract engineering-oriented quality information from quality demands expressed in the marketplace in the form of customer verbatims, and (2) how to make a demanded quality deployment chart. We then explained how to use this quality chart. In Chapter 2, we described how quality charts are used in developing product quality plans. In the remainder of this chapter we will discuss technology deployment as a continuation of this process.

An outline of technology deployment is shown in Figure 6.1. The upper left portion of the chart is the part that we explained in Chapters 1 and 2. The lower portions indicate the quality characteristic weights, which were determined by the proportional distribution method described below. For example, the demanded quality weight (8.4) for the "easy to hold" line on Chart 1-I in Figure 6.1 is proportionally distributed as 3:2:1 for ◎, ○, Δ. In this case,

$$= 0.65 \text{ points}$$
$$(0.65 \times 2) = \text{approximately } 1.29 \text{ points}$$
$$(0.65 \times 3) = \text{approximately } 1.94 \text{ points}$$

Figure 6.1 does not show everything, but the total for this line will come to 8.4. The quality characteristic weight is a result of proportionally distributing the other lines in this same way and then adding them up vertically. A large value shows a strong relationship to an important demanded quality.

We can use this method (of assigning values of 3 points, 2 points, and 1 point, respectively, to ◎, ○, and Δ in more than one way. If these points are distributed *after* direct multiplication by 8.4, it is called an independent point distribution method. Figure 6.1 shows an example of the proportional distribution method, but experience shows that the independent point distribution method is generally better. It also seems to be better than just assigning 5 points to ◎, 3 points to ○ and 1 point to Δ. Whichever method is used, I would like to make it clear that the above methods are only approximations. They serve as a general guide, but they are by no means absolute indicators.

As we mentioned in Chapter 2, when we compared our product with those of our competitors, we found that the quality demand "easy to hold" was lacking in our product. In our product planning, we decided to raise the level of this quality by 1.67 and to make this a major sales point. Now I would like to explain the process for resolving the technical aspects of the "easy to hold" requirement.

Technology Deployment

The basic function of the radio controller is to move an object such as a model plane or car that is at a distance from the user without using a wire. This function can be expressed as "move an object." In realizing this function, the controller's housing plays a very important role, which we can deploy further to such functions as "hold the main unit" and "protect the components."

Then there is a need to "communicate hand movement to the distant object." This can be deployed into functions such as "generate signals" or "send out radio waves." These functions, however, have nothing to do with the user. The user is satisfied as long as he or she can "communicate hand movement" to the distant object and will not care whether a laser or some other system is used instead of radio waves. Although it doesn't matter to the user, this difference in technology represents a crucial difference in the design of the remote control product, since it is one of its fundamental aspects. We will see later on that the design cannot be based solely on user-demanded items — but first we must clarify the basic function of the remote control device.

Using a method described previously, the function weight was derived from the demanded quality weight in Chart 2'-I — which is a matrix made up of from the demanded quality deployment chart and the function deployment chart. Chart 6.1, which is an expanded version of Chart 2'-I, enables us to see that the functions "hold the main body" and "protect the components" correspond to the "easy to hold" demand. Thus, our job becomes a matter of realizing these functions. This matrix plays an important role in enabling a company to realize user demands by relating them to the company's special technology.

We cannot stop at the deployment of demanded quality, however. We still have to determine the priorities of functions from a technical standpoint, using the function evaluation methods described previously, and then show which functions are most important to the design.

Mechanism Deployment

Even when demanded quality is converted and the product functions are spelled out clearly, it is not necessarily easy to connect them with the current level of technology. We have to determine what kind of mechanism can be used to build the required functions into the product.

Conversion of functions into mechanisms is particularly important with machines or assembled electronic products. Chart 1-II in Figure 6.1 shows one part of the mechanism deployment. The basic mechanisms of a radio-controlled product are the transmitter, the receiver, and the servo mechanism, with the addition of auxiliary mechanisms. The transmitter, for example, can be further divided into a control mechanism, a signal-generation mechanism, and a radio wave transmission mechanism.

"Seed information" (such as new technology) should be put into this mechanism deployment chart for future use. Consumer demands are input at the beginning of quality deployment. "Seeds" are input at the beginning of technology deployment. Then, we try to determine whether new technology, new materials, or new mechanisms can be used in some way in the remote control products. It is important to note that, contrary to what one would expect, needs are often discovered through these seeds. This is especially important when you are creating an entirely new product.

As Chart 2-II of Figure 6.1 shows, a matrix is made from the function deployment chart and the mechanism deployment chart. In order to realize the product functions, they must be converted into mechanisms. The "radio wave transmission" mechanism, which corresponds to the "transmit signals" function, is a more specific deployment. Of course, the "hold the main body" function mentioned previously corresponds to the mechanism that will house the parts. Chart 2-II is used not only to clarify relationships between functions and mechanisms, but to convert functional priority to mechanical priority, that is, mechanical weights.

Detecting Engineering Bottlenecks

Every company has its own system of classifying technical standards and technical data and works hard to compile this information. It is usually appropriate to include technical standards and data in the mechanism deployment portion of the technology deployment system. In most cases technical standards are compiled for functional parts, component units, and the like, but they are not compiled in a way that allows the company to accumulate technology when changes are made as the product changes.

If you can create classifications that apply within a mechanism, then technology can be accumulated even when the parts are changed. In order to achieve a particular function, we can look at a matrix of functional deployment and mechanism deployment for a similar model or product and find a corresponding mechanism. In determining whether it is possible to achieve the required function with your company's special technology capability, if you find that achievement is likely to be very difficult, this situation should be designated an engineering bottleneck. Detecting bottlenecks throughout the technology deployment chart is the most important point of technology deployment.

Let me give you a concrete example of improving quality, using the "easy to hold" example. When the product quality plan item "easy to hold" (quality level 5) is converted to a quality characteristic in quality chart 1-I in Figure 6.1, it is called "portability," a second-level characteristic pertaining to maneuverability. As you can see in the bottom row of Chart 1-I, the quality characteristic weight is derived from the demanded quality weight, and in this case is 6.28. In Chart 6.2, portability is divided at the third level into "weight", "shape", and "measurements". Although portability has been assigned a point value of 1.0, the third-level weights have been determined by experience to be 0.5, 0.1, 0.2, and so on. When you multiply these by 6.28, the respective weights become 3.14, 0.63, 1.26, and so on. It should be obvious that in order to improve portability, the emphasis must be placed on "weight".

Let us suppose that we have determined the design quality level for this characteristic to be 400 grams, as contrasted to the present value of 500 grams. The matrix shown in chart 2-II is made up of a characteristics deployment chart and a mechanism deployment chart. Let's focus on the parts housing mechanism. The unit currently has a handle made of metal. Since the weight we have targeted is difficult to obtain by an extension of our present technology, we enter "weight reduction engineering" in the chart as bottleneck engineering. In this way we specify that this design quality characteristic is relatively difficult to achieve, and we call it a bottleneck characteristic. It is important here to assign a number to each bottleneck item and to establish a plan of action to resolve each problem — and, of course, to follow through.

Investigating Engineering Bottlenecks: Using the Reviewed Dendrogram

There are a number of ways to deal with engineering bottlenecks, including PDPC and the reviewed dendrogram (RD). I would like to discuss the use of the latter.

Figure 6.3 gives the results of a case study in which a reviewed dendrogram was used to achieve weight reduction engineering for a radio-controlled product. First, we need to have some idea or plan for weight reduction. Questions should be repeated until a satisfactory answer is reached. For example, "change the material to a resin" can be reviewed by asking "what about durability," which could be answered "satisfactory when compared to the previous type." ("Review" here means asking a question or pointing something out.) As a result of asking these questions, after investigating resin-based materials, the idea of combining the outer housing and handle into one unit occurred to us as a solution, and we achieved the targeted weight reduction without using metal parts. (For more details on how this method was used, please refer to the Kohate-Oke reference at the end of this chapter.)

Summary

We have introduced the process of detecting engineering bottlenecks using the case of a radio-controlled product. New product development requires a flow of both material and information. The material is a problem for special technology. The information flow is a problem for control engineering. Quality information flow is quality deployment. Technical information flow is technology deployment. Identifying what is important in this flow is a particular problem for control engineering. Early discovery of solutions to engineering bottlenecks is the key to successful technology deployment. I want to emphasize the importance of this point in building a rational, systematic plan for technology deployment.

Quality Function Deployment to Understand Customer Needs: The Case of Taikisha, Ltd.

The main business of Taikisha, Ltd., is the use of heat, air, and water technology to design and build air conditioning equipment and painting equipment. The company manufactures a wide variety of equipment designed to conform to customer needs, which may vary with each project. Thus, quality deployment charts are very effective tools in helping the company understand and meet their customers' needs.

The Meaning of Quality Deployment Charts

In our company, using quality charts has the following benefits:

- They help us quantify demanded qualities and relate them to the company's special technology.
- They increase the efficiency of technology development, shorten the development process, and reduce the number of design processes.
- As a result, the company finds it easier and faster to realize the customers' demanded quality.
- They enhance our company's ability to systematize its special engineering capabilities and thus accumulate technology.

Quality Function Deployment at Various Design Levels

At Taikisha, quality function deployment is used at every step of the design development and execution stages. Here we will discuss an example of its use at the design stage.

Problems in Design Work

The following problems have plagued our design work for some time.

- Customer verbatims about quality demands and their relative importance often lack cohesion, objectivity, and comprehension, and the designers — even with their capabilities — have trouble understanding them.
- Designs are easily influenced by the capacity, technical ability, and creativity of the designers.
- The ability to interpret and review drawings and related materials depends heavily, at any particular time, on the intuition and experience of a limited number of senior members of the company.
- Quality-related information provided by users, and gained through design work and accumulating technical data, is not always sufficiently organized.

If we want to deal with the very complex process of satisfying customer quality demands, we must solve these problems.

Making Quality Charts and QA System Diagrams

For the reasons just spelled out, Taikisha requires — as a systematic activity related to design — the development of quality charts at every step of the QA system. Figure 6.4 summarizes Taikisha's QA system. They use QA at each step in establishing target qualities and then complete their design activities by using quality chart II, described as follows:

Quality Chart I: Quality characteristic values are determined for customer-demanded qualities and other requirements that relate to each room and each manufacturing process being designed. These requirements are converted into design conditions, and design targets are determined.

Quality Chart II: A system is then constructed by correlating the design conditions specified in quality chart I with the company's unique technology and the corresponding engineering for each of the rooms or manufacturing process under consideration.

Quality Chart III: The design steps for which corresponding engineering was specified in quality chart II are clarified and incorporated into the blueprints, plans, and other detailed documentation.

Quality Chart IV: Drawings and plans made at each design step are inspected and examined to make sure they have realized the customer-demanded quality.

Making a Four-Dimensional Matrix Quality Chart

After quality charts I through IV have been separately drawn up and deployed and are actually being used in design activities, it is often difficult for the individual design groups to pick out the parts of each of the four charts that are most relevant to their own activities. To solve this problem, we adopted a four-dimensional matrix quality chart that combines charts I through IV for each type of design function. Figure 6.5 illustrates this concept.

Using the Four-dimensional Matrix Quality Chart to Design Clean Room Facilities

Recently the demand for "clean rooms" has increased because they are used in semiconductor manufacturing. Every manufacturer of clean rooms is striving to acquire a high level of experience with quality and reliability. Taikisha, too, has experienced a marked increase in designs and orders from customers for clean rooms, and we offer the following observations.

1. To take advantage of the sudden increase in demand, the time period between receiving the customer's plans and starting production has been shortened, which means that the time period allocated to design has had to be shortened as well. Such changes have turned this new business into a large-scale operation.
2. A high level of special technology for the design and manufacture of clean room facilities has become indispensable in order to meet the requirements of the highly integrated semiconductor industry.
3. Manufacturers of clean rooms must ensure that all key participants in the design and production process have a common, uniform understanding of information about design conditions learned from discussions with the customer.

To respond to this situation in an economic, accurate, and timely manner, we developed — and now are using effectively — the four-dimensional matrix quality chart shown in Figure 6.6 for clean rooms at semiconductor facilities.

In quality chart I of the four-dimensional matrix, for example, we looked at the wafer-polishing process and a counterpart quality characteristic value — the need to reduce dust of specified particle sizes ranging from x to y microns. Other necessary functions and their counterpart quality characteristic values are also shown in quality chart I.

In quality chart II, you can see that a company's special technology is necessary to achieve the counterpart quality characteristic values required for the wafer-polishing process. We could meet these requirements by providing an air-change frequency of 35 to 80 times per hour, or a 0.3 micron final filter, or an inlet/exhaust system with ceiling inlet and floor exhaust, for example. In quality chart III you can see which of the company's special (or relationship) technologies must be clarified, and whether such clarification should take place at, for example, a meeting with a customer or a design policy meeting during the design process.

In quality chart IV we see which customer-demanded functions must be confirmed at each step of the design process.

The Results of Using a Four-dimensional Quality Chart

Using the four-dimensional quality chart has led to increased customer satisfaction, according to the results of a Taikisha customer satisfaction survey that showed an improvement in customer evaluations. Because of progress in raising the level of cleanness, there is also a reduction in overall design labor hours, in spite of an increase in the number of design examinations and inspections.

Three-dimensional Relationship Technology Chart

Background for Making the Chart

When we are designing air conditioning equipment, we often find it very difficult to decide how to fit the related technology from quality chart II into the design. The difficulty arises because different kinds of related technologies are available and because so many factors are involved in making a decision.

For example, the choice of technology for the refrigeration equipment — which plays a major role in air conditioning systems — depends on its energy source (electricity, oil, or gas), the type of system (central or individual units), the cooling method (such as centrifugal, compression method, or absorption method), and other factors. Dozens of different types of units may be available, such as turbocharged refrigeration units, absorption refrigeration units, package air conditioners, and room coolers. From among these many types, we must select the one most appropriate to meet the customer's demanded quality.

In such a situation, we are using the three-dimensional relationship technology chart as a tool to help us fit the related technology into the design in such a way that the resulting air conditioning system will be suitable for each clean room and the manufacturing process carried out there. By assigning numeric values to the relationships between the customer-demanded qualities and the various clean rooms and manufacturing processes, the relationship between the customer-demanded quality and the corresponding technology can be more easily analyzed and this analysis can be performed in a comprehensive and a consistent way.

Structure

As shown in Figure 6.7, a three-dimensional relationship technology chart is a matrix made up of three elements. The first element is the demanded quality as expressed in the customer's own words, the customer verbatim. The demanded quality is then deployed in words that express the customer's demands in terms of what the company finds necessary. The second element is the customer's clean room names and the manufacturing processes that are carried out in those rooms. The third element is a comprehensive knowledge of the technologies that could be used to meet the customer's requirements.

Chart A. Enter each item of the demanded quality for each of the rooms and manufacturing processes and evaluate each item on a 0-to-5 scale, according to degree of importance. These entries can be based on the quality deployment chart classified by building use, which contains the customer specifications, the company's standards, and so on. For example, in Figure 6.8, the intersection of item 11 "quiet" and "halls" is given 5 points.

Chart B. Using the relationship technology deployment chart, evaluate each item of technology that might be applicable on a 0-to-5 scale according to its suitability for realizing each of the demanded qualities. For example, in Figure 6.8 the intersection of "is quiet" and "AHU (CAV) air handling unit (constant air volume type)" is given 5 points.

Chart C. The values determined from charts A and B are then calculated according to the methods shown in Figure 6.7.

$$C_{jk} = \quad (A_{ij} \times B_{ik})$$

In Figure 6.8, for example, the relationship between the two lines, room line $j = 4$ (hallway system) and corresponding technology $k = 1$ "AHU (CAV) air handling unit" is depicted with the following equation:

$$C_{41} = 5 \times 4 + 0 \times 2 + 2 \times 2 + \ldots 5 \times 3 = 353$$

With a calculation like this, one can find the degree of relationship between each room or manufacturing process and the corresponding technology. These calculated values can then be used to identify the most appropriate technologies for each of the rooms or manufacturing processes. These choices are then incorporated into the design.

In this way, such factors as building and operational costs can be compared for several types of technologies that have been identified as appropriate for each room or manufacturing process, and the optimal technologies can then be selected.

We can summarize this procedure by saying that in the three-dimensional relationship technology chart, numeric values representing evaluation points are used to identify the most appropriate technology. This makes it easier to gain customer approval.

An Application

Figure 6.8 is a three-dimensional relationship technology chart that enables us to identify the most appropriate air handling unit equipment (interior load processing) for the interior of a particular building. One can see that a constant air volume type of air handling unit (AHU/CAV) has the highest degree of correspondence for the hallway system. The package-type air conditioner (No. 12) has a high degree of correspondence with the computer rooms. This chart makes it easy to see the degree of relationship for each room.

Benefits of Using the Three-dimensional Relationship Technology Chart

Using the three-dimensional relationship technology chart allows more effective use of the four-dimensional matrix quality chart, improvement in design quality, and a reduction in the number of design processes. When one of these charts is presented to a customer, it makes it easier to explain the reasons for various design decisions in a way that the customer can readily accept. This, in turn, increases the value of our drawings and plans in the customer's eyes.

Future Topics

Quality deployment charts must be regularly reviewed — if they are to maintain precise correspondence with ever-changing customer demands and thereby help us improve our designs and products. Inconveniences, gaps, defects, and other problems in using a quality function deployment chart should be recorded as soon as they are discovered, and a continuous flow of such information should be fed back in a timely manner to the appropriate departments.

Meanwhile, we must issue clear directives regarding the priorities to be established for the scope of projects and products for the development of quality deployment charts — priorities relating to both individual products and the scope of various projects.

References

Akao, Yoji; Kamizawa, Norio (1979). "Quality Function Deployment and FMEA." *Quality Control*, Vol. 30, No. 8, pp. 12-18, JUSE.

Akao, Yoji; Ono, Sadatoshi; Harada, Akira; Tanaka, Hinenori; Iwasawa, Kazuo (1983). "Quality Deployment including Cost, Reliability, and Technology (Parts 1 & 2)." *Quality*, Vol. 13, No. 3, pp. 61-77, JSQC.

Furukawa, Yasushi; Ikeshoji, Hindenori; Ishizuchi, H.; et al; (1981). "Theoretical Research regarding the Structure of Quality Control Systems (Reports 1 & 2)." *Quality*, Vol. 11, No. 2, pp. 30-42, JSQC.

Ishizu, Ikuzo (1980). "Use of Production Engineering Charts in Advance Development Systems." *Quality Control*, Vol. 31, Nov. special issue, pp. 43-45, JUSE.

Kano, Noriaki; Sera Nobuhiko; Takahashi, Fumio; Tsuji, Shinichi (1984). "Attractive Quality and Must-Be Quality." *Quality*, Vol. 14, No. 2, pp. 145-156, JSQC.

Kume, Hitoshi et al (1982). "Effectiveness and Limits of Quality Deployment." *Quality Control*, Vol. 133, No. 5, pp. 36-42, JUSE.

Matsumoto, K. (1985). "Use of Quality Deployment Charts at Taikisha Company." *Quality Control*, Vol. 36, No. 5, pp. 34-40, JUSE.

Miake, Shinichiro (1983). "Use of Three-Dimensional Relationship Technology Matrix in Air-Conditioning Equipment Design." *Quality Control*, Vol. 34, Nov. special issue, pp. 283-285, JUSE.

Mizuno, Shigeru; Akao, Yoji (1978). *Quality Function Deployment*. JUSE.

Nakui, Satoshi (1987). "Applying AHP to Weighting and Functional Classification in Function Deployment." JSQC 31st Research Committee Abstract.

Obata, Akira; Oke, M. (1980). "About the Reviewed Dendrogram System: Systematic Deployment of Development/Design/Planning." *Quality Control*, Vol. 31, Nov. special issue, pp. 37-42, JUSE.

QC Methods Development Dept. (1979). *Seven Tools for New QC for Controllers and Staff*. JUSE.

Sato, Katsuaki (1982). "Use of Quality Charts in Air-Conditioning Equipment Design." *Quality Control*, Vol. 33, Nov. special issue, pp. 303-306, JUSE.

Tone, Kaoru (1986). *Game-Like Decision Making*. JUSE.

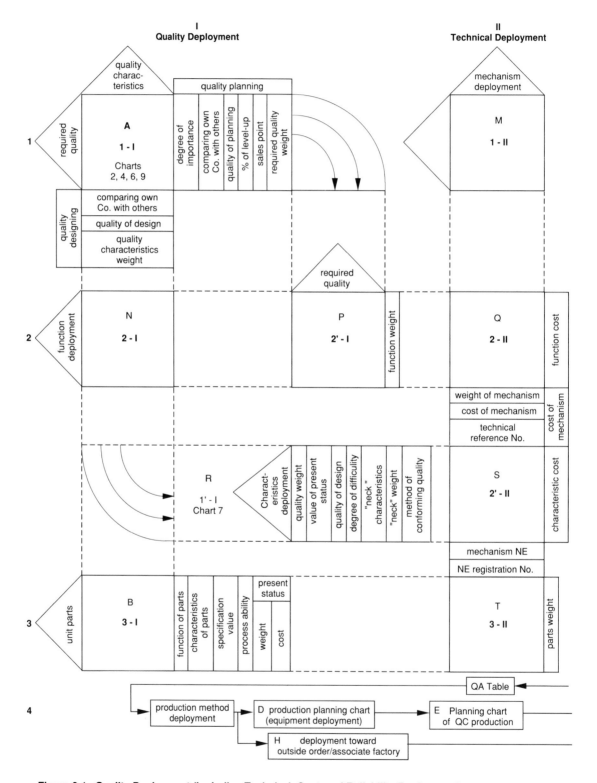

Figure 6-1. Quality Deployment (Including Technical, Cost, and Reliability Deployment)

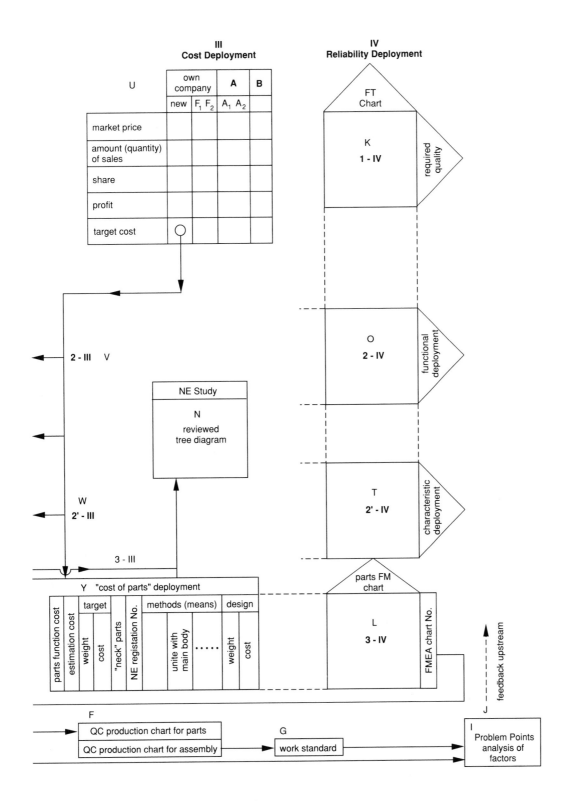

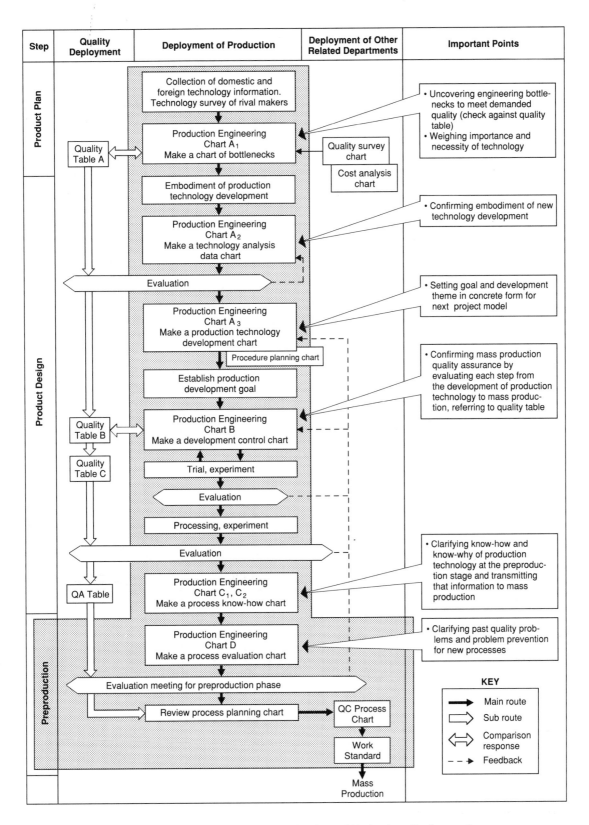

Figure 6-2. System Chart for Production Engineering (Quality and Technology Deployment)

1-I chart

demanded quality (1st level)	demanded quality (2nd level)	electrical performance (TRS characteristics / R characteristics)	mechanical performance	maneuverability (portability, stick characteristics, switch characteristics, antenna characteristics, stability, functionality)	common use availability	...	rate of importance	own company	company Y	company Z	quality planning	% of level up	sales point	absolute weight	demanded quality weight
1. precision movement	1.1 does not make wrong movement	△ 0.12 ◎ 1.85					4	5	4	4	5	1.0	◎	6.0	6.8
	1.4 stability of performance	◎ 1.06 ◎ 1.06					5	4	4	3	5	1.25	○	7.5	8.4
3. easy to maneuver	3.1 easy to understand how to maneuver			○ 0.85 ◎ 1.28 ◎ 1.28			3	4	5	3	5	1.25	○	4.5	5.1
	3.4 easy to hold			◎ 1.94 ○ 1.29 ◎ 1.94			3	3	4	4	5	1.67	◎	7.5	8.4
	Quality chart wt 100	3 52 5 10		6.28 4.12 3.90 2.27 6.98 11.97										88.8	100

quality characteristics — 1st level / 2nd level

quality planning — comparative analysis — planning — weight — other

function deployment chart

2 - I chart

2 - I chart

demanded quality weight

demanded quality deployment chart

move the objects	protect main parts	hold the main body in hand		◎	
		protect parts		○	
	convey the movement of hands	generate signals	○	◎ ○ ○ △ △	
		transmit radio waves	○	◎ ◎ ◎	

Chart 6-1. Technology Deployment

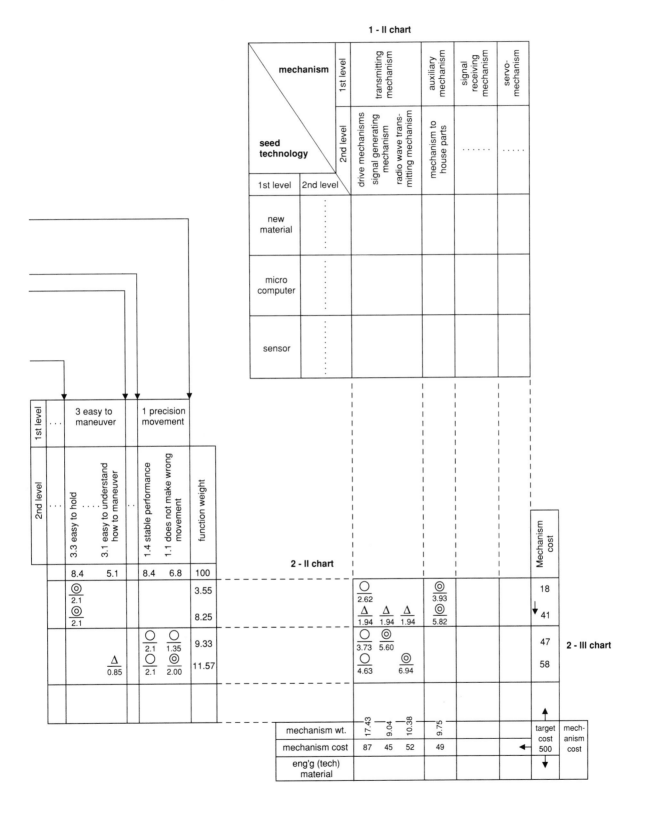

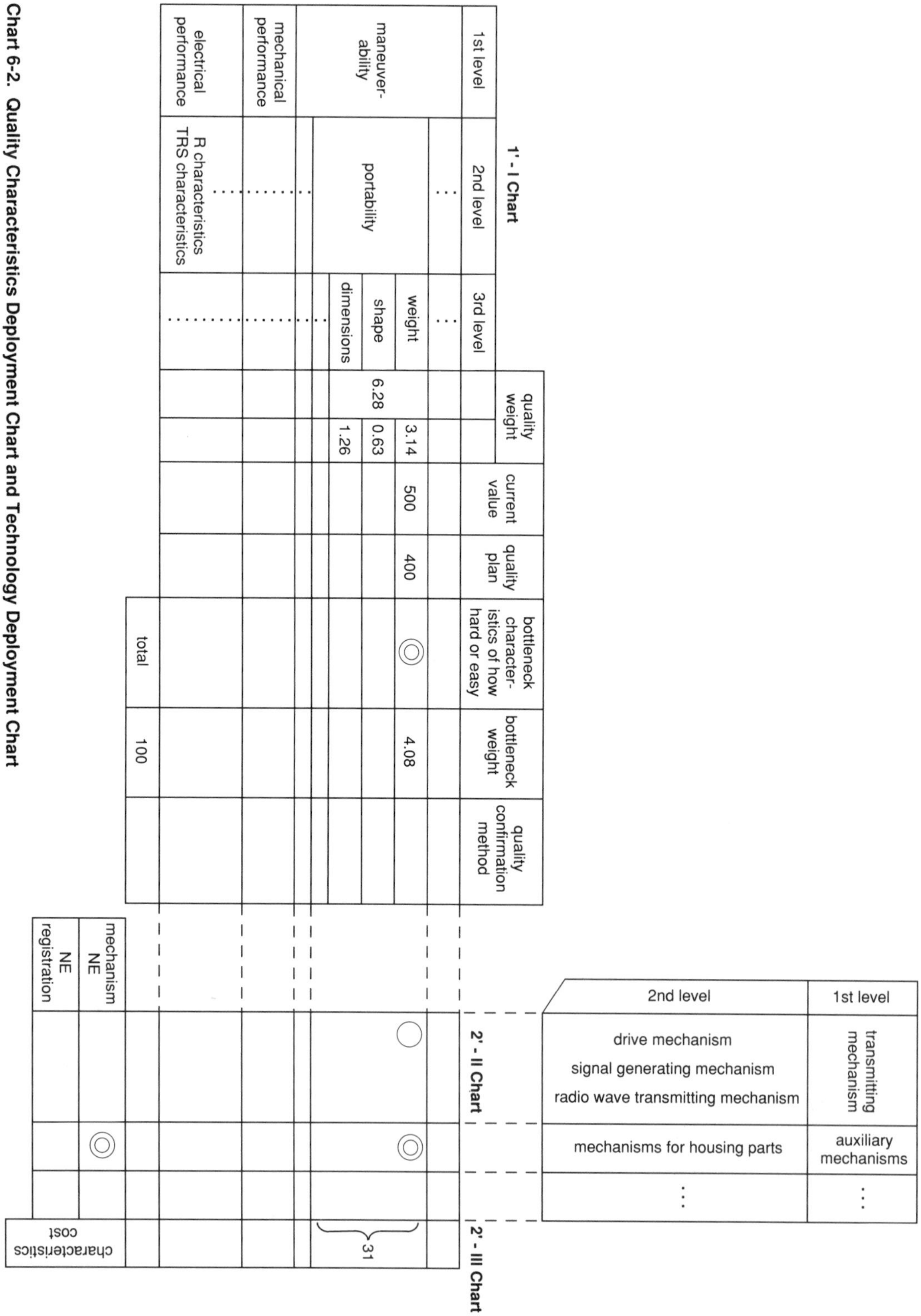

Chart 6-2. Quality Characteristics Deployment Chart and Technology Deployment Chart

1'- I Chart

1st level	2nd level	3rd level	quality weight	current value	quality plan	bottleneck character-istics of how hard or easy	bottleneck weight	quality confirmation method
maneuver-ability	portability	dimensions	6.28					
		shape	3.14					
		weight	1.26 / 0.63	500	400	◎	4.08	
mechanical performance	R characteristics	··········						
electrical performance	TRS characteristics	··········						
	total				100			

1'- II Chart

2nd level	1st level
drive mechanism signal generating mechanism radio wave transmitting mechanism	transmitting mechanism
mechanisms for housing parts	auxiliary mechanisms
⋮	⋮

2'- II Chart / **2'- III Chart**

	mechanism NE	NE registration	characteristics cost
	○		31
		◎	
	◎		

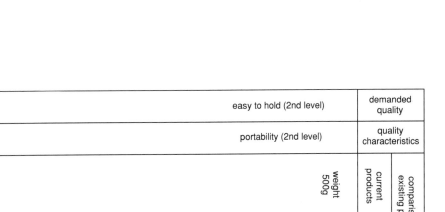

Figure 6-3. Reviewed Dendrogram Searching for Weight Reduction

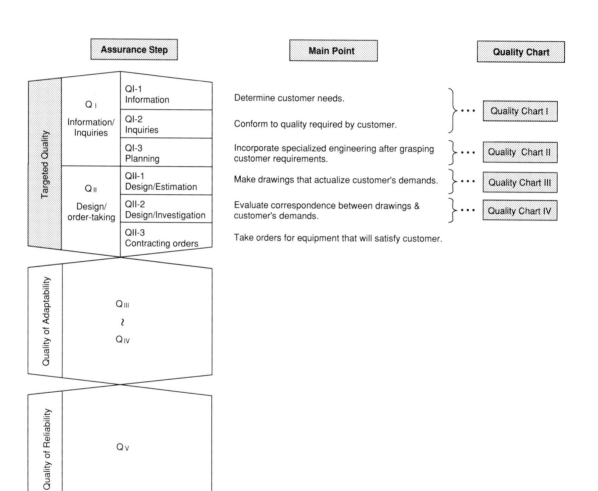

Figure 6-4. Relationship Between QA System and Quality Charts

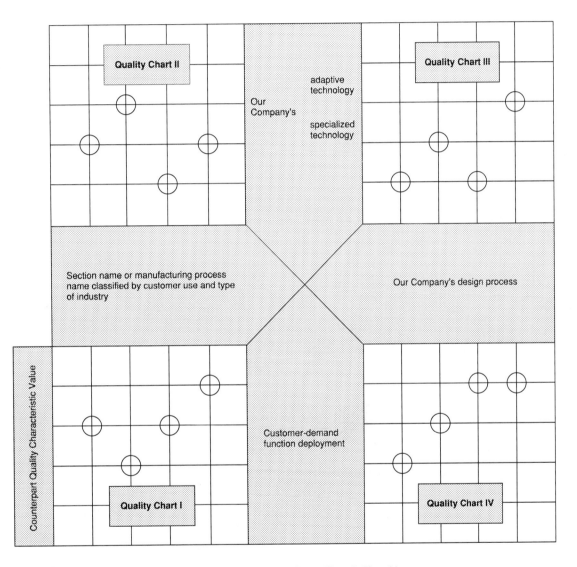

Figure 6-5. Structure of Four-dimensional Matrix Quality Chart (Rough Sketch)

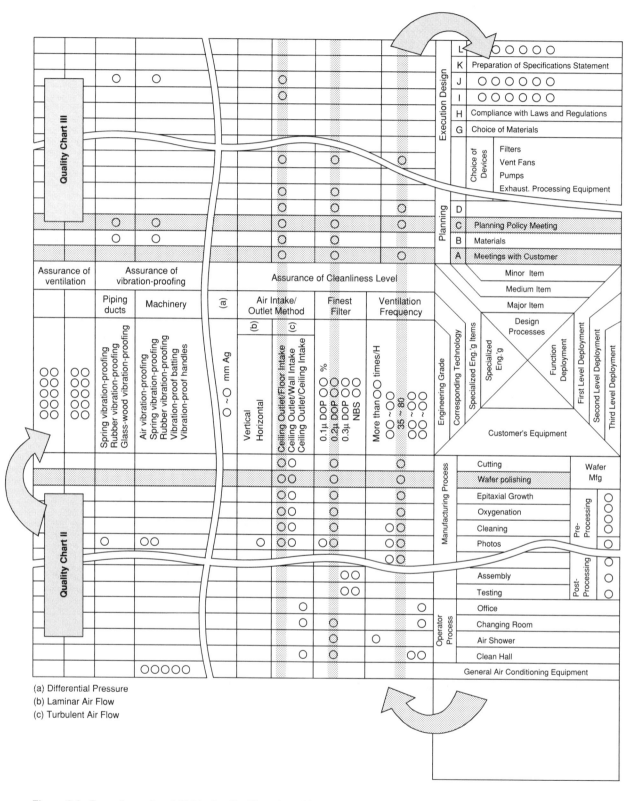

(a) Differential Pressure
(b) Laminar Air Flow
(c) Turbulent Air Flow

Figure 6-6. Four-dimensional Matrix Quality Chart for a "Clean Room"

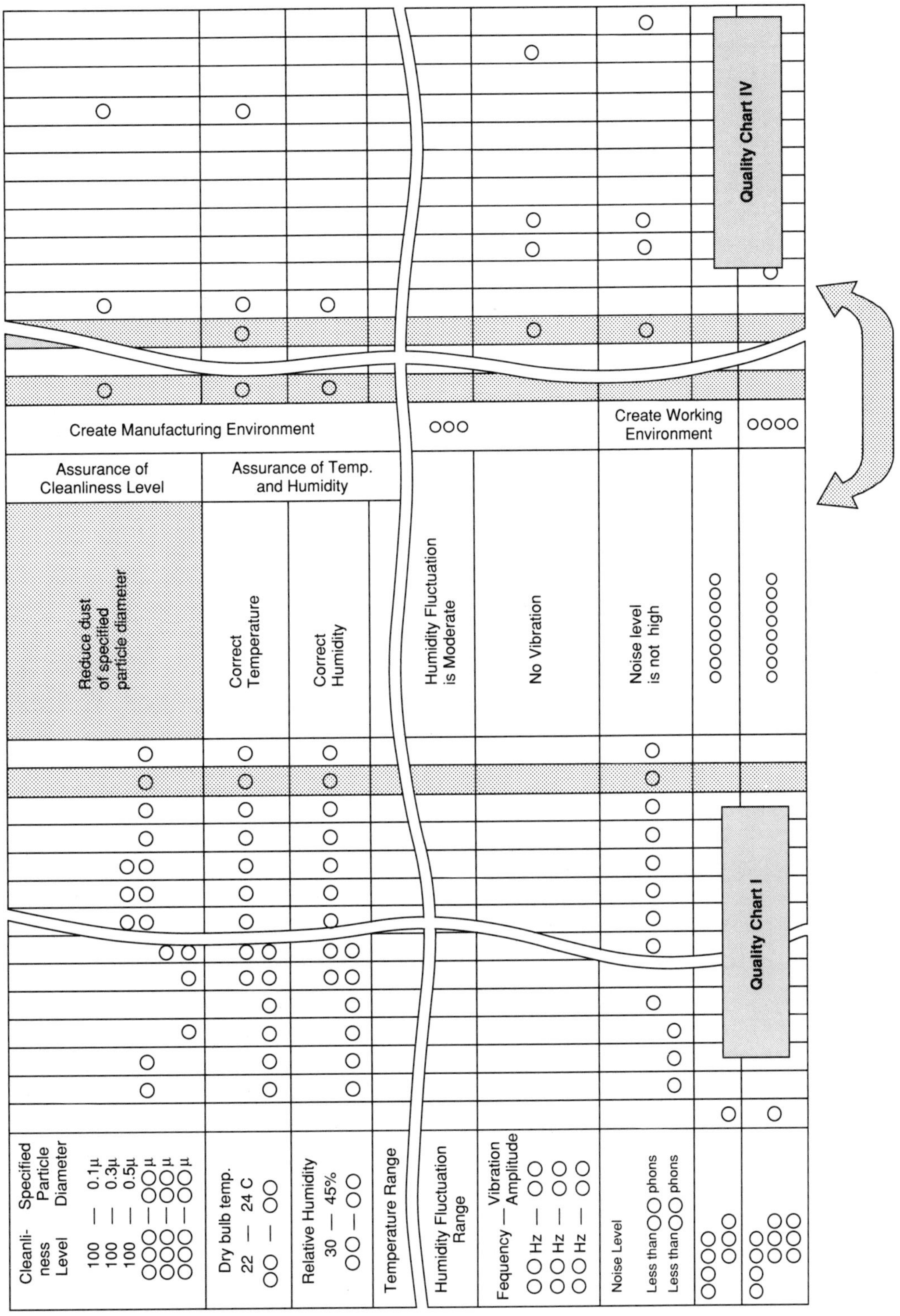

Quality Chart IV
Create Manufacturing Environment
Create Working Environment
Assurance of Cleanliness Level
Assurance of Temp. and Humidity
Reduce dust of specified particle diameter
Correct Temperature
Correct Humidity
Humidity Fluctuation is Moderate
No Vibration
Noise level is not high
Quality Chart I
Cleanli-ness Level
Specified Particle Diameter
100 — 0.1μ
100 — 0.3μ
100 — 0.5μ
Dry bulb temp.
22 — 24 C
Relative Humidity
30 — 45%
Temperature Range
Humidity Fluctuation Range
Fequency — Vibration Amplitude
Noise Level
Less than ○○ phons
Less than ○○ phons

Standards for Evaluation Points

Chart A	Evaluation Points	Chart B
Requirement for the room is		As a corresponding technology for the requirement
strong	5	excellent
↕	4	↕
average	3	average
↕	2	↕
unnecessary	1	inferior
negative	0	bad

Calculation method for C_{jk}: $C_{jk} = \sum\limits_{i=1}^{n} (A_{ij} \times B_{ik})$

Example of calculation when $i = 5$:

$$C_{22} = A_{12} \cdot B_{12} + A_{22} \cdot B_{22} + \cdots + A_{52} \cdot B_{52}$$

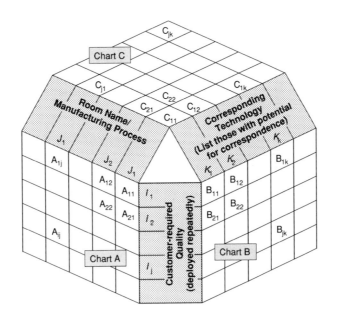

Figure 6-7. Structure of a Three-dimensional Relationship Technology Chart

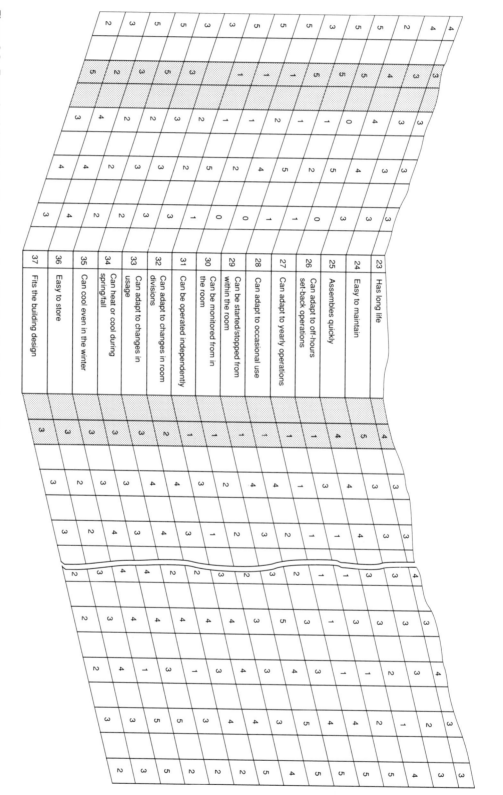

Figure 6-8. Example of the Use of a Three-dimensional Relationship Technology Chart

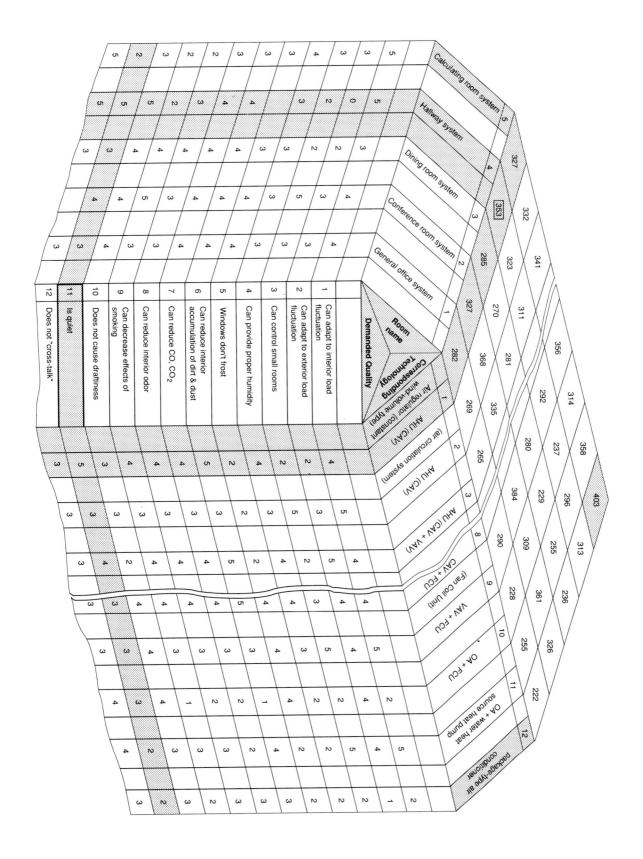

CHAPTER 7

Quality Deployment and Reliability Deployment

*Nobuo Takezawa, Executive Director, Toyota Auto Body;
and Masayuki Takahashi, Plant Control Manager,
Koyama Plant, Komatsu Manufacturing*

In the world of consumer products we often hear comments from customers expressed in such simple terms as, "This is good," "It's easy to use," or "The merchandise I buy at this department store or at any established store has better guarantees," or "Products from these large manufacturers are more reliable." Much research has been conducted on the problem of reliability, and in this chapter we will learn how to treat reliability within the framework of quality function deployment.

Customer Expectations

Very often when we are deploying quality in order to clarify quality, we find ourselves deploying the basic functions of the product. Sometimes the word *quality* is used in the broad sense — when referring to merchandise that is full of defects, for example. In narrow usage, phrases like "long-lasting shine," or "an unbreakable mirror" can be treated as top selling features in quality deployment. I think it better, however, to understand quality deployment in the way I will now describe.

When customer expectations for a product are sorted and arranged as items of current and future value, the result will look like Chart 7.1. The second item in the list of functions, durability, tells us how long customers think the basic functions of an item should last. We can think of durability as product life, but it is also reliability, in the narrow sense. We define reliability as the ability of a product to perform its functions long after it has been purchased. The third item in the chart, safety, must be examined from a totally different angle, but we should treat this item the same as product life. The fourth item, maintainability, or ease of maintenance, while not a major goal, is still one of the basic aspects of a product.

Special Aspects of Reliability

When we speak of the reliability of a product, we are really talking about the life of each of the product's basic functions. In other words, we need to consider the following aspects of reliability:

- Reliability means that the product as a whole continues to function.
- A product may include several functions, each of which has its own lifespan. Each quality characteristic of the product described in Chart 7.1, which we will call Product A, will change over time, according to the amount of use. In mathematical terms, $a_1, a_2, \ldots a_n$ can be expected to change to $a'_1, a'_2, \ldots a'_n$. But the degree to which they diminish over a given time period is not always the same.
- Although a product has a number of quality features, the life of a product really means the life of the product's main function. For example, even though the surface of a painted product may fade over time, the fading may not affect the performance of that product.
- The lifespans of the various quality features will differ according to how the product is used and maintained, and in relation to the environmental conditions under which it is used.

- With products subject to fashion trends, the lifespan of the fashion trend may be a more important factor than the life of the product's quality characteristics.

When we talk about the lifespan of a product in light of the points, we should ask the following questions:

- What special quality features do we need to pay attention to?
- What can we expect in terms of product life?
- How can we expect varying conditions of use and environmental conditions to affect product life?

Setting Targets

The reason for conducting research on product life is to develop the ability to manufacture products that will satisfy the target value for product life. Therefore, it is very important to have a process that enables us to assess what that life should be. Needless to say, the targets for product life will differ according to various factors such as design, production, and usage. So the probability of a breakdown occurring must be assessed after some consideration of the conditions under which the product will be used. For example, the breakdown rate might be once in 200,000 hours, or once in 6,000 hours.

It is generally desirable to be able to repair or recondition a product or its parts. When some products cannot be repaired, however, defective units are thrown away. Therefore, in making our decisions about reliability, we need to consider two basically different types of products and related factors:

- Products that are impossible to repair → product life which can be measured by success ratio, survival probability which can be measured by mean time to failure (MTTF).
- Products that can be repaired → required intervals for maintenance (time, cycles, travel), elimination of circumstances that cause failure, decreasing function (redundancy, etc.) which can be measured by mean time between failures (MTBF).

Promoting Reliability

Establishing reliability is not simply making a product according to plan or making sure it is used according to the instructions. Ideally, we could say that we need to develop and produce a product that is built in such a way that even if a failure were to occur in some function it would not greatly interfere with the function of the product as a whole; it would still maintain the reliability target that we had originally established. Reliability can be maintained only if certain activities are performed, beginning at the product planning and design stage and continuing throughout the entire manufacturing stage. In these high-tech times, when we are trying to achieve the utmost of every design, two activities are key to this reliability:

1. the design stage
2. the prototype and production prototype stages

Let's look at this more closely, using two examples to show us how to deploy reliability.

Reliability Deployment in Automobile Body Manufacturing: The Case of Toyota Auto Body

Building a Deployment System

First we need to clarify the quality targets that we have already been pursuing, and then try to deploy quality in a way that will allow us to achieve these targets with assurance. We try to deploy simultaneously all the items important to reliability that are listed among the other items in the quality deployment chart. As targets are set, the means (steps) to achieve them bring forth secondary (or more specific) targets, and the means to achieve these bring forth even more specific targets.

This method helps to identify the measures needed to achieve reliability, and it can be used for deploying every item. It can also be used in establishing the reliability targets for each characteristic and in assuring the achievement of those targets.

As we have said before, reliability means guaranteeing that the basic functional quality features of a product will last over a certain time period. Therefore, as we move through our deployment of the basic functions, we should be considering reliability as well. Figure 7.2 is a schematic representation of the relationship between these two deployment activities. The process flow in this figure is based on Figure 1.4 in Chapter 1, and the activities designated as 1-1, 2-1, 1-IV, and 2-IV in this figure also correspond to Figure 1.4. It is sometimes easier to understand the interrelationships with the deployment chart by depicting them in a tree format instead of a two-dimensional matrix, but they are substantially the same.

In Figure 7.2, the demanded quality column in the quality deployment shows a "comfortable cab" item; reliability in relation to this quality means to maintain the comfort over a certain timespan. We need to determine what this timespan is. As we continue with our deployment, this will require us to clarify our demanded qualities, which means determining their quality elements.

When deploying reliability, we need to identify quality elements for those characteristics whose quality could be difficult to maintain over the desired timespan. In the effort to identify them, it is helpful to consider an analyses of past complaints and quality problems that have occurred — or are recurring — during process control. With new products, especially, lack of experience in new applications of new technology, new materials, or new mechanisms increases the likelihood of reliability problems. We have found that failure mode effect analysis (FMEA) and similar analyses are effective in preventing these problems.

We now continue our deployment to measures that will allow us to assure the reliability characteristics. When we ask what we need to do in order to have this assurance — in other words, when we ask what reliability function deployment consists of — we see that reliability mechanism deployment attempts to specify the construction design that will realize these functions. Also, certain component FMEA charts deal with the quality of component parts.

In conducting reliability deployment, there are two methods for deploying the measures shown in the lower section of Figure 7.2 — by combining the deployment shown in both the upper and the lower panel or by considering the cost. The first of these deals directly with achieving reliability objectives by improving the product's operation — improving the smoothness of an operation by preventing friction, for example, or raising baking temperatures to obtain a tougher finish, or avoiding concentrating such a heavy load on one spot that one creates the possibility of fatigue failure, or making the diameter of a shaft bigger. The other method is based on the proposition that if there is a one-in-a-million chance of a failure occurring due to friction, and we need to maintain smooth operation, perhaps we can switch to an auxiliary system or find a method of bypassing the problem or fitting the mechanism with an additional support structure. We must realize, however, that the solutions may greatly increase the cost even though the probability of function loss is greatly reduced.

Reliability Deployment Using Fault Tree Analysis (Analyzing the System)

In order to accurately deploy the high-priority quality items in quality function deployment, we cannot just look at the relationships between the quality items. We must look into the relationships between the assurance characteristics and the primary cause characteristics. For example, when establishing tolerances using the rules of variance and variance synthesis, or when handling engineering characteristics, the relationships among the various product features in a mechanism consisting of assembled mechanical components are tested to confirm their repeatability. An experimental formula is then used to express the relational formula of the characteristics.

In reliability deployment, the characteristic values near the top event use failure probability. In the past, fault tree (FT) charts have been made in electrical systems using the logical symbols that link the relationships of the top event to the basic event. The FT chart shows this product system. As shown in Figure 7.3, if we know the probability of failure occurrence for individual parts a, b, and c, we can calculate the probability of the top event.

Stated in terms of reliability, this means that the reliability of the components will assure the target reliability of the whole system, or product. We can calculate this by means of Boolean algebra based on the set theory and by using a formula that expresses the relationship in logical symbols. Figure 7.4 is a FTA of the "comfortable cab" example shown in Figure 7.2. Using negative terms to express such targets is very common.

Reliability Deployment at the Component Level

As we have just observed, product reliability has two aspects: (1) minimizing the effects of system failures and (2) finding more effective ways to increase the reliability of the system components or parts.

Now I would like to discuss methods for examining reliability in structural components. Generally speaking, a new design is made by analyzing past experiences and smoothing over rough spots at the design stage using information recorded in the engineering manual. It is commonly done so systematically that any omissions that have occurred in the past are prevented from occurring again and more effective ways to plan can be devised. In this example, FMEA is used quite often. FMEA differs from FTA in that it is a qualitative, rather than a quantitative, method. It focuses on preventing failure modes that we know about from our past experiences.

For more detailed information on the use of FMEA, I can recommend the Suzuki textbook listed at the end of this chapter, but I will briefly explain here how this procedure is followed.

1. Clarify the function of each component part.
2. Investigate the factors that are apt to cause problems.
   - Check the environment and use conditions.
   - Identify failure modes.
3. Study the extent of effects produced by problems that have occurred, and look for important causal factors.
4. For problems that have produced significant effects, select countermeasures or, if the nature of the problem is unclear, explore the relationships between effects and their causes using failure analysis methods.

The purpose of this example is to show how to organize and maintain know-how in the failure mode chart. In this chart, all failures are classified by the type of characteristic and by the kind of problem, and information about the circumstances and conditions of use under which the problem occurred is included. This information comes from maintenance record cards filled out at the factory. We need to determine which of the structural parts will be included in the chart and what level of detail will be included. Figure 7.5 shows how the primary FMEA chart can be used to single out the parts that should be analyzed in detail because their failures produce important affects. Using FMEA to identify these critical parts and then perform a more detailed (or secondary) FMEA on them enables us to achieve better reliability assurance.

The Value of Our System (Combining FTA and FMEA)

Even in new product development one can usually find some experimental data or work records to help us in reliability deployment. Similar products may exist, or there may be at least some connection with an existing product structure or parts. This means that it is usually possible to have some concept of the structure of the new product at the design planning stage. Using FTA to show the relationships between the reliability of parts and the reliability targets for the systems they make up, we can gain some knowledge of the product's reliability. For example, in the process of clarifying new targets we might find that the reliability of one or more structural parts will need improvement. In that case, we would apply FMEA, develop some plans for improvement, and select the one that comes closest to meeting our cost requirements. The FTA results can then be evaluated in light of the new targets, and the real design work can begin. The FTA chart is a very effective aid for accurately analyzing the results of trial evaluations and manufacturing evaluations.

Reliability Deployment: The Case of Komatsu Manufacturing, Koyama Plant

Generally speaking, automobiles and trucks are designed to run on highways and are not intended to crash into obstructions. But construction machinery is required to work repeatedly at crushing, digging, and scraping the earth. Thus, the demand for reliability in the construction machinery market is very high — often higher than demands for efficiency in other functions. The reliability of the diesel engines used in this machinery is a major discussion topic, and diesel engine development consumes about two-thirds of all the time and money allocated for design preparation. I would like to introduce the quality deployment and reliability deployment methods being used at our Koyama Plant.

Quality Deployment and Reliability Deployment

The left half of Figure 7.6 represents deployment of the users' demanded qualities; the right half represents reliability deployment and shows how reliability is integrated at each step.

Our first step is to assign weights to the user quality demands collected by our sales and engineering departments. They have been deployed in a quality chart for each section or part of the diesel engine. Then we determine the final selling points and deploy them into quality targets — which are determined after considering our current machines, our competitors' current machines, predicted future moves by our competitors, and our own potential for mechanical improvements.

In this case, since we are developing the construction machinery, we are determining the selling points for the first time. We use the technology deployment chart to deploy the quality target values into engineering components and their characteristics. However, since incompatibilities may exist among the basic component functions, their quality characteristics, and the quality target items, we combine several component items and apply a simulation analysis technique called system analysis. Various combinations of component items can be analyzed. We try to select the most appropriate combination, and the one we select becomes what we call the "reliability evaluation standard." The reliability targets established for each component are deployed in relation to the standard with reliability allocation.

Reliability Evaluation Standard

In our company, all market reliability data is stored in a data base that is accessible for on-line analysis. Our system is called the SEARCH system. Anyone can access it and the data, which can be analyzed and sorted for up to 28 parameters, such as machine, geographical, and use classifications. All failure experiences for our company — about 3,000 modes in the past twenty years — are stored in this data base, along with any related failure data. With this failure mode information, we can identify the most important quality problems for any period and then use the thirteen steps defined in the failure analysis to thoroughly analyze the information. This allows us to investigate the real causes of the failure modes.

One of the most important steps in this failure analysis program is a reproducibility test based on-site usage conditions. Here, the relationships between the failure modes and the true causes become apparent, and when this information is combined with other mechanical reliability data stored in SEARCH, we can get a failure ratio. We then prepare a feature correlation diagram and explain the limits on the reliability target values for each component in this chart. This is the reliability evaluation standard, and it becomes an accumulation of the reliability know-how of our company.

Reliability Allocation Chart

In reliability deployment, failures are classified as A, B, or C failures to promote easy understanding of all failure events (modes) of all engines (before and after model changes, if there has been one). In this case, an A failure is one in which the engine must be removed to be repaired; a B failure is one in which the engine is inoperable, but can be repaired while it is still attached to the chassis; and a C failure is one that will not fault the engine's operation, but must be repaired before further deterioration occurs. Reliability targets are then established for each failure A, failure B, failure C, and so on. Accumulating these, we have the reliability targets for the entire engine.

Reliability allocation is another way to establish reliability targets for an engine under development. The reliability allocation chart (see the right side of Figure 7.6) shows the reliability experience and characteristic values of engines similar to the one being developed. By studying the characteristic values (the numerical values assigned to characteristics during technology deployment) and the reliability target values of similar engines, we can establish the reliability targets for each component of the engine being developed.

Design Concept Deployment

We use the concept deployment chart, which is based on component feature values that have been deployed as we have been doing to investigate the concept behind each component and determine our design policy.

The details of the component features to be examined are refined using FMEA and other analysis methods, and test items are established. At this step of the detailed design, the component specifications are developed from the FMEA and reliability allocation chart, and the development engineers and design element engineers who will actually design the components look at different possibilities for realizing these specifications and establish the final values. During this, all component items and feature values are determined, and engineering bottlenecks that will be key targets for research and deployment become apparent.

Confirming Quality

In order to confirm that reliability actually exists in the design that has been deployed, a quality confirmation item evaluation chart is made from the quality confirmation section of the component specification chart. This chart enables us to determine whether any failure mode items have been missed. We use our SEARCH system and the quality confirmation forms to do this. This chart also lists evaluation features for each confirmation item (failure mode) and allows us to see whether the expected and the actual values match. It also explicitly specifies which test codes should be used in making final evaluations. Along with this reliability confirmation program, we conduct quality confirmation, and where the expected and actual measurements do not match, we immediately feed this information back into a revised expectation program. We then evaluate each confirmation item again. Engines deployed in this way are then test marketed and a final evaluation is performed using SEARCH.

Figure 7.7 summarizes the way this system is used. These engines have been mass produced for the past three years and are receiving very high marks for being one of the most reliable engines in the marketplace.

Conclusion

Reliability assurance programs are in some respects still at the stage of experimental element engineering. Conducting reliability assurance with a simple reliability deployment method is difficult unless records of daily activities are maintained and great efforts are made to collect market reliability information. Only with such information can we thoroughly investigate the causes of problems using failure analysis. We can then combine the results of these two efforts and use them to establish revised reliability evaluation standards. Quality assurance based on reliability evaluation becomes an everyday activity and should be added to the new product development system to enhance the reliability deployment program.

References

Reliability Management Handbook (1985). Japan Standards Association, p. 512.
Suzuki et al. *FMEA FTA Enforcement Method* (1982). JUSE.

	Function	Example	Note
1	Basic functions	Convenience, esthetics Easy handling	
2	Durability	Extended use; life at least 11 years	Reliability items
3	Safety	No danger, harmless	
4	Maintenance	Parts can be easily replaced	

Chart 7-1. Customer Expectations

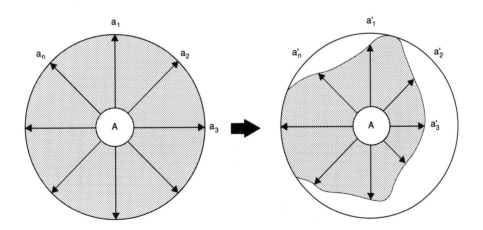

Quality characteristics change as time passes.
(The quality characteristics of Product A ~ a_1, a_2, a_n will change to a'_1, a'_2, a'_n.)

Figure 7-1. Quality Characteristics

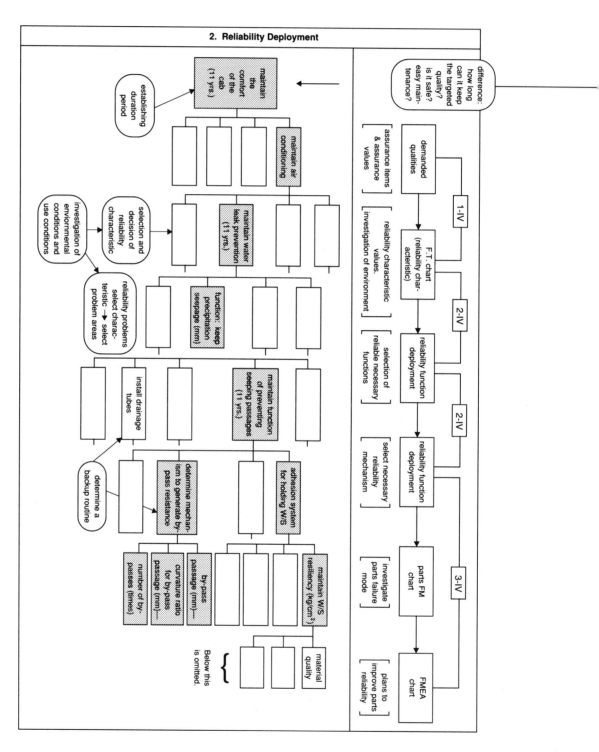

Figure 7-2. Reliability Deployment

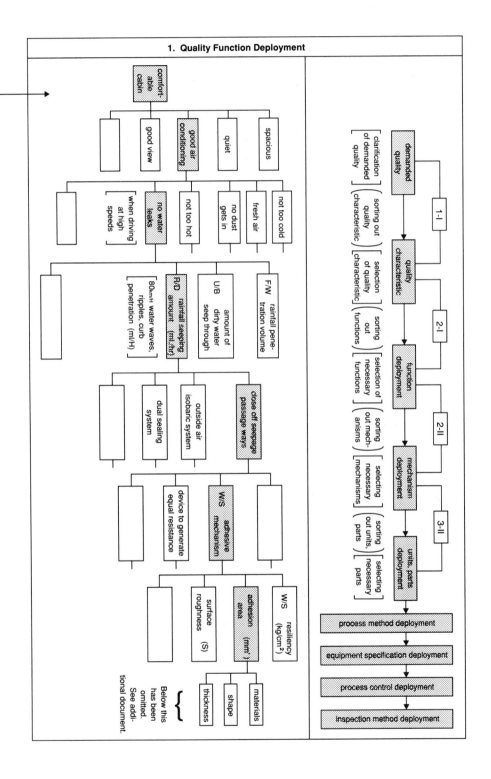

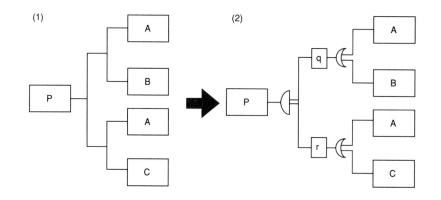

Theme: When the part failure occurrence probability (A) — (C) is known, the system failure occurrence probability can be calculated.

Solution: q = A + B, r = A + C . . . OR gate

$$P = q \times r . . . .\ AND\ gate$$

therefore

$$\therefore P = (A + B) \times (A + C)$$

$$= A \times A + A \times B + A \times C + B \times C$$

When this is transformed using the basics of Boolean algebra:

$$P = A + B \times C$$

when the failure occurrence probability of parts A, B, C is assumed 0.02, the faiilure occurrence probability of system P is calculated thus:

$$P = 0.02 + (0.02)\ Q = 0.0204$$

Figure 7-3. Using FTA to Calculate Reliability
   (1) Relationship shown by FT diagram
   (2) Arranges like logic circuits

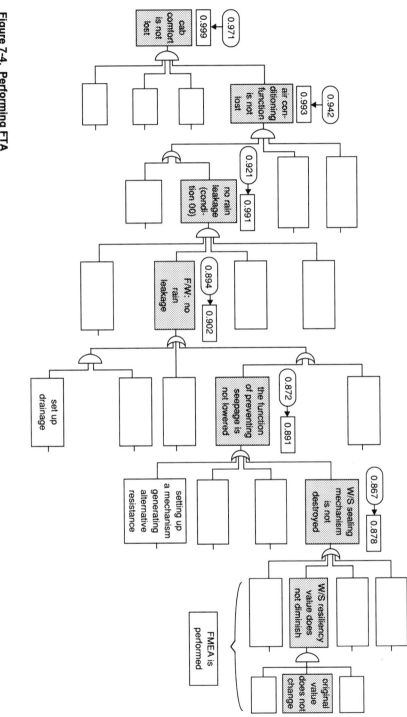

Figure 7-4. Performing FTA
(Figure 7-2. Reliability Deployment ⟶ FTA Chart)

Primary FMEA

Title	Rotary Index							
No.	Block Titles	Function	Failure Mode	Possible Cause	Effect	Detection Method	Failure Class.	Prevention Strategy
1	rotor sub-assembly	transfer	poor speed control. motion unreliable	foreign particles attached slide friction	lower production	cycle indicator	II	prevent powdered dust
2	stopper sub-assembly	positioning	big impact, skips positions; unreliable sliding	worn out springs, abrasion, large clearance	system stops	alarm	I	strong improvement, prevent powdered dust
3	puller sub-assembly	speed					III	
4								

Secondary FMEA

Title	Stopper sub-assembly							
No.	Parts Names	Function	Failure Mode	Possible Cause	Effect	Detection Method	Failure Class.	Plan for Improvement
1	hone sub-assembly	set position	wear	small pressure resisting area	poor precision	honing scale	I	enlarge area shape of hone (R-type)
2	slide mechanism	retain hone	scuffing abrasion wear	metal contacts lots of powdered dust	position uncertain	slide position	II	lubrication control slide cover installed
3	spring	normal: pulled out	fatigue	large contortion			III	
4	female							

Figure 7-5. Performing FMEA

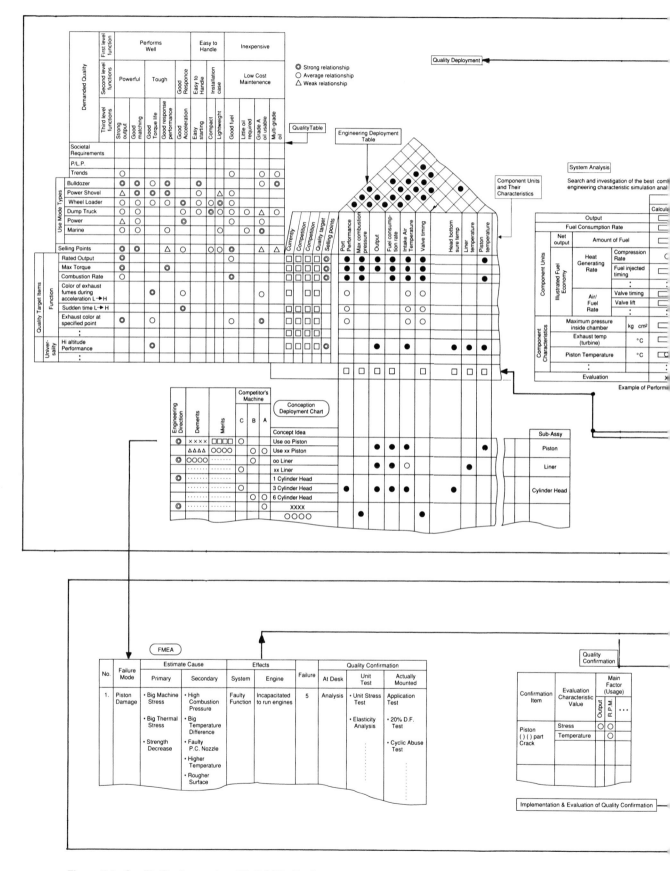

Figure 7-6. Quality Deployment and Reliability Deployment

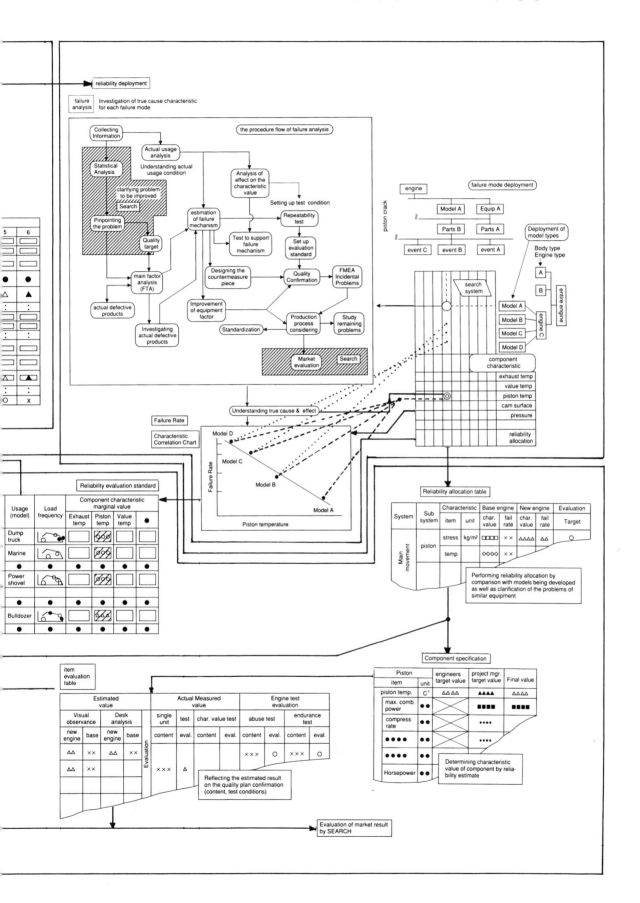

Legend:
◎ Strong relationship
○ Average relationship
△ Weak relationship

Demanded Quality

First level function		Performs Well				Easy to Handle		Inexpensive			
Second level functions	Powerful		Tough		Good Responce	Easy to Handle	Installation case	Low Cost Maintenence			
Third level functions	Strong output	Good matching	Good Torque life	Good response performance	Good Acceleration	Easy starting	Compact	Lightweight	Good fuel	Little oil required	Grade A oil usable	Multi-grade oil
---	---	---	---	---	---	---	---	---	---	---	---	---
Societal Requirements												
P/L.P.												
Trends	○								○		○	○
Bulldozer	◎	◎	○	◎		◎					○	◎
Power Shovel	△	◎	◎	◎		○		△	○			
Wheel Loader	○	○	○	○	◎	○	○	◎	○			
Dump Truck	○	○			○	○	◎	○	○	○	△	○
Power	△	○			◎				○		○	
Marine	○	○		○			○				○	◎
Selling Points	◎	◎		△	○		○	○	◎		△	△

QualityTable → Engineering Deployment Table

Quality Target Items

Function	Strong output	Good matching	Good Torque life	Good response performance	Good Acceleration	Easy starting	Compact	Lightweight	Good fuel	Little oil required	Grade A oil usable	Multi-grade oil	Currently	Competition	Competition	Quality target	Selling points	Port Performance	Max combustion pressure	Output	Fuel consumption rate	Intake Air Temperature	Valve timing
Rated Output	◎						○						□	□	□	□	◎	●	●	●	●	●	●
Max Torque	◎		◎										□	□	□	□	◎	●	●	●	●	●	●
Combustion Rate	○						◎						□	□	□	□	◎	●	●		●	●	●
Color of exhaust fumes during acceleration L→H			◎		○						○		□		□	□		○				○	○
Sudden time L→H					◎								□	□	□	□		○				○	○
Exhaust color at specified point	◎	○					○				◎		□	□	□	□		○				○	○
:													□	□	□	□							
Universality — Hi altitude Performance			◎										□	□	□	□	◎			●		●	

Conception Deployment Chart

Engineering Direction	Demerits	Merits	Competitor's Machine C	B	A	Concept Idea	Port Performance	Max combustion pressure	Output	Fuel consumption rate	Intake Air Temperature	Valve timing
◎	××××	□□□□	○			Use oo Piston						
	△△△△	○○○○		○	○	Use xx Piston			●	●	●	
◎	○○○○	....		○		oo Liner			●	●	○	
	....	....	○			xx Liner			●	●	○	
◎	....	....				1 Cylinder Head						
	....	....		○		3 Cylinder Head	●		●	●	●	
	....	....		○	○	6 Cylinder Head						
◎	....	....			○	XXXX		●				●
						OOOO		●				●

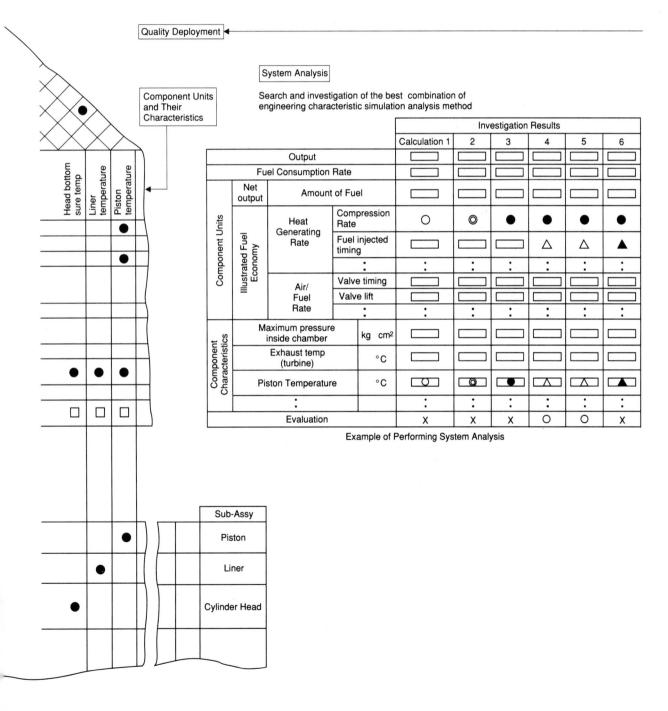

Example of Performing System Analysis

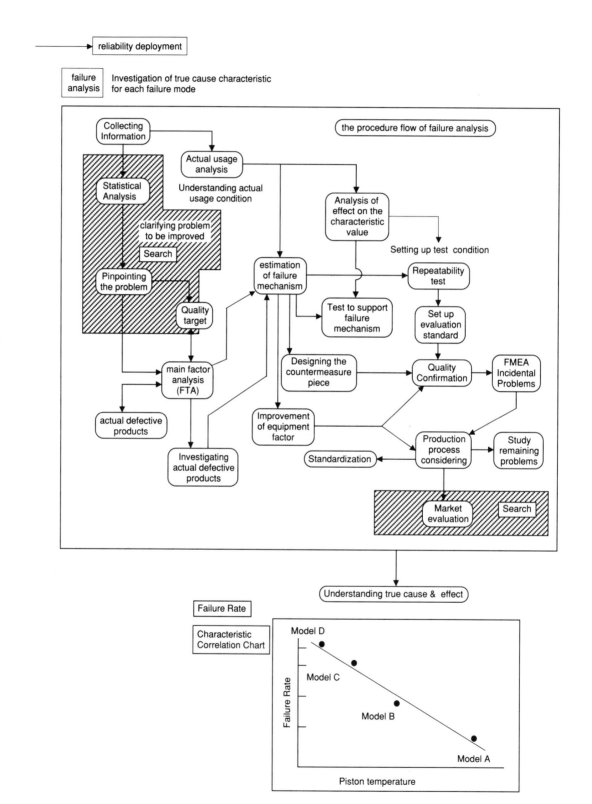

reliability deployment

failure analysis | Investigation of true cause characteristic for each failure mode

the procedure flow of failure analysis

Collecting Information

Actual usage analysis

Understanding actual usage condition

Statistical Analysis

clarifying problem to be improved

Search

Pinpointing the problem

Quality target

Analysis of effect on the characteristic value

Setting up test condition

estimation of failure mechanism

Repeatability test

Test to support failure mechanism

Set up evaluation standard

main factor analysis (FTA)

Designing the countermeasure piece

Quality Confirmation

FMEA Incidental Problems

actual defective products

Improvement of equipment factor

Production process considering

Study remaining problems

Investigating actual defective products

Standardization

Market evaluation | Search

Understanding true cause & effect

Failure Rate

Characteristic Correlation Chart

Model D

Model C

Failure Rate

Model B

Model A

Piston temperature

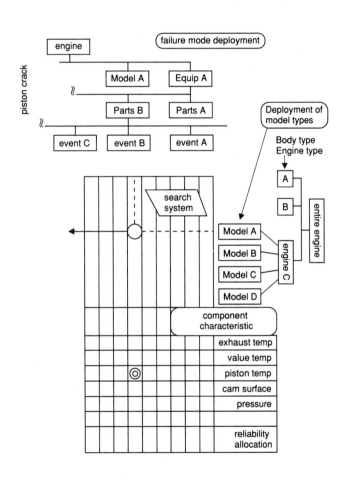

Reliability evaluation standard

Load rate	Usage (model)	Load frequency	Component characteristic marginal value			
			Exhaust temp	Piston temp	Value temp	●
Below % Light	Dump truck					
	Marine					
	●	●	●	●	●	●
Below % Medium	Power shovel					
	●	●	●	●	●	●
Over % Heavy	Bulldozer					
	●	●	●	●	●	●

item evaluation table

Estimated value							Actual Measured value				Engine test evaluation			
Visual observance		Desk analysis			single unit	test	char. value test		abuse test		endurance test			
new engine	base	new engine	base	Evaluation	content	eval.	content	eval.	content	eval.	content	eval.		
ΔΔ	××	ΔΔ	××						×××	○	×××	○		
ΔΔ	××				×××	Δ								

Reflecting the estimated result on the quality plan confirmation (content, test conditions)

Reliability allocation table

| System | Sub system | Characteristic | | Base engine | | New engine | | Evaluation |
		item	unit	char. value	fail rate	char. value	fail rate	Target
Main movement	piston	stress	kg/m²	□□□□	××	△△△△	△△	○
		temp		◇◇◇◇	××			

Performing reliability allocation by comparison with models being developed as well as clarification of the problems of similar equipment

Component specification

| Piston | | engineers target value | project mgr. target value | Final value |
item	unit			
piston temp.	C°	△△ △△	▲▲▲▲	△△△△
max. comb. power	●●		■■■■	■■■■
compress rate	●●		••••	
••••	●●		••••	
••••	●●			
Horsepower	●●			

Determining characteristic value of component by relia-bility estimate

Evaluation of market result by SEARCH

FMEA

No.	Failure Mode	Estimate Cause		Effects		Failure	Quality Confirmation		
		Primary	Secondary	System	Engine		At Desk	Unit Test	Actually Mounted
1.	Piston Damage	• Big Machine Stress	• High Combustion Pressure	Faulty Function	Incapacitated to run engines	5	Analysis	• Unit Stress Test	Application Test
		• Big Thermal Stress	• Big Temperature Difference					• Elasticity Analysis	• 20% D.F. Test
		• Strength Decrease	• Faulty P.C. Nozzle						• Cyclic Abuse Test
			• Higher Temperature						
			• Rougher Surface						

Quality
Confirmation

Confirmation Item	Evaluation Characteristic Value	Main Factor (Usage)		
		Output	R.P.M.	...
Piston ( ) ( ) part Crack	Stress	O	O	
	Temperature		O	

Implementation & Evaluation of Quality Confirmation

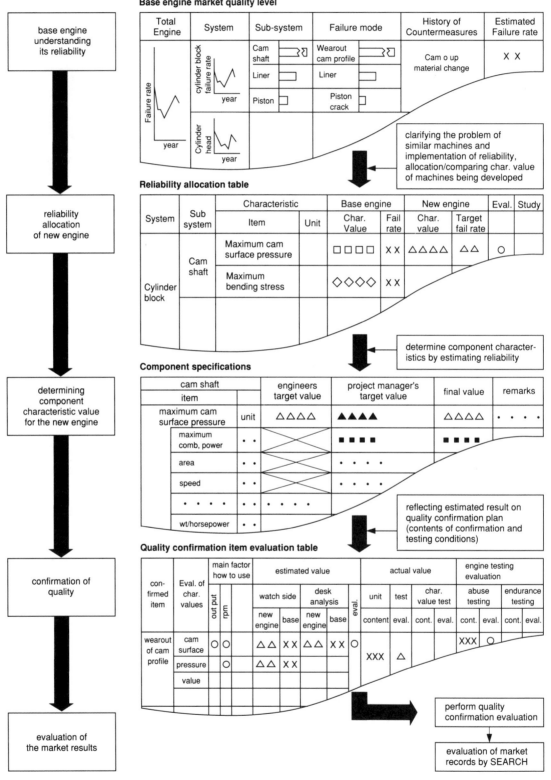

Figure 7-7. An Application Example of Use at the Development Stage of a New Line of Engines

CHAPTER 8

Quality Deployment and Cost Deployment

Yoshitomo Maekawa, Total Quality Manager, Design Department,
Yokohama Works, Nippon Steel Works,
and Ken Ohta, Manager, Engineering Section #1,
Toyoda Machine Works Ltd.

It has not been that long since the first and second oil crises and again we are faced with problems. A strong yen, coupled with the trade imbalance, has recently produced rather severe circumstances. Many firms are deploying survival tactics in order to stay alive these days. Our firm is experiencing these pressures, and I think many of our readers are as well.

While most survival tactics differ according to company, new product development is common to all and is being given priority. A new product must meet the quality and cost requirements of the market and also consider the timeliness of its introduction to the market.

Our company's new products are supposed to be competitive with those of other firms but we are experiencing many problems, including (1) poor sales despite high product performance and (2) exceeding planned costs by the time development is completed. (Planned cost is the cost determined by repeatedly forecasting the timing and effect of a cost reduction plan established through cost planning activities designed to determine the achievability of a product's target cost.) Chart 8.1 summarizes these problems. I should add here that some of these problems are peculiar to our company because, in the case of unique problems, we cannot rely on the experience of other companies with similar products to identify quality and cost problems at the initial stage of new product development. Solving these problems is crucial.

Cost Deployment Based on Quality Deployment

While the general theory of quality function deployment was outlined in Chapter 1, this chapter will deal with another aspect — cost deployment based on quality deployment.

The purpose of cost deployment is to build into the engineering process a systematic way to reduce product cost while maintaining a balance with quality. Many companies are very serious about this effort, although their approaches may differ. It is important to note that blind cost reduction can create more problems than it solves — such as cost reduction efforts being disproportionate to the results or causing unanticipated customer complaints and warranty claims and undermining customers' trust. Thus, if we want to reduce costs by improving our engineering of the product, we need a logical system for selecting the product features to which this cost reduction engineering effort can be most advantageously applied.

Value engineering (VE) was the first method to be introduced as a logical system for studying cost reduction. The focus of VE is implementing improvement plans in such as way as to ensure achievement of the necessary functions — in either products or services — at the minimum life-cycle cost. This type of function analysis is based on the customers' quality demands, however, and thus is not a suitable cost reduction method for new product development. The importance of cost deployment that starts with quality deployment will become clearer as we outline its steps in the following pages.

Cost Deployment Using the CR-QA Chart

We use a cost reduction/quality assurance (CR-QA) chart at our Hiroshima plant. When our analysis of user needs conducted at the time an order is placed shows that new quality levels are required, we construct the CR-QA chart to serve as a basis for the product quality plan. We do this by preparing a product quality plan chart, a quality prediction chart, and new design notice. The CR-QA chart also enables us to analyze and establish target costs that will help us meet our overall cost reduction goal and CR targets for each product or part — and to establish all of these in relation to the quantity of the order received.

The CR targets and CR plan for each department must be accompanied by objective back-up data that addresses quality assurance issues. Our "upstream" departments use a CR-QA chart such as the one shown in Figure 8.1 for back-up data. For example, in order to predict problems with strength or some other characteristic, we might use FEM (Finite Element Method) to analyze a current product configuration. Then we would check the results of these analyses against the CR proposal for, say, reducing wall thickness or outer diameter. This check enables us to prevent a predictable problem and thereby enhances our quality assurance. This example, however, does not cover the selection of parts that is to be the subject of cost reduction.

Cost Deployment through Quality/Cost Technology Deployment

In general, our company resolves technology problems by clarifying the correlation of planned quality extracted from the quality deployment based on demanded quality. We apply company-specific technology to the subject mechanism, and then systematically solve technical problems through bottleneck engineering (BNE). Bottleneck engineering is engineering that is applied to technical problems that must be solved in order to implement quality and cost targets, but that cannot be resolved with our current technology — as applied in our usual ways.

However, there is a strong need to ensure at the product planning stage our ability to achieve expected costs or target costs while keeping a balance between quality and cost. After repeated attempts to do this, we usually detect some bottlenecks — engineering barriers to achievement of our target cost. We have discovered that the most effective way is to develop what we call quality/cost technology deployment charts, in which cost deployment is based on quality deployment. The six-step system for constructing a quality/ cost engineering chart is illustrated in Figure 8.2. The next section provides more details.

Six Steps for Constructing a Quality/Cost Engineering Chart

1. *Weighing demanded quality.* A demanded quality is weighted by considering the customer comparison of our planned product with other manufacturers'

products, future market needs, and the sales points. In other words, this weight indicates the relative value of each demanded quality, as viewed by the customers.

2. *Demanded quality cost.* When a target cost is divided among the various demanded qualities, the weight of each demanded quality can then be expressed as a unit of cost. We call this demanded quality cost.

3. *Function cost.* When a demanded quality is translated into its individual functions in the function deployment chart, the demanded quality cost is divided among the various functions. The function cost, as we call it, is based on the relationships between the demanded quality and the function and the weighing of that function.

4. *Mechanism cost.* The method we use to establish function cost can also be used to establish mechanism costs.

5. *Part cost (target value).* The target cost of a mechanism's parts can be established by dividing the target mechanism cost among its parts — which are listed in the part deployment chart that we prepare as part of quality deployment. In other words, the "should be" cost of parts is analyzed from the mechanism viewpoint.

6. *Detecting engineering bottlenecks in order to attain target costs.* If with current engineering capabilities, the quoted cost of a part is higher than the target cost of the part, this part becomes a candidate for bottleneck engineering. We must study both the function and the mechanism again to solve this problem. Engineering bottlenecks generally can be solved by using QC and related methods. The solutions can then be accumulated in the mechanism engineering to be used again in future new product development.

Remember that when you are assessing the degree of importance customers have assigned to various demanded qualities, the customers may have neglected to mention some functionally necessary quality that they take for granted. We recommend that in the effort to establish functional costs and part costs, you study the degree of functional importance not only from the customers' perspective, but also from the technical point of view. In Chapter 6, we briefly mention using AHP for this purpose.

Development of an Ultra-Compact Injection Molding Machine
Based on Quality/Cost Technology Deployment:
The Case of Nippon Steel Works

Our company's line of industrial machines includes injection molding machines ranging in size from small (17 tons) to ultra-large (6,000 tons). At one point we decided to develop an ultra-compact (less than 15 tons) injection molding machine that would be suitable for molding small precision parts for our office automation equipment. This decision was part of an effort to anticipate customers' needs and the success of the project was due to our implementing quality deployment and cost deployment, as we explain in the following case study.

Advance Overall Deployment Activity

In this company, the challenge of establishing and meeting quality and cost targets begins when new product development begins. To achieve these objectives in a timely manner, we promote advance overall development activities. These activities may be deployed:

1. for projects that have been designated as high priority in the plant superintendent's annual operational directive,
2. to help us attain established strategic targets,
3. in an advanced overall manner at the product planning stage,
4. by using the best engineering capabilities of the plant,
5. using quality/cost technology deployment and design review as basic tools,
6. by detecting engineering bottlenecks and looking for solutions, and
7. for performing quality assurance at the source stage.

Quality/cost technology deployment is a tool for both new product development and advance overall development activity. It is a method for detecting engineering bottlenecks by establishing product planning quality and target costs and then deploying them into the details, as we have already described.

Quality Deployment for the Ultra-Compact Injection Molding Machine

Since we have already presented many examples of quality deployment in the foregoing chapters, in this section I would like to talk more specifically about cost deployment.

1. Demanded Quality Deployment and Weighting

The demanded quality deployment chart is the starting point not only for quality/cost technology deployment, but also for quality deployment and cost deployment. Therefore, preparation of demanded quality deployment charts should be as unbiased and as accurate as possible. It should be based on all the available data and research results that have been compiled by the company.

Weighing demanded quality is the important process by which we evaluate quality demands made by the customer. To establish the degree of importance of a demanded quality, we first conduct an in-house study to evaluate the customers' future needs. We use a 1-to-5 rating system to indicate the degree of importance of each demanded quality. Then, to establish the target quality, we study the quality levels of our competitors' products, decide what percentage of improvement we want to achieve, and determine the sales points for this quality level. Now we can quantitatively determine demanded quality weights on the basis of these items. For example, in Figure 8.4, the relative weight of 5.9 assigned to the demanded quality "small injection capacity" was calculated as follows:

(degree of importance × percentage of improvement × sales points)
$\div \Sigma$ absolute evaluation × 100 Σ
= $(5 \times 2 \times 1.5) \div 255 \times 100 = 5.9$

That is, the demanded quality weight for "small injection capacity" is 5.9 percent that of total demanded quality.

2. *Detecting Engineering Bottlenecks from Quality Deployment*

A quality chart is prepared from the demanded quality deployment chart and quality characteristics deployment chart, and the strength of the correlation is indicated by symbols whose values can be expressed as a ratio:

$$\textcircled{\odot} : \bigcirc : \Delta = 4:2:1$$

Once the quality characteristics have been weighted, we can compare the planned values and current values, and can rank the weighted quality characteristics from highest to lowest in order to determine where bottleneck engineering is warranted.

For example, in Figure 8.4 we see that the quality characteristic "screw diameter" has a planned value of 10, but the current value is 20 and its weight is high — 1.01. We designate it a bottleneck engineering problem requiring resolution. When we consider "screw diameter" in relation to the various mechanisms that make up the machine, we find that this characteristic is strongly related to the "molten resin injection mechanism." So the improvement of the "molten resin injection mechanism" becomes a bottleneck engineering item — and then we discover that improving this mechanism also requires improving the "screw cylinder," which has a strong relationship to "screw diameter."

Detecting Engineering Bottlenecks during Cost Deployment

In the "Advanced Overall Deployment Activity" section of this chapter, we mentioned establishing and meeting target costs in order to put our company at the top of our industry. Our efforts to attain these target costs are based on detecting engineering bottlenecks through the cost deployment part of quality/cost technology deployment — and then solving these problems.

For example, the cost of the demanded quality "high die mating rigidity" is:

relative evaluation × target cost ÷ 100
= $3.5 \times 60 \div 100$
= 2.1

where, the relative evaluation is 3.5 and the target cost is 60. That is, the cost of "high die mating rigidity" is 2.1 percent of the target cost 60, as shown in Figure 8.5.

Next we perform a similar conversion of relative evaluation of demanded quality into the quality characteristic weights. It is converted into function cost, mechanism cost, and then further into parts cost by ratings with ◎, ○, and Δ. For example, the cost 2.1 of demanded quality "high die mating rigidity" has a strong correlation with "clamping against internal pressure," so 1.3 is assigned to it. (This value comes from proportioning. The total cost of the demanded quality "high die mating rigidity," 2.1, is distributed between the two functions that correlate strongly with it — "clamping against internal pressures" and "match dies accurately." Distribution is made according to the 4:2:1 ratio for ◎, ○, and Δ. Next, the "clamping against internal pressure" function cost gets a 7.0 score (1.3 + 0.1 = 1.4, multiplied by 5, the total importance score) and 1.0 is assigned to the "hydraulic power mechanism" in the vertical column of the mechanism deployment section of the chart. Summing horizontally, the "hydraulic power mechanism" has a mechanism cost of 3.1.

Further, the correlation of this item to the correlated parts indicates a strong relationship with the "hydraulic unit" (◎ = (2.4), etc.). Next, summing vertically for "hydraulic unit" gives us a total of 9.3, which indicates that the part cost of the "hydraulic unit" is 9.3. In other words, the part cost (9.3) can be expressed as a deployment of the demanded quality weight — the value that corresponds to the users' needs. However, because the quoted cost (16.4) of the hydraulic unit is much higher than the part cost necessary for cost reduction activity, the hydraulic unit becomes a bottleneck engineering item.

Future Work

Quality/cost technology deployment charts are still in the developmental stage and have the problems discussed below.

- It is often difficult to adequately evaluate the data at the time the demanded quality deployment charts are being prepared.
- The weighting of a demanded quality may vary considerably, according to the needs of different customers.
- Even when there is a big difference between the targeted part cost and the current quoted cost, we may not be able to reduce cost below the quoted cost. Much time will be lost and cost reduction efforts will be wasted on parts that cannot be improved unless this problem is identified at the planning stage.

Summary

The theme of this chapter is quality deployment and cost deployment, yet, as we have explained in this section, cost deployment based on quality deployment might be a more accurate description of this activity. Unlike the well-arranged system used in quality deployment, the cost deployment system is still in the trial stage. We hope that readers will do a lot to develop this subject.

Design and Development of a Machining Center: The Case of Toyoda Machine Works

Our firm produces and sells machine tools such as grinders, machining centers for the automotive industry, and other mechatronic products like robots and measuring and control equipment. Recent market demands for machine tools have been in the area of factory automation with systematic integration of element engineering which permits greater accuracy and productivity, electronics engineering for CNC, and software engineering for machinery with diagnostic intelligence. Our company has been active in new product development in order to respond to these market needs — especially since the introduction of TQC and other concepts like "quality first," "market-in," and "source control."

In this section we will present an outline of quality deployment undertaken to determine appropriate quality targets and cost targets for the development of a horizontal machining center, the FH40.

Quality Deployment I: Demanded Quality Deployment and Establishing Commercial Product Planning Specifications

Figure 8.6 shows the process outline for our development of the FH40 machining center. At the product planning stage, market research provided the basis for establishing the major specifications for the FH40. We developed a list of desired features for a machining center through market research (MR) that used questionnaires to obtain the customer verbatims (their exact comments) and understand their requirements. The customers' requirements are diverse, but they can be grouped into about twenty representative items. Our questionnaire was designed to investigate the level of demand for each of these questionnaire items. As Figure 8.7 shows, the demand level was converted into degrees of importance for approximately 100 demanded quality items, which were then arranged through demanded quality deployment. We then designated the demanded qualities with the highest degree of importance as the target qualities, that is, the qualities most attractive to our customers.

Using a matrix that deployed these demanded qualities into major specifications for the machining center (quality characteristics), we translated the degree of importance assigned to each demanded quality into the degree of importance for each major specification. The basic specifications for the product under development (product planning specifications) were based on (1) the degree of importance and (2) a comparison of our current products with those of other manufacturers. We subjected the planning specifications to a second market research study to evaluate customer satisfaction with them, and then finalized them after making any necessary modifications.

For example, we selected "high machinery efficiency" — a demanded quality strongly related to the customer-demanded quality "improvement in high speed cutting" — because its degree of importance was a high 4. Next, we selected from the group of major specifications "fast feed speed," which was related to "high machinery efficiency" and whose degree of importance was also 4. Since the customer evaluation gave our product a lower rating on this demand than our competitors' existing products, we assigned it a high 4 in the quality plan in order to strive for improvement.

Quality Deployment II: Deploying Quality Characteristics and Establishing Design Target Values

During the second stage of quality deployment, we deployed the specifications drafted during product planning into more detailed machine specifications and target performance values. Figure 8.8 shows how we deployed both cost and quality characteristics in such a way as to connect the deployment with the prototype design. The specifications and performance of the machining center were deployed in considerable detail to the third level of quality characteristics. The degree of importance for each demanded quality was converted into a degree of importance for each quality characteristic of a machining center by merging this deployment matrix with the demanded quality deployment chart prepared previously. For example, the degree of importance for "ATC time" — a third-level quality characteristic of "fast feed speed" — was set at 3. Quality characteristics with a high degree of importance were designated as sales points. In order to establish target values that would reflect both this degree of importance and the sales points, each characteristic value was studied by comparing our current models with those of our competitors and then comparing two-year predictions of each. In addition, engineering problems were evaluated by comparing the target value with the current level and using bottleneck engineering to solve any problems.

We set cost targets by deploying the machining center into its subassembly units. In this example, we selected the "ATC part" and converted the degree of importance for the quality characteristics into the degree of necessity for the assembly unit (38). This was done by combining a matrix of this deployment with the quality characteristics deployment chart (see Figure 8.8).

A target cost for the FH40 had been set separately by market research, and we made the target cost for the assembly unit proportional to the degree of necessity of the assembly unit. We compared this proportional value and the estimated proportional value of a conventional model, and where great differences existed, we identified bottleneck engineering items to become the focus of our VE activity. As Figure 8.8 indicates, the ATC was selected as an engineering bottleneck for cost reasons. The first-stage design (the basic drawing) was developed on the basis of these quality characteristic values and cost target values. After evaluation and correction through design review, we moved on to the prototype design stage.

Cost Bottleneck Engineering and Value Engineering Activity

The cost of the items identified as engineering bottlenecks with the aid of the quality deployment II chart allowed us to focus our attention on developing a few ideas for solving the bottleneck and then comparing their respective quality and costs. We summarized these in a BNE cost study report in order to narrow our choices to those ideas that were most compatible with the basic design (see Figure 8.9). In this case, since "adoption not permitted" meant "not feasible," we tried to solve the cost bottleneck by conducting further VE activities. At the prototype design stage, we performed function deployment for each equipment unit and conducted VE using the procedure illustrated in Figure 8.10.

1. *Mechanism analysis:* Calculate cost of equipment analyzed down to the part level.
2. *Function analysis:* Analyze the function of equipment right down to its ultimate function.
3. *Function evaluation:* Determine the degree to which each of the parts contributes to the end function, and multiply this by the unit cost of the part, thereby proportioning the part cost to the end function. Calculate the estimated cost per end function unit to determine which functions should be improved. In this case, an "unnecessary function" gained number one priority for improvement.
4. *Generating ideas:* By brainstorming, we came up with ideas for improving each function and summarized those that could be adopted.
5. *Evaluating the ideas and determining which ones to adopt:* We compared quality and cost and evaluated each idea to determine which ideas were most suitable in terms of target quality and cost. By redoing the concept design and going through the study described above, we were able to achieve the initial target cost, and our development was a success.

Conclusion

The foregoing example shows how to use quality deployment at the planning stage for developing a machining center. We consider quality deployment work to be very effective in improving our ability to reflect the needs of customers. It is more objective than strictly quantitative planning, which has always tended to be somewhat dogmatic. We want to thank the many people who have guided us in our application of quality deployment. We intend to keep up this work in the future.

References

Hasegawa, Akira; Maekawa, Yoshitomo; Aizawa, Kenji (1983). "Quality/ Cost Technology Deployment Chart for New Product Development." *Quality*, Vol. 13, No. 3, pp. 92-97, JSQC.

Kawai, Toshio (1980). "Design Activity by Combining Use of FTA, QA-VE, VE Chart, 2-Step FMEA Wiper Design." *Quality Control*, November special issue, pp. 129-131, JUSE.

Maekawa, Yoshitomo; Sano, Hiroaki (1985). "Development of Ultra-Compact Injection Molder." *Quality Control*, Vol. 36, No. 7, pp. 29-35, JUSE.

Yasumori, Takehiro (1979). "CR-QA Activity in Product Design." *Quality Control*, Vol. 30, November special issue, pp. 297-302, JUSE

	Quality	Cost
Product Planning	• Market and in-house evaluation are not in agreement. — Inadequate understanding of environmental use — Inadequate understanding of level of market requirement • Rough quality target. • Vague sales point.	• Vague cost target.
Product Design	• Inadequate quality prediction engineering. • Weakness in establishing quality level. • No utilization of accumulated engineering. • Poor communication of design quality downstream.	• Lack of cost deployment. • Imprecise cost reduction targets. • Lack of understanding of cost prediction.
Prototyping	• Trial production does not reflect normal production.	• Poor evaluation of cost prediction.
Preproduction	• Insufficient understanding of critical characteristics. • Inadequate conversion of characteristic values. • Poor understanding of process capability.	• Vague measures for cost reduction target. • Lack of correlation between cost reduction and quality analysis.

Chart 8-1. Reflections on New Product Development

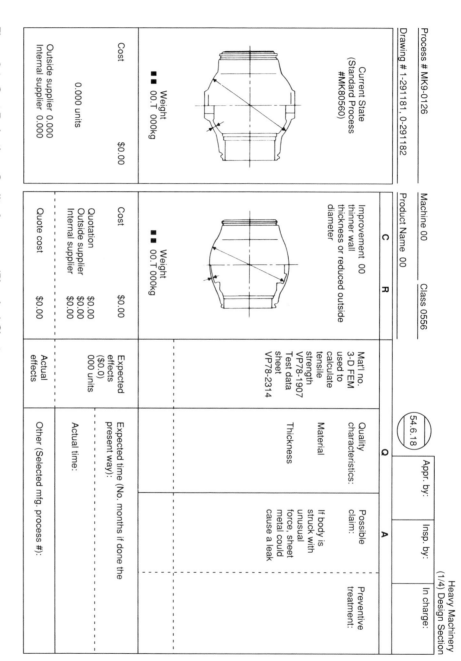

Figure 8-1. Cost Reduction - Quality Assurance (Planning) Chart

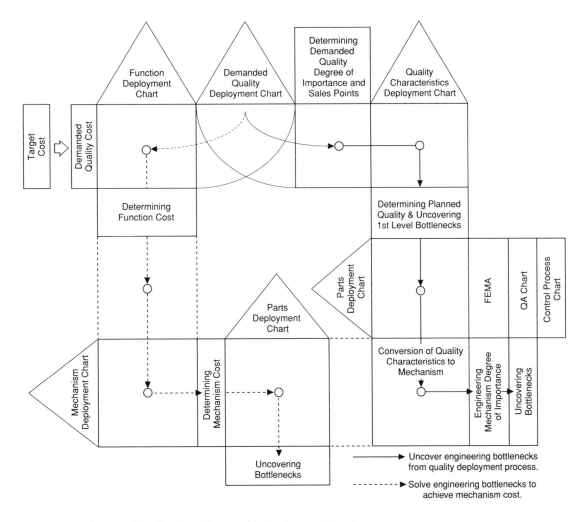

Figure 8-2. System of Quality/Cost Engineering Deployment Chart

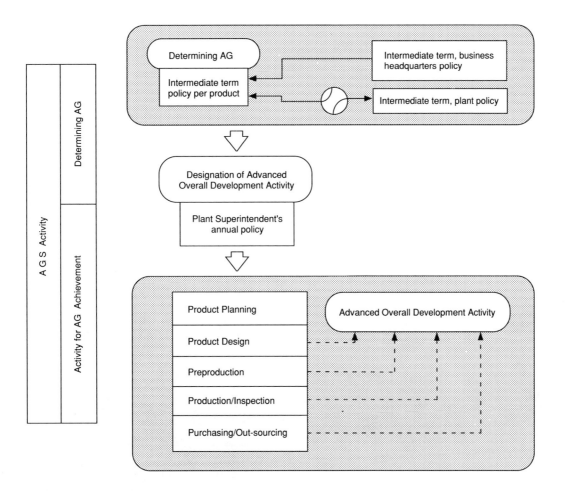

Figure 8-3. The Concept of Advanced Overall Deployment Activity

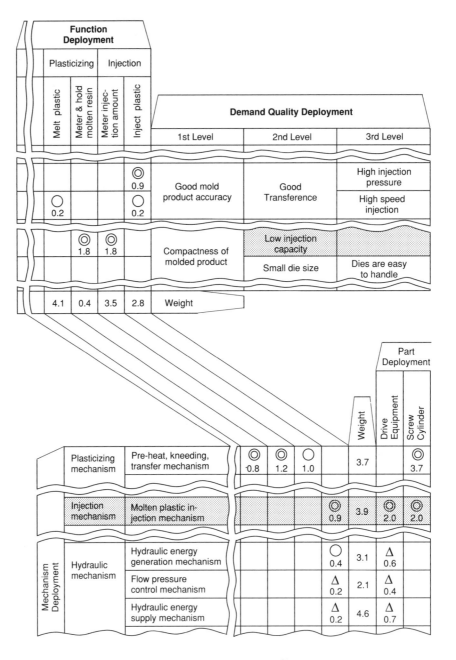

Figure 8-4. Quality Cost Engineering Deployment Chart

	Weighting Demanded Quality												Quality Characteristics		
	Evaluation of degree of importance				Comparison with other makers and target weight										
	Customer evaluation	In-house evaluation	Future needs	Degree of importance	Own firm	Co. S	Co. T	Target weight	Rate of level up	Sales Point	Absolute evaluation	Relative evaluation		Cylinder temperature	Screw diameter	Screw rpm
											255	100		C°	mm	rpm
	5	5	5	5		5	5	5			5	2			◯ 0.33	
	4	4	4	4		4	4	4			4	1.6				
	4	4	5	5		4	4	4	2	1.5	15	5.9			◎ 0.32	◯ 1.16
	4	4	4	4		4	4	4	1.5	1.2	7.2	2.8				

		Weight	2.31	1.01	19
		Planned value		10	200 650
		Current value		20	
		Engineering bottleneck	Δ	×	Δ
		Weight	2.31	3.03	1.9

Molding clamping equipment	Registration #							
	UNEI — 209			8.54	12.8			
				2.47	3.7			
Δ 0.6				2.95	4.42		◯ 1.01	
Δ 0.4				2.92	4.38			◯ 0.95
Δ 0.7				1.99	2.98			

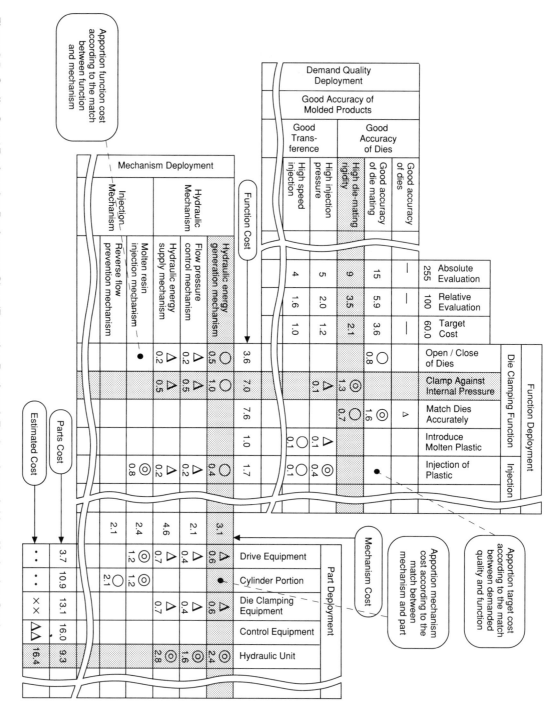

Figure 8-5. Quality Cost / Engineering Deployment Chart (Extracting Bottleneck Engineering to Achieve Mechanism Cost)

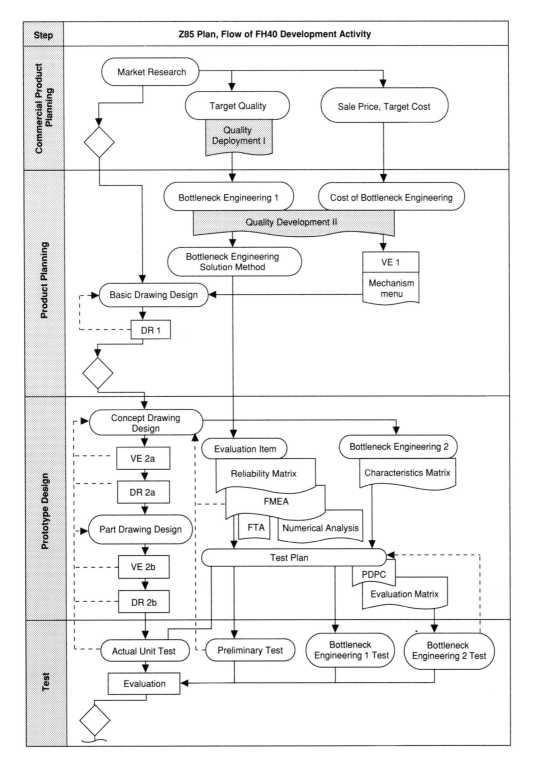

Figure 8-6. Flow of FH40 Development Activity

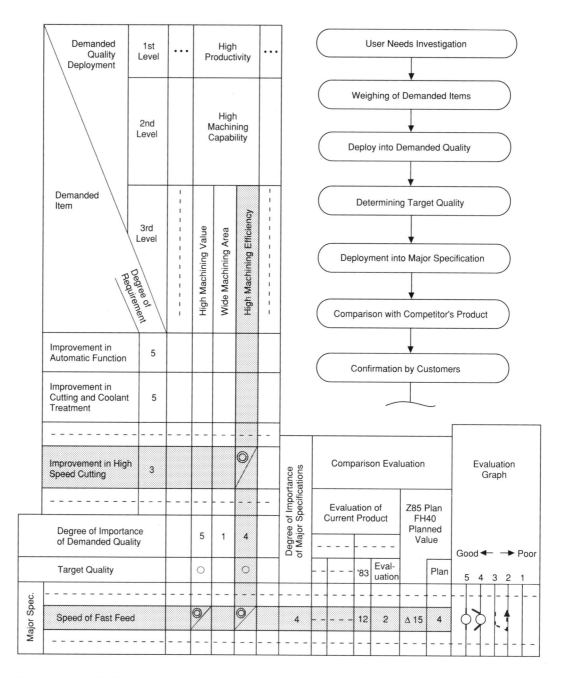

Figure 8-7. Quality Deployment I

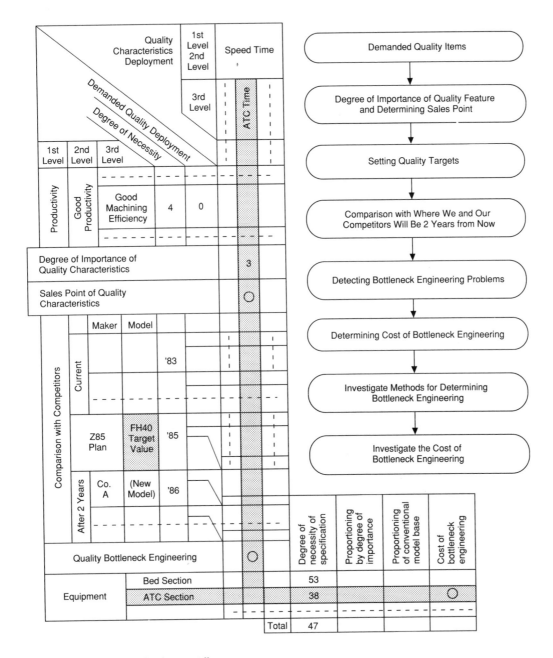

Figure 8-8. Quality Deployment II

BNE Cost Study Report

Chart Structure Comparison

O : 3 Points
Δ : 2 Points
× : 1 Point

Comparison Item (Quality Characteristics)	Degree of Importance	Sketches	Idea ① (Type FHN40 II)		Idea ②		Idea ③	
1. Speed of table setting	4	(Sketch Omitted)	× ...... sec	4	Δ ...... sec	8	O ...... sec	12
2. Chart clamp force	4		Δ ...... kg	4	O ...... kg	6	O ...... kg	6
3. Pallet clamp force	2		Δ ...... kg	4	O ...... kg	6	O ...... kg	6
4. Chart loading weight	2		O ...... kg	6	O ...... kg	6	O ...... kg	6
5. Reliability of table setting	5		Δ miss	10	Δ miss	10	O	15
6. Accuracy of table setting	4		O ± a°	12	O ± a°	12	O ± a°	12
7. Maintenance within table	5		O	15	O	15	O	15
Total			×	55	Δ	63		72
Target			Unit: 1000 Yen		Unit: 1000 Yen		Unit: 1000 Yen	
Estimate			Unit: 1000 Yen		Unit: 1000 Yen		Unit: 1000 Yen	
			×		×		Δ	
Summary			Adoption not permitted		Adoption unfeasible			

Q (items 1–7)
C (Target / Estimate)

(Study Items)

1. ....
2. ....
3. ....
4. ....

(Conclusions)

....
....
....
....

Figure 8-9. BNE Cost Study Report

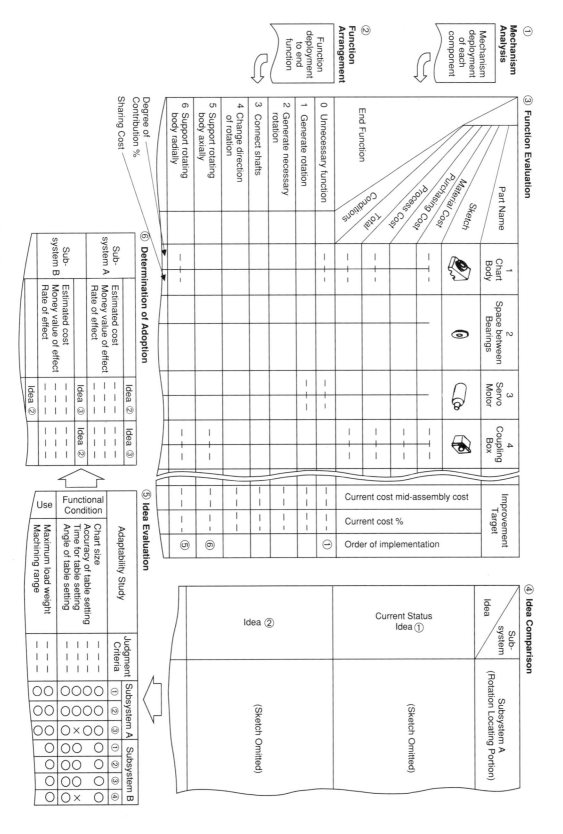

Figure 8-10. Value Engineering by Functional Engineering

CHAPTER 9

Quality Function Deployment in Process Industries

Masahiko Koyatzu, Promotion Manager,
Refresh Zeon, Nippon Zeon Company;
and Isuke Kubota, Production Engineering Manager,
Electrode Business Group, Nippon Carbon Company

In applying quality function deployment to a process industry, we need to be aware of two major differences between a process industry and machine and assembly industries. The first difference (as Chapters 3 and 4 have made clear) is that, generally, in machine and assembly industries a demanded quality for a total system can be deployed into successively smaller subsystems. This is possible because the structure of one subsystem does not affect the functional aspects of other subsystems. In process industries, however, a mechanism that is necessary to realize some demanded quality cannot function independently of other necessary mechanisms and functions. The second difference is that in most process industries — such as raw material industries, whose role is to offer material rather than parts, to other industries — the raw material by itself does not have full function; it is only an intermediate product in a process that will eventually allow the material to exhibit its function. As an example, let us use the case of synthetic rubber.

In our company, synthetic rubber exhibits its function only when it is processed and formed by the user, a tire maker, into tires. Functions such as a good ride and not slipping on wet pavement can be exhibited only after the tire has been manufactured. These are the demanded qualities for tires. In a direct sense, however, they are also the demanded qualities for the raw material, because they are necessary to be able to fulfill these requirements for tires. In other words, the demanded quality being deployed of the raw material, including its performance, will be exhibited after processing and forming by the tire manufacturer.

With these observations in mind, in this chapter we will explain quality function deployment for the production of raw material in a process industry. The first half of the chapter will deal with the general concepts for preparing charts; the second half will introduce some case studies from the Nippon Zeon and Nippon Carbon companies.

Quality Chart

The purpose of the quality chart is to correlate the quality demanded by the manufacturer with measurable quality characteristics (counterpart characteristics) and to provide a logical framework for establishing a target to be achieved for each characteristic. Figure 9.1 shows an example of a quality chart for raw materials.

Here, the demanded quality deployment includes both the quality demanded for (1) the manufacturer's process and forming stages, and (2) the post-processing stage. The quality characteristics are deployed as characteristics that will be the result of combining our raw material with other materials that we assume will be used by the manufacturer in a certain manner; in other words, the quality characteristics of the final product are not deployed as the characteristics of the raw material itself.

Here, the method of accommodation is determined by the processors who are the manufacturers, not by the raw material producers.

Since the deployed demanded quality can be attained only after the compounding and further transformation of the raw material in the manufacturer's process, the quality chart for the raw material must be prepared in cooperation with others. Figure 9.2 shows how to prepare a general quality chart for raw material producers — through a cycle that includes arranging past experiences into the first-stage quality chart, taking it to the manufacturer to be revised, integrating new information and confirming it by testing, and resubmitting it to the user. This process is called the "design quality upgrade cycle" and is described in the next section of this chapter.

We can describe the properties of machinery and other constructions with design drawings, but there is no easy way to describe the properties of raw materials. Thus, accurate information on the demanded quality or the method of use of the raw material being developed is not readily available. Similarly, data or explanations submitted by a raw material producer will not provide sufficient and necessary information to the manufacturers. For these reasons, a dialogue between the manufacturer and the raw material producer is essential when the quality charts are being developed. In other words, these two parties need to collaborate in order to set the development targets and realize the demanded quality.

The quality chart for raw material serves as a device for improving communication with the manufacturer, and in this context can be effectively used not only to attain higher efficiency in new product development but also to enhance sales activities.

Structure Deployment

The point of product development is to convert demanded quality into counterpart characteristics, to use the counterpart characteristics to quantify targets, and then to determine what kind of structures would be most suitable for implementing the characteristics. In our company, we call the stage in raw material development that corresponds to mechanism deployment in the machine and assembly industries "mechanism deployment."

In the machine and assembly industries, the necessary functions are deployed into a mechanism for implementation. This is done for each unit that makes up the mechanism. With raw materials, the structure of the raw material corresponds to this mechanism and cannot be determined independently for each individual quality characteristic.

Figure 9.3 shows an example of structure deployment. In this chart we deployed the demanded qualities into necessary functions like "tensile stress," which is an important quality characteristic. We then related this characteristic to polymer structure, which is the structural factor that can produce this characteristic. The goal of this stage of our product development was to solve the problem of finding polymer structures suitable for particular functions as well as the problem of dysfunctional interactions among polymer structures, where achieving one function hinders the achievement of another. The purpose of structure deployment is to thoroughly understand the bottleneck engineering points before beginning the development work. That is, we cannot establish targets for the raw material producer until the bottlenecks have been identified.

Process Deployment

The best structure for deploying demanded quality in a process industry is a matrix arrangement of demanded quality and production engineering factors. We call this process deployment. An example is given in Figure 9.4.

This example shows the relationship between various production engineering factors, such as the amount of primary and secondary raw materials to be used, the reaction conditions (temperature, pressure, etc.), and the means to obtain the quality characteristics, such as the necessary molecular structure. This deployment chart enables us to design an efficient test for determining the appropriate level of various production technology factors; it also enables us to prepare proper QA charts to be issued to the plant. Arranging the development chart like this also helps improve the efficiency of the development, because it necessarily leads our researchers to correlating structural factors with production technology factors. In other words, the deployment chart has an additional role — it is a tool for compiling economies gained from company-specific technology.

Summary

Figure 9.5 summarizes the steps taken in quality function deployment, from the deployment of demanded quality at the beginning to establishing the production technology that will deliver the demanded quality characteristics.

Through its TQC activities, our firm learned a method for developing new raw materials called quality-technology deployment. This deployment helped rearrange past technology and experiences, and clarified the bottleneck engineering necessary to solve current problems.

But this is only one model. Even within the process industry, the mix of products, sales, and engineering differs from company to company. Since, for each company, quality function deployment is a mixture of company-specific technology and control technology, the results should reflect the firm's own characteristics. In this context, we hope that this chapter will be of some help to those involved in similar activities.

New Product Development Using Quality Technology Deployment: The Case of Nippon Zeon

Our company's main product is a high molecular material made of synthetic rubber and plastic. The high molecular material is a raw material that is offered to the market only after it undergoes a process selected by our direct customer-users. The demanded qualities for the raw material are always changing in response to changing market demands. At our company, we have implemented TQC in order to respond to these changing needs, to develop products that will satisfy the users in a timely way, and then to ensure our capacity to provide a stable supply of these products. As we mentioned in the preceding section, we call our method of material design "quality-technology deployment." This method deploys demanded quality into material characteristics in order to determine production conditions for new material development.

In this case study we will explain how we used quality-technology deployment successfully to develop a K-application vinyl chloride plastic.

Applying Quality-Technology Deployment in the Development of K-Application Vinyl Chloride Plastic

K-application is an area of the market we expect will grow in the future. Expanding our company's business into this area is important, so we are bringing out new products. Applying quality-technology deployment to this project has led to very efficient product development. As shown in Figure 9.6, we prepared for quality-technology deployment by translating the demanded quality derived from user information (for example, "allowable amounts of filler to be compounded") into a quality characteristic (characteristic P). We did this by relating such quality characteristics to polymer structure factors (for example, particle size distribution), and then further relating these factors to production technology factors (for example, amount of secondary material F). This procedure has unified the basis of raw material development and made it more efficient by requiring the parallel activities of understanding demanded quality, design, and prototyping. We will now explain the procedure.

1. Setting Quality Targets

We prepared the first-level quality chart by arranging market information in a demanded quality deployment chart and relating the demanded qualities to quality characteristics. This chart was then improved by communicating with our customers — using this quality chart as a basis for discussion (see Figure 9.7). The dialogue with our users, recorded below, came about in the course of using the quality chart to clarify our targets.

Sample Discussion with Customer A

Producer: "The emphasis on 'high speed processing' seems opposite to our demanded quality X. Isn't that a problem?"

Customer: "Yes. It can't be tolerated."

Producer: "We weren't told this was an important demand."

Customer: "We didn't emphasize it because we took it for granted."

Sample Discussion with Customer B

> *Producer:* "We think we could increase the amount of the filler."
>
> *Customer:* "Well, please do so then."
>
> *Producer:* "Why didn't you mention this before? Wasn't it a very important re-quirement?"
>
> *Customer:* "We didn't think that both this requirement and requirement X could be met at the same time."

This kind of dialogue arises only through the use of a quality chart. In raw material development, where there is no drawing that can be used to communicate quality, this chart becomes an important device for enhancing communication between producers and manufacturers (users) who are jointly involved in developing the material. And in raw material, many items of demanded quality cannot be achieved independently. This makes a comprehensive dialogue using a quality chart very important, because it is the only way one can understand in detail what the manufacturer-user wishes to accomplish. Such dialogue can also help prevent omission of necessary quality items that the customer has neglected to mention, and can prevent the waste of resources that occurs as a result of discovering unexpected problems at a much later stage, when the manufacturer-user is evaluating the prototype sample.

In this example, improving characteristic P was identified as a problem to be resolved in order to meet the demand for larger allowable amounts of filler, while keeping a balance between this and other demands.

2. Deploying Quality Characteristics to Polymer Structure Factors

In order to deploy quality characteristics to polymer structure factors, we must identify the structural characteristics of a polymer that will enable us to realize the quality characteristics. To do this, we translate quality characteristics into polymer design concepts that are based on past findings, hypotheses, or model tests. Then we can define — and develop, if necessary — the suitable polymer structure (see Figure 9.8A).

In this example, we used a model test to determine the particle size distribution that would be required to improve characteristic P. The test results indicated that a certain distribution of molecular weights was necessary, and we realized that increasing particle size was one of the polymer structure factors that would improve characteristic P.

3. Deploying Polymer Structure Factors Into Production Technology Factors

In order to deploy polymer structure factors into production engineering factors, we first identify the production engineering factors related to large particle size (see Figure 9.8B). We arrange the relationships between the production engineering factors and polymer structure factors in a matrix, which helps to clarify the task of increasing polymer chain length while maintaining the required polymer structure. With the help of the matrix, we came up with an efficient solution for this engineering bottleneck and prepared a PDPC for the introduction of secondary material F. This deployment enabled us to achieve efficient development of the K-application vinyl chloride plastic.

Summary

We consider quality-technology deployment to be a very effective methodology for new product development at this time for the two following reasons.

1. People involved in development can view the total picture, including both demanded quality and production engineering. This enables them to establish rational development routines.
2. People participating in this development work with shared information and a common understanding.

Even after we started production, and discovered some production problems, the effects of the problems on the demanded quality could be assessed by tracing back through the QC process chart and the quality technology deployment. This, in turn, helped us gain a thorough understanding of the way we were building quality into the production process.

The real advantage of quality-technology deployment is that it can be applied to the next development by allowing technological experience to be accumulated in it. We hope to further improve this method so that we can respond to customer needs quicker and more appropriately.

Using Quality Function Deployment: The Case of Nippon Carbon

Nippon Carbon, a manufacturer of carbon products, has been active since its beginning in new product development. The current president of our company, after becoming head of the research laboratory, expanded our research activities according to the following concepts: (1) "From Organic to Inorganic" (resulting in the development of carbon fiber in 1962, for example), and (2) "From Simple to Composite" (resulting in the development of silicon carbide for rotary engines in 1966, for example). These two concepts led to the development of our silicon carbide fiber "Nicalon" and its application products in 1983.

Prior to the introduction of TQC in 1979, we actively used the test plan method, but we lacked a company-wide system for research and development. After 1979, we began introducing quality function deployment to address high-priority quality problems in the development of Nicalon. As a result, we have put together a QA system based on quality function deployment that covers every step from the target quality upgrading process to QA process charts (see Figure 9.9). The main points of this system with examples follow.

Quality Assurance by Quality Function Deployment

The carbon industry is both a raw material and a parts industry. Our firm's new product development activities are designed to find apparent and latent market demands for products with particular qualities, to develop carbon products that will meet these demands, and to expand into new markets. Silicon carbide carbon for rotary engines is one example. We are in a period of expanding production of our new material Nicalon in order to meet unsatisfied needs for carbon fiber, such as the need for fibers that are compatible with metals and resist oxidation.

Even though carbon products are widely used in industry, there are still many unexplored potential niches in the market. In order to quickly develop products for these markets, research based on a "needs map" must be conducted in cooperation with one's manufacturing partner from the initial period of development. In the case of Nicalon, we did this with Dow Corning and Rolls Royce. We based the first-level quality chart on the qualities demanded by the manufacturing partner, and after we had submitted several samples for testing, evaluation, and revision, we made the quality chart, which became the basis for our quality design. The "quality target upgrading process" (see Figure 9.9, right side) is a summary of this work. Because of the great effect of equipment specifications on product quality, we built a pilot plant to test the development concepts at this stage.

In addition to new products based on the advanced "seed" type of technology mentioned above, our firm also develops types of product that meet a specific customer's needs — the needs of a chemical plant that uses a high heat-resistant, nonpermeable graphite, for example — as well as the type of product that improves upon our current major product, electrodes. Each requires certain means of development. We see in Figure 9.9 a development system in which selection I directs us toward either improvement of current products or "seeds and needs" products. Selection II then takes us in the direction of either "seeds" or "needs" product development projects.

Figure 9.9 (left) shows the flow of development from the quality chart (step 2) through quality design (step 4) for the new products we select for development that represent improvement of current products or do not need basic research. Step 3 indicates a decision made in cooperation with customers regarding whether to proceed with product development and QA based on quality function deployment after the target upgrade process. Figure 9.10 shows an example of quality function deployment for Nicalon at the prototyping stage.

Because equipment operating conditions (temperature, pressure, time, etc.) have a strong influence on product quality, after preproduction prototyping we establish engineering standards for process conditions in order to assure large-scale design quality improvements in the development of raw material facilities and processes (step 5 in Figure 9.9). Next, we indicate the control points and inspection points on the QA chart (step 7). Then we prepare the QC process chart (step 8) for controllers and the QA process chart (step 9) for workers. Using the process chart, we review work standards (step 10) in order to ensure early stabilization of process and maintenance control.

Market evaluation (step 11) is performed at engineering meetings (step 12) with the customer, and is based on quality evaluation standards. The information from such meetings is then fed back to the quality charts and so on.

Quality Target Upgrade Cycle

The side to the right of selection II of Figure 9.9 shows how we handle technology seeds for new material development. We prepare a first-level quality chart based on predicted needs and establish quality target #1 before we test market the sample. The original quality target is then modified in response to the market evaluation (step 1). Unexpected new needs may be discovered at this stage, which will lead to establishing a new quality target (step 2). At this point, we undertake corrective actions for bottleneck engineering problems, and then offer a sample to the market again. In this way, we upgrade the quality target and respond to expanded needs. We call this process the quality target upgrade cycle. We can see that raw materials development differs from the development of products like automobiles or home appliances, which have clearly defined applications at the development planning stage.

Figure 9.11 shows the development process for Nicalon. The main predicted need for the Nicalon NL100 we marketed in 1983 was for use in fiber-reinforced metal (FRM). However, as a result of test marketing, we found that the composite strength of Nicalon-reinforced metal was not what we had expected. As a result, we determined that the matrix (base material) of the composite should be ceramic instead of metal.

Next, we added the requirement "should not react with base material and should not deteriorate" (see Figure 9.11B) and we stablished a quality target to meet this new requirement. Then we used bottleneck engineering to solve the problem of matrix-fiber boundary reaction, and finally we successfully marketed a new grade of Nicalon, NL200. More recently, an entirely new quality requirement has appeared to be added to the list of qualities required for the conventional reinforcing fibers. This new requirement arises from a new function that is based on the shapes of the fibers in the product — which is one of the basic physical characteristics of Nicalon. We met this need with a new Nicalon product, NL300.

The production and engineering for Nicalon NL300 was different from the production and engineering used for fibrous reinforcing materials based on conventional strength concepts. Once in the market, a product must lend itself to various applications. Such a product is "needs-responsive" (in Figure 9.9, follow the arrow to the left of Selection II). Development of a needs-responsive product in a process industry follows a path that is close to conventional quality function deployment. (For more information on this subject, see the Ishikawa-Kobayashi and Osaki-Kobayashi references at the end of this chapter.) In general, new materials often have the potential for wider application than is originally predicted. We systematically expanded the applications for our Nicalon product in the field of FRM by "seeds/needs deployment," in which we matched the FRM characteristics (characteristics and functions) to needs through trial marketing. (This subject is covered in the Hayase-Tanaka article cited in this chapter's reference list.)

Quality Improvement for Electrodes Used in Electric Steel-Making Furnaces

Electrodes are used to create an electric charge in an electric furnace, whose function is to melt and refine scrap iron. The main functional requirements for an electrode in such a furnace are to be "capable of charging a large amount of electricity," "difficult to break," and "resistant to wear and tear." In recent years particularly, customers have been looking for high operating efficiency in electric furnaces, so the demand is very great for more durable electrodes to lessen the frequency of sudden down time.

After comparing the breakdown frequency of our electrodes and those of our competitors, we decided to aim for a 50-percent reduction in electrode failure, with less than a $\bigcirc\bigcirc$ increase in cost. We allowed ourselves X years to achieve this target. We began by using the quality chart shown in Figure 9.12, the design standards, and simulation analyses. Then we established a target of 25 percent improvement in the quality characteristic X — bending strength. Next, we calculated that Y should be increased by $\triangle\triangle$ percent over the current engineering standard because of the specific gravity, $\bigcirc\bigcirc$. The effect of Y on process D is shown in the QA chart in Figure 9.12, and the relationship between Y and X is indicated in the matrix by the intersection of characteristic Y and checkpoint X_1. This relationship is expressed as an engineering standard in Figure 9.13.

We created an implementation plan by prioritizing the major factors, analyzing their interactions, making cost comparisons, identifying engineering difficulties, and studying other factors with the aid of matrix charts in which we expressed the expected effects in the following form:

$$X_1 \text{ is changed from } \bigcirc_1\bigcirc_1 \text{ to } \triangle_1\triangle_1 \ldots$$
$$X_2 \text{ is changed from } \bigcirc_2\bigcirc_1 \text{ to } \triangle_2\triangle_2 \ldots$$
$$\vdots \qquad\qquad\qquad \vdots$$

total expected effect › $\triangle\triangle$
total cost ‹ $\bigcirc\bigcirc$

(In practice, some factors are not directly related, so the expression must be in this complex regression form.)

We used a reviewed dendrogram to efficiently identify solutions for engineering bottlenecks. After implementing these solutions, we confirmed the effects of the solution on Y and the effects of Y on bending strength. Finally, we test marketed a sample with a 25-percent increase in bending strength. We were able to reduce the test error through the use of measuring electric furnaces (step 12 in Figure 9.9) and to reduce the test period through cooperative discussions with our customers. After confirming our market evaluation, we revised the work standards (step 10 in Figure 9.9) and incorporated the results of this initial improvement phase into our regular production.

Conclusion

The carbon industry has a wide range of products and a wide-ranging market. The use of quality function deployment enabled us to do research and development that were more directly related to the market than would otherwise have been possible, and to more clearly determine the requirements for production preparation, production, and service. Quality function deployment is required to respond to ever more diverse social needs. Identification of common engineering factors, advocated by Professor Shigero Mizuno, is becoming increasingly important in the process industry. Our wish is to develop better QA for this industry based on a better correlation with quality function deployment.

References

Hayase, Tokuji; Tanaka, Yoshikazu (1984). "Quality Design for New Material Development: Approach from Seeds to Needs." *Quality Control*, Vol. 35, November special issue, pp. 304-309, JUSE.

Hayase, Tokuji; Yamazoe, Hiroshi (1986). "Quality Target Up-Grade Cycle for New Material Deployment." *Quality Control*, Vol. 37, May special issue, pp. 72-74, JUSE.

Ichikawa, Hiroshi; Kobayashi, Tadashi (1985). "Quality Control Development Chart at Nippon Carbon Company: Application Example of Production of New Material Nicalon." *Quality Control*, Vol. 36, No. 5, pp. 19-25, JUSE.

Ishikawa, Toshisuke; Nagaoki, Toru (1986). *New Carbon Industry*. edit.

Kano, Noriako. "Attractive Quality and Must-Be Quality." *Quality*, Vol. 14, No. 2, JSQC.

Kusaki, Eiich; Kobayashi, Tadashi (1985). "Trial for Better Process Control: Deployment from Review of QC Process Chart to QA Process Chart." *Quality Control*, Vol. 36, May special issue, pp. 91-97, JUSE.

Mizuno, Shigeru (1984). *Company-Wide* QC. JUSE.

Mizuno, Shigeru; Akao, Yoji (1978). *Quality Function Deployment*. JUSE.

Obata, Akira; Toyomori, T. (1980). "On RD System (Reviewed Dendrogram): Systematic Deployment of Developmental Design Plan." *Quality Control*, Vol. 31, November special issue, pp. 37-42, JUSE.

Teranishi, Haruo; Akao, Yoji (1986). *Quality Deployment in Material Industry*. JSQC, No. 29, Conference Proceedings, JSQC.

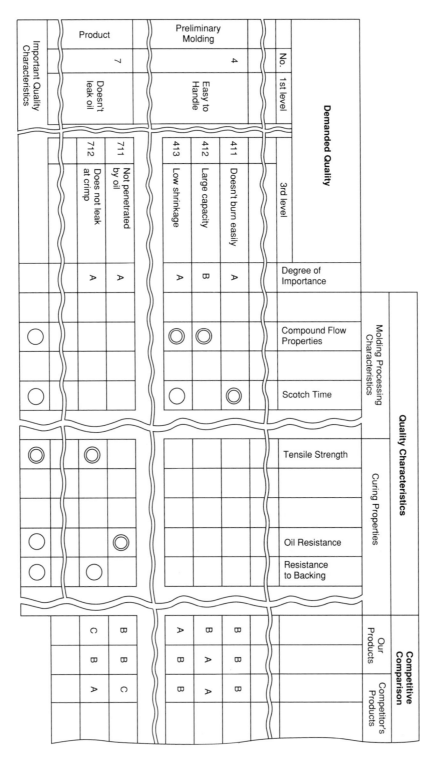

Figure 9-1. Quality Chart for Oil-resistant Synthetic Rubber (NBR), (Nippon Zeon)

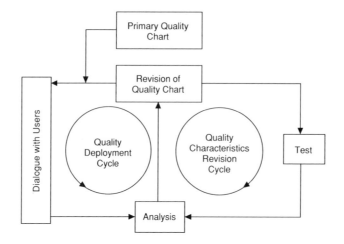

Figure 9-2. Quality Chart Revisions Built-in to Quality Deployment Cycle

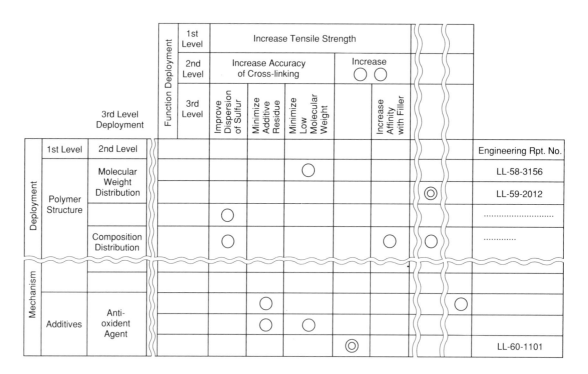

Figure 9-3. Structure Deployment of Synthetic Rubber for Oil Hose (Nippon Zeon)

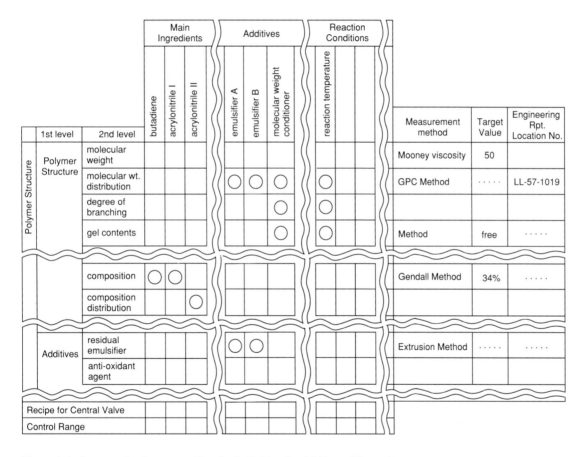

Figure 9-4. Process Deployment of Synthetic Rubber for Oil Hose (Nippon Zeon)

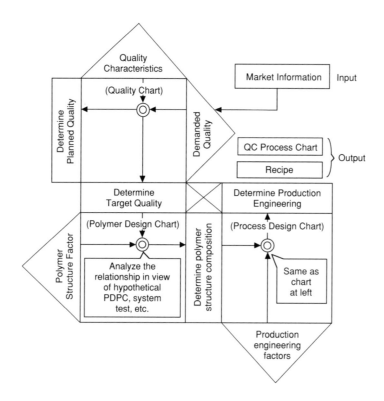

Figure 9-5. Concept Diagram of Quality Engineering Deployment

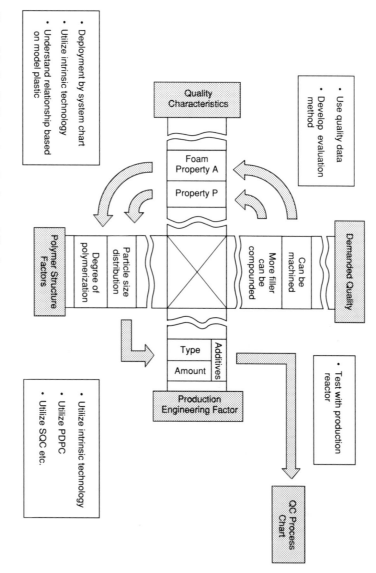

Figure 9-6. Quality/Technology Deployment Chart

Demanded Quality			Degree of Importance	Counterpart Characteristics						
1st Level	2nd Level	3rd Level		Y_1	Foaming Property	Y_3	Y_4	Characteristic P	Y_5	···
	Easy to form into sheets	Can be processed at high speeds	A			◯				
		X_{112}	Ⓐ			◯				
		X_{113}	B							
		⋮								
		Large amount of filler can be compounded	Ⓐ		◯			◯		
		X_{112}	B							
		X_{123}	A					◯		

Figure 9-7. Quality Chart

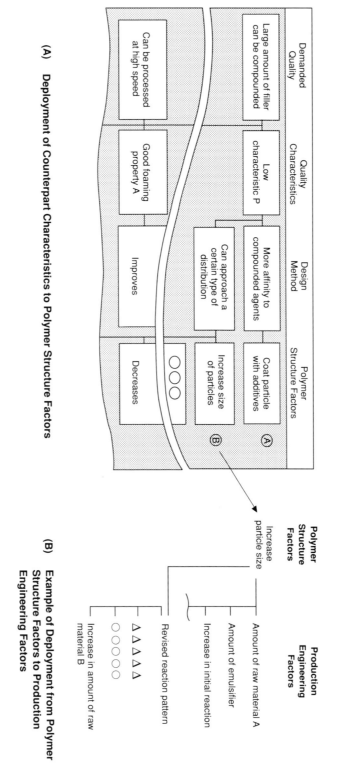

 Figure 9-8.

(A) Deployment of Counterpart Characteristics to Polymer Structure Factors

(B) Example of Deployment from Polymer Structure Factors to Production Engineering Factors

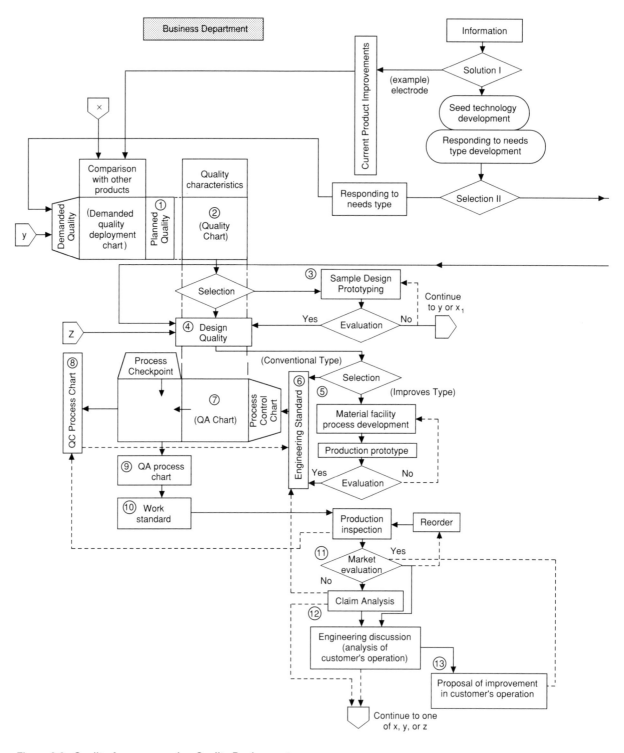

Figure 9-9. Quality Assurance using Quality Deployment

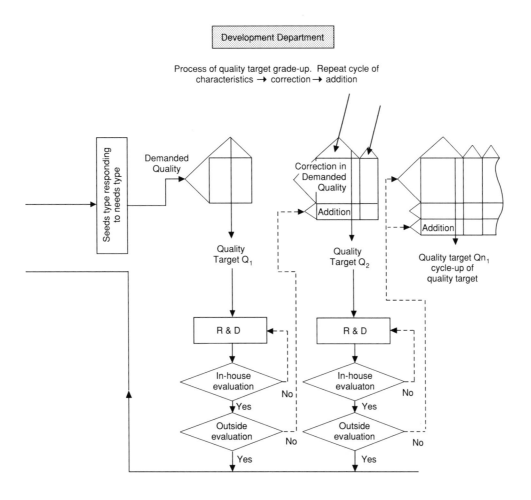

Development Department

Process of quality target grade-up. Repeat cycle of
characteristics → correction → addition

Seeds type responding to needs type

Demanded Quality

Correction in Demanded Quality

Addition

Addition

Quality Target Q_1

Quality Target Q_2

Quality target Qn_1 cycle-up of quality target

R & D

R & D

In-house evaluation

No

In-house evaluaton

No

Yes

Yes

Outside evaluation

No

Outside evaluation

No

Yes

Yes

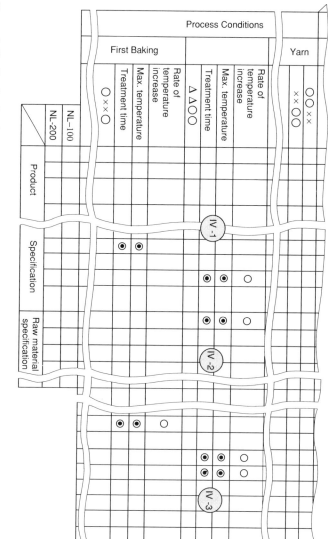

Figure 9-10. Quality Deployment Chart at the Prototyping Stage

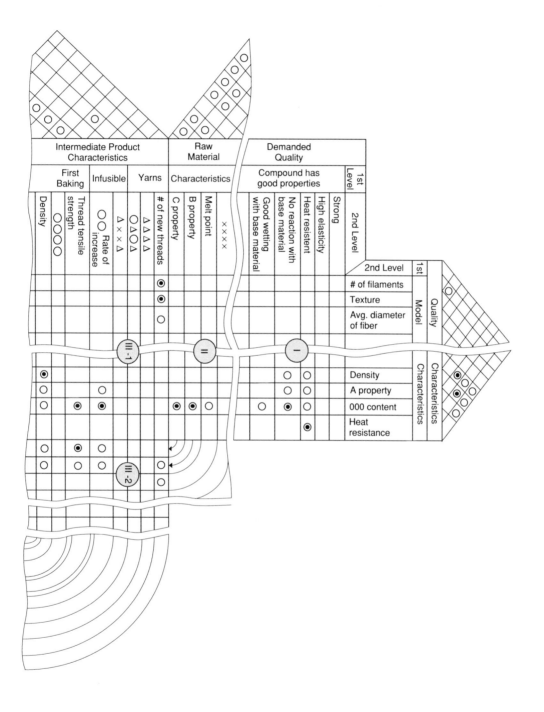

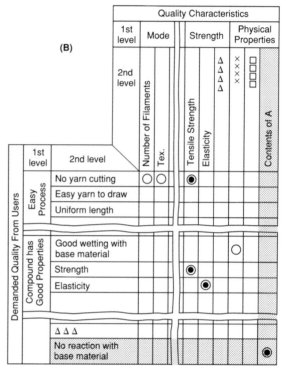

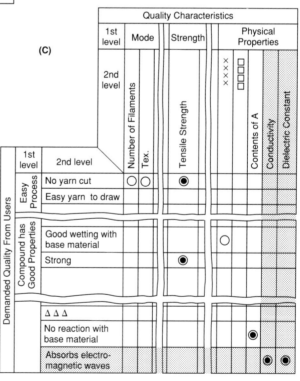

(A) NL - 100 Quality Chart
(B) NL - 200 Quality Chart
(C) NL - 300 Quality Chart

Figure 9-11. Quality Target Upgrade Scale For Nicalon

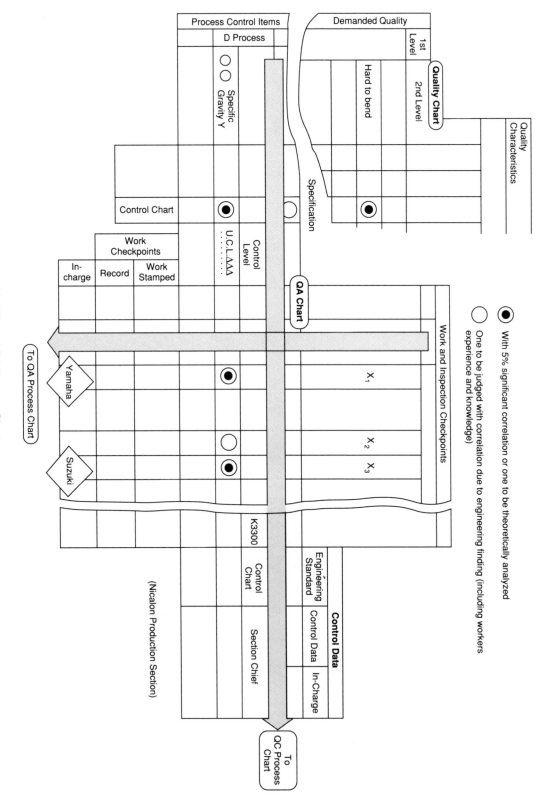

Figure 9-12. The Relationship Among Quality Charts, QA, QC, and QA Process Charts

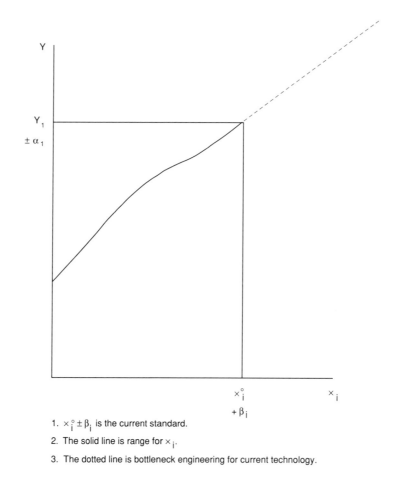

1. $x_i^\circ \pm \beta_i$ is the current standard.
2. The solid line is range for x_i.
3. The dotted line is bottleneck engineering for current technology.

Figure 9-13. The Relationship Between X_1 and Y

CHAPTER 10

Quality Development in the Construction Industry

*Jun Shiino, Development Manager, Taisei Pre-Fab Company;
and Ryoji Nishihara, Production Control Manager,
Engineering Development Center, Shimizu Construction Company*

Total quality control (TQC) has recently and rapidly become popular in the construction industry, and quality function deployment is also being applied. There are many reports and examples of applications (see the references at the end of this chapter). This chapter will present examples of quality function deployment in factory-manufactured multiple-family housing, using a systematic methodology. These examples should help you understand how quality function deployment has been adapted to and used in this industry. We will also refer to a report by Imazu *et al* for an example of general construction.

Quality Function Deployment for Factory-Manufactured Multiple-Family Housing

The Flow of Quality Function Deployment

Figure 10.1 broadly illustrates the flow of quality function deployment for factory-manufactured multiple-family housing. Here the requirements of the buyer (user) — the demanded qualities — are deployed into components, materials, and construction processes for the house. It is necessary to extract those components, materials, and processes that are important for satisfying the user's requirements. The left-hand column of this figure shows the flow of quality development in the narrow sense.

The middle column of Figure 10.1 shows the flow of function deployment, where the functions of the housing are built into a quality design based on company-specific technology and the design targets are communicated downstream for engineering implementation. The right-hand column shows the flow of reliability deployment, where claim information is deployed into components, materials, and processes reflecting an analysis and a detailed understanding of the claims. Quality function deployment for factory-manufactured multiple-family housing consists of these three types of flows.

Quality Deployment

Chart 1 of Figure 10.1 is the demanded quality/quality element deployment chart, which converts the quality demanded by the users into the quality of the housing. This generally is called the quality chart. The most desirable way to express housing quality is to use measurable quality characteristics, but that is not always feasible. Thus, design elements that will actualize the demanded qualities are used in place of quality characteristics. Since these elements also serve as the tools for quality evaluation, they are called quality elements.

Chart 2 is the housing component/quality element deployment chart. For each structural component listed in this chart, we assign values representing the degree of importance of each of its quality elements.

Chart 3 is the housing element materials/component deployment chart. It matches the building materials of each housing element to the functional components of the housing.

Chart 4 is the housing element materials/housing quality element deployment chart. In it, we identify for each housing element the building materials that are most strongly related to the user's requirements.

Chart 5 is the material characteristics/housing quality element deployment chart. We make one of the charts for each material that is selected. In this chart, we translate the degree of importance of each housing quality element into quality characteristics for the materials.

Chart 6 is the material manufacturing process/material characteristics deployment chart. It enables us to identify the processes critical to quality and to prepare the QC process chart.

Chart 7 is the construction process/housing quality element deployment chart, which relates the degrees of importance of each housing quality element to construction processes.

Chart 8 is the construction component characteristics/housing quality element deployment chart for specific construction components. In this chart we convert the degree of importance of the housing quality elements into the degree of importance for construction characteristics.

Chart 9 is the construction process/construction component characteristics deployment chart. It enables us to identify important construction processes and to prepare QC process charts.

In the next section of this chapter about the Taisei Pre-Fab Construction Company, we will detail the narrow definition of quality deployment that can be applied for these factory-manufactured multiple-family housing units.

Function Deployment

The quality function deployment system mentioned above may be effective for translating user requirements into housing quality, but that alone cannot build a house. For example, the user expects the quality of the foundation of a building to be adequate and generally does not express much interest in it. It is therefore not that important in quality deployment. Since the foundation is an important component of the building, however, we must remember that the necessary qualities of housing must be figured into the engineering, regardless of the user's demand.

Chart I of Figure 10.1 is the demanded quality/housing function deployment chart, which translates user demands into housing functions and from which the design information based on company-specific technology for realizing these demands can be obtained. Chart III is the technology deployment chart, which helps to actualize the housing functions that have been weighted according to housing quality demands in Chart I. Charts II, IV, and VII are housing component, material, and construction process deployments that correspond to Charts 2, 4, and 7 of quality deployment, respectively. They deploy the degrees of importance for the various housing functions downstream and carry the information through to the QC process charts.

For more details about function deployment, interested readers are referred to pages 95-113 of the 1986 MITI article listed at the end of this chapter.

Reliability Deployment

Quality deployment and function deployment each deploy demanded quality and technical information (architectural design and construction engineering) into details and carry this through to the QC process charts. When we are assessing negative quality, such as defects, however, the information on each specific defect must be understood accurately and arranged into failure modes for deployment into detail. Then the related QA points must be carried over to the QC process charts. The next section of this chapter will deal with the specifics of this deployment.

Quality Function Deployment in General Construction

The Akao-Shiino article cited in the reference list explains the report by Imazu, which describes the use of quality function deployment as a system for general construction. The system is composed of the following three subsystems, which are also shown in Figure 10.2:

1. demanded quality deployment flow
2. technology study flow
3. construction control flow

Construction is a term that applies to a wide variety of structures, ranging from those that can be built as an extension of conventional technology to those that would be equivalent to new product development in general manufacturing, such as building liquified gas tanks or an LSI plant. The three subsystems listed above allow us to accommodate almost any project within this range as Figure 10.2 shows.

First, we can choose a system that either divides up or integrates planning and construction. In the latter case, we can make further selections as indicated by cases 1, 2, and 3 in the demanded quality column. Case 1, the confirming demanded-quality deployment flow, corresponds to new product development mentioned above. Case 3 is a situation in which conventional engineering suffices; case 2 is a situation somewhere between these two. The selection is made for each engineering study and construction control flow. There is one more type in addition to the above. (Refer to the forthcoming section on designing an LNG underground tank for an example in the general construction industry.)

Quality Function Deployment in Multiple-Family Housing: The Case of Taisei Pre-Fab Construction Company

We described an outline of quality function deployment (broadly defined) for factory-manufactured multiple-family housing. In this section we will deal with the specifics of quality deployment (narrowly defined), such as converting the degree of importance of demanded quality into the degree of importance of the quality element, preparing a QC process chart based on the results of quality deployment, and establishing checkpoints.

Preparing the Quality Chart

One portion of a quality chart showing the relationship between demanded quality and housing quality elements (the demanded quality/quality element deployment chart) is shown in Figure 10.1 and in Chart 1 of Figure 10.3. The left side of this chart is the demanded quality deployment chart. It is an arrangement of reworded quality demands that indicates the requirements of owners, agents, and residents of property lots and rental apartments. Degrees of importance are based on the repeated frequency with which a given demand was mentioned — the number of instances per 1,000 respondents. (The 1986 MITI publication cited at the end of this chapter gives details.) The horizontal top portion of the chart is the quality elements deployment, in which the elements indicate the quality of housing.

The symbols ◎, ○, and Δ in the chart indicate the strength of the correlation between the demanded quality and design elements. They are given 5, 3, and 1 points, respectively. The degree of importance of a demanded quality is converted to the degree of importance of the quality element by what we call the independent scoring method. For example, "maintain privacy" carries a degree of importance of 6.9. Since it intersects with "sound insulation," "floor impact sound insulation," and "quietness of facilities," each of which has a score of ◎, we can calculate the degree of importance for each of these to be (6.9 × 5 =) 34.5. The strength of the correlation at the intersection with "openness" is ○, so we calculate the degree of importance there as (6.9 × 3 =) 20.7. Since the correlation strength at the intersection with both "ventilation" and "air circulation" is a Δ, the score for each is (6.9 × 1 =) 6.9. These scores are then summed up for each quality element, and the degree of importance for each quality element (rate/1000) is calculated. An example for "sound insulation" is a degree of importance of 17.8.

Degree of Importance of Components

Our next step is to convert the degree of importance of each housing quality element into a degree of importance for each component within the house. Chart 2 in Figures 10.1 and 10.3 shows that "sound insulation" is among the quality elements having the highest degree of importance. At its intersection with "external furnishings" we find a ◎. The degree of importance indicated by this intersection can therefore be calculated as (17.5 × 5 =) 89.0. Next, the intersection with "internal furnishings" is a ○ and that with "internal staircase" is a Δ, so these points are scored as (17.8 × 3 =) 53.4 and (17.8 × 1 =) 17.8, respectively.

The importance of each quality element is calculated the same way and the scores summed up horizontally to obtain the degree of importance (rate/1000) for each component. For example, the degree of importance of "external furnishings" is high — 76.4.

Calculating the Degree of Importance of Building Materials and Preparing QC Process Charts for Manufacturing Building Materials

Chart 4 is a material quality element deployment chart. This chart converts the degree of importance of quality elements to the housing components.

The strengths of the correlations between "sound insulation" and "floor PC (precast concrete) panel," "wall PC panel," and "roof PC panel" are given $\bigcirc$, $\circledcirc$, and Δ marks, respectively. These marks give us scores of $(17.8 \times 3 =)$ 53.4 and $(17.8 \times 1 =)$ 17.8, respectively. These calculations are similar to the ones we did in the previous section, and the results are summed in order to find the degree of importance for the materials. In this case, the degree of importance for "wall PC panel" is highest, at 35.4.

Figure 10.3's Chart 5 picks up the PC panel that has received the highest importance rating in Chart 4 (which includes wall, floor, and roof PC panels), extracts its material characteristics, and puts them into the deployment chart which is then combined with the quality element deployment chart to make a matrix. This new chart translates the degree of importance of each quality element into material characteristics.

In this chart "sound insulation" intersects with "broken pieces" and "cracks" which are marked $\circledcirc$ and $\bigcirc$, respectively. The correlation strengths at these intersections can therefore be calculated as $(17.8 \times 5 =)$ 89.0 and $(17.8 \times 3 =)$ 53.4, respectively. This calculation is repeated to compute the degrees of importance for each of the material characteristics. Here the degrees of importance for "cracks" and "breaks" are high — at 108.3 and 110.19.

Chart 6 shows the material manufacturing process/material characteristics deployment chart for PC panels. This chart relates each degree of importance of the material characteristic to the material manufacturing process.

"Cracks" on the chart has a $\circledcirc$ at the intersections with the processes "interim finish," "partial demolding," and "final finish." Each of these intersections thus scores $(108.3 \times 5 =)$ 541.5. This calculation is repeated for each material characteristic, and the results are summed up to compute the degree of importance for the material manufacturing process. In this case, the degree of importance of "partial demolding" is 15.7.

The next step is to prepare the QC process chart on the basis of the importance ratings calculated in chart 6. Check points are filled in with the $\circledcirc$ marks derived from chart 6. For example, the intersections between "partial removal from mold" and "cracks," "breakage," and "rough surface" are marked with $\circledcirc$'s. Therefore, "cracks," "breakage," and "finish of a piece prematurely demolded" will become check items in this process. A checksheet showing the control levels is used to inspect "cracks" and "broken pieces," and a routine operator check is performed for "unevenness," "defect," and "poor finish" later on so that repairs can be made manually if necessary.

Expressing the Degree of Importance of the Construction Process in the QC Process Chart

Chart 7 is a construction process/quality element level deployment chart. It converts quality element degree of importance to construction processes, and forms the basis for the QC process chart. "Sound insulation" on this chart has a ⊚, 2 ○s and a △ where it intersects with the "erection of PC panel walls," "construction of cast-in-place concrete joints," "erection of PC floor panels," and "PC roof panel construction," respectively. These points can be scored at $(17.8 \times 5 =) 89.0$, $(17.8 \times 3 =) 53.4$, and $(17.8 \times 1 =) 17.8$, respectively. The same calculation is repeated to compute the construction process degree of importance. Here, the QC process chart is prepared for "construction of roof panel" because it has the highest degree of importance.

The most logical way to prepare QC process charts for construction processes is to first make a construction component characteristics/quality element deployment chart (Chart 8 of Figure 10.11). This is done by identifying construction component characteristics (in this case, roof characteristics) and forming a matrix with quality elements. Then we relate the quality element degree of importance to the construction component characteristics. Next, we make a construction process/ construction component characteristics deployment chart (Chart 9 of Figure 10.1) and prepare a QC process chart for construction processes, following the example of the PC panel manufacturing process in the previous section. This will help us determine the checkpoints for the process. Here we show only the QC process chart.

Reliability Deployment

In this section we will describe reliability deployment as it corresponds to the quality function deployment mentioned above. First, we collected claim information and converted it into failure modes as shown in Figure 10.4. This is called a failure mode (FM) chart. In it, failure modes are deployed in tree form. Next, we make a demanded quality/failure mode deployment chart with an FM chart at the top and the demanded quality deployment chart on the left (Chart i of Figure 10.1) for converting the demanded quality degree of importance into failure mode degree of importance (chart omitted). We arrange the degree of importance of claims (in this case, the claim-handling cost × claim frequency) into a claim degree of importance chart in Figure 10.2 parallel to this.

Figure 10.1 chart iii-i and Figure 10.4 chart iii-ii are the quality element/failure mode deployment chart and function/failure mode deployment chart, respectively. They are used to relate the degree of importance of the failure modes of housing into quality elements and housing functions.

Chart ii in Figures 10.1 and 10.4 is a component/failure mode deployment chart that communicates the degree of importance of the failure mode for the components. Chart iv is the component/failure mode deployment chart that selects the most important components in relation to the failure mode. This chart is then used in preparing the FMEA chart.

Chart vii of Figure 10.1 is a construction process/failure mode deployment chart, which enables us to perform an FMEA on the process or processes associated with each important failure mode and to prepare a QC process chart that will help us to prevent failure. (I thank Kenji Tojo for making charts i-vii of Figure 10.3 available.)

Quality Function Deployment for Civil Engineering: The Case of Shimizu Construction

Our firm works mainly on client or owner custom-order civil engineering and general construction. Due to changes in society's needs, we have had to change from a passive role to a more active one in which we develop new types of structures or buildings in cooperation with the client or by ourselves. Quality function deployment has proved to be the most suitable method for achieving this new development role, and although we are still at a very low level of skill, we have seen some results that we would like to introduce here.

Designing an LNG Underground Tank

Liquified natural gas (LNG) underground tanks are large underground structures with a capacity of over 100,000 kiloliters designed to store liquified gas at −162° C. Because of the nature of the substance being stored, the structures must be able to withstand earthquakes. This requirement and that of maintaining low-temperature storage conditions are new experiences for us in civil engineering and construction.

Applying past technology to this product is extremely difficult. Our design approach has to be based on a thorough study of the demanded quality and on deployment of appropriate technology.

Figure 10.5 is an outline of this approach and Chart 10.1 shows some of the details. The basic steps of the approach will be described briefly.

1. The owner's demanded quality (Q) is translated into quality characteristics (HA) — which in this case are more like functions. These functions are then correlated with the structural components (L) in a three-element chart (HA-Q,L chart).
2. The characteristics (HA = functions) to be assured at the design stage and the elements of the corresponding design engineering are defined as quality characteristics of design engineering (SA) and are added to the three-element chart as an axis.
3. Next, technology elements are added to the construction engineering (PA) quality characteristics as another axis of the three-element chart.
4. The relationships among HA, SA and PA are clarified so that an HA level can be established on the basis of PA and SA.
5. With SA and PA as back-up, we can add construction method deployment in order to compare construction methods with different combinations of components.
6. After completing these studies we go back to the HA for specifications and adjust the quality characteristic values for each item. These items are deployed to between three and five levels of detail, which results in a very large deployment chart. We have had to develop a computer program — a paperless system — to speed up data handling, search, and revision, as well as deletion of data at the final phase.

Chart 10.1 is part of the HA-Q,L deployment chart and Chart 10.2 is a part of the HA-SA deployment chart in which the strength of the correlation is not graded, but is expressed as 1 or 0. Basically, in this type of technology deployment, instead of deploying the correlation of quality elements/quality characteristics, we use design engineering and construction engineering quality characteristics.

This arrangement might be considered an irregular type of quality function deployment, but it has made classification and correlation of quality possible, as well as clarification of the correlation between engineering and quality and between established quality characteristics and target levels in the final design phase.

Improving the Layout of Multiple-Family Housing

Our firm designs, builds, and sells apartment buildings to purchasers who are unspecified users and multiple users. An important sales point is the balance between quality and price. Achieving this balance is definitely not the typical strength of a custom-client-order general contractor, but we have been improving our residential units over the past ten years in response to changes in the times and changes in needs. The following example shows how we use quality function deployment to improve the layout of a house.

Chart 10.3 is an overall deployment flow. We start with the upper left deployment and the correlation of demanded quality and quality elements. Whether the building is to be a single detached house or multiple-family housing, "ease of use" (second-level detail) is the item of greatest interest to users who have mentioned "pleasant living" as a demand (first-level detail).

On the other hand, the quality element corresponding to this demand — "layout" (second-level detail) — is of the highest significance among the elements corresponding to the functions (first-level details) of the whole house. It is stronger than the significance of other second-level detail elements, such as hot and cold water supply to the kitchen and bathroom, and so forth (according to the overall quality function deployment chart for housing).

These second-level items are deployed to the third level and weighted by the independent scoring method. This is the matrix chart in the upper left corner of Chart 10.3. It shows that in order to respond to the demands for "ease of use," improvements in the layout should focus on "functional independence," "accessibility," and "area ratio," because their point values for degrees of importance are 77, 59, and 57, respectively. However, this focus will not by itself result in specific design improvements.

The various spaces for different uses within a housing unit were grouped together in a category called "room type per (as defined by) usage," which was added to the deployment chart's lower left corner in chart 10.3. Demanded quality was then correlated with "room type per usage" to determine the weight that should be assigned to each type of room in order to satisfy the demand (see section I of the chart). Next, for each type of room we determined the appropriate level of improvement for each quality element (section II of chart). The results show that both common spaces for the family and home task space are important and that the same items — "family space," "utility room," and "bathroom space" — are important in relation to the quality elements.

Next, we studied specific improvements for the three quality elements that we focused on at the starting point of the work flow, as shown in the upper right column of Chart 10.3. Figure 10.6 shows the layouts before and after improvements. With the aid of these layouts, we can compare the combinations of various room types, paying special attention to: (1) expansion of the dining-living space (measured as a percentage of total area); (2) equalization of distance from living room to utility room and bathroom space (accessibility among room types); (3) reduction of distance between kitchen and laundry room (accessibility among room types); (4) separation of kitchen and living-dining space (functional independence); and (5) component change of one Japanese-type room (increase in area percentage for private life and greater functional independence). These items are arranged on the right-hand side of Chart 10.3 so that we can evaluate the improvements.

The example described above introduces the concept "room type defined by use/purpose" and also introduces a method that enables us to evaluate the extent to which we can meet custom-order requirements by comparing two-dimensional view drawings of the proposed housing without having to express quality elements in characteristic values.

Whether the concept of room type defined by use/purpose belongs to function deployment or technology deployment is a question that remains to be answered and requires further experience and study.

References

Akao, Yoji; Kawamura, Hisashi; Inoue, Katsuyuki (1982). *Required Quality Deployment for Pre-Fab Housings*. 23rd Conference, Abstracts, JSQC.

Akao, Yoji; Shino, Jun (1986). "Current Status of Quality Deployment in the Construction Industry." *Quality*, Vol. 15, No. 4, pp. 299-307, JSQC.

Imazu, Hideyuki; Tateishi, Naruo; Kameda, Kazuo; Terada, H. (1982). "Application of a Quality Transmission Deployment System and Examples." *Quality Control*, Vol. 33, November special issue, pp. 912-916, JUSE.

Kikuchi, Tsutomu; Sasaki, Masaaki; Shiino, Jun; Ishiguro, Tsutomu (1986). "Study of the Use of Quality Charts for New Series Development of Standard Rental Condominiums." *Quality Control*, Vol. 37, May special issue, pp. 197-201, JUSE.

Kitamura, Takao; Shiino, Jun; Gomi, Noriaki; Akao, Yoji (1986). "QA by Use of Quality Deployment Chart for Condominiums." *Quality Control*, Vol. 37, May special issue, pp. 179-182, JUSE.

Kitamura, Takao; Shiino, Jun; Takahara, Sampei; Akao, Yoji; Inoue, Masao (1986). 29th Conference, Abstracts, pp. 37-40, JSQC.

MITI: Seikatsu Sangyo Kyoku Housing Division, eds. (1986). "Quality Deployment for Industrial Production Housings." Housing Industry Quality Improvement Committee.

_____ . (1976). "QC Study Group Report."

_____ . (1982). "QC at Building Construction Site." Japan Standards Association.

_____ . (1975). "QC at Housing Components Plant." Japan Standards Association.

_____ . (1986). "Quality Deployment for Industrial Production Housings." Housing Industry Improvement Committee Report, pp. 181-197.

Nakazawa, Ryo; Nakajima, Takashi (1984). "Improvement in Quality Function Systems for LNG Underground Tanks." *Quality Control*, Vol. 35, May special issue, pp. 37-40, JUSE.

Nakui, Satoshi; Kamano, Hiromi; Tezuka, Misao; Akao, Yoji; Onishi, Masahiro (1986). 29th Conference, Abstracts, pp. 33-36, JSQC.

Shiino, Jun (1977). "QC Systemization for PC Pre-Fab Buildings." *SEKOU*, 128, pp. 189-200.

Shiino, Jun; Akao, Yoji (1986). "QC in Condominiums." 2nd Symposium on Construction and Control Techniques, Proceedings, pp. 101-104, Nippon Kenchiku Sakkai.

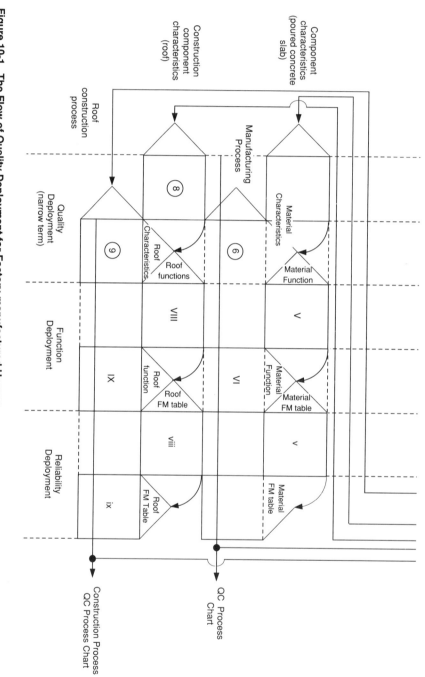

Figure 10-1. The Flow of Quality Deployment for Factory-manufactured Houses

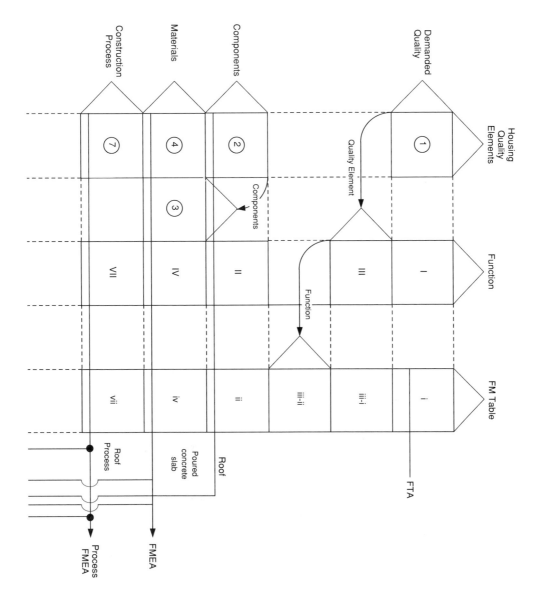

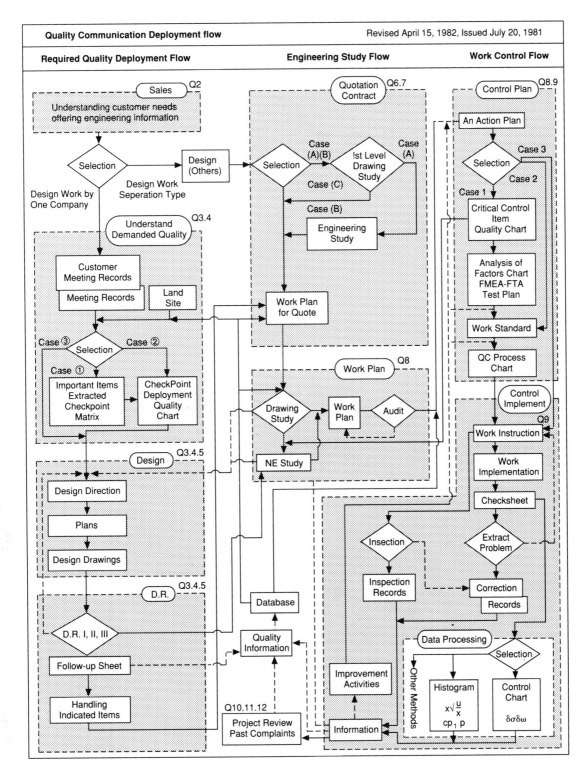

Figure 10-2. Quality Function Deployment Flow

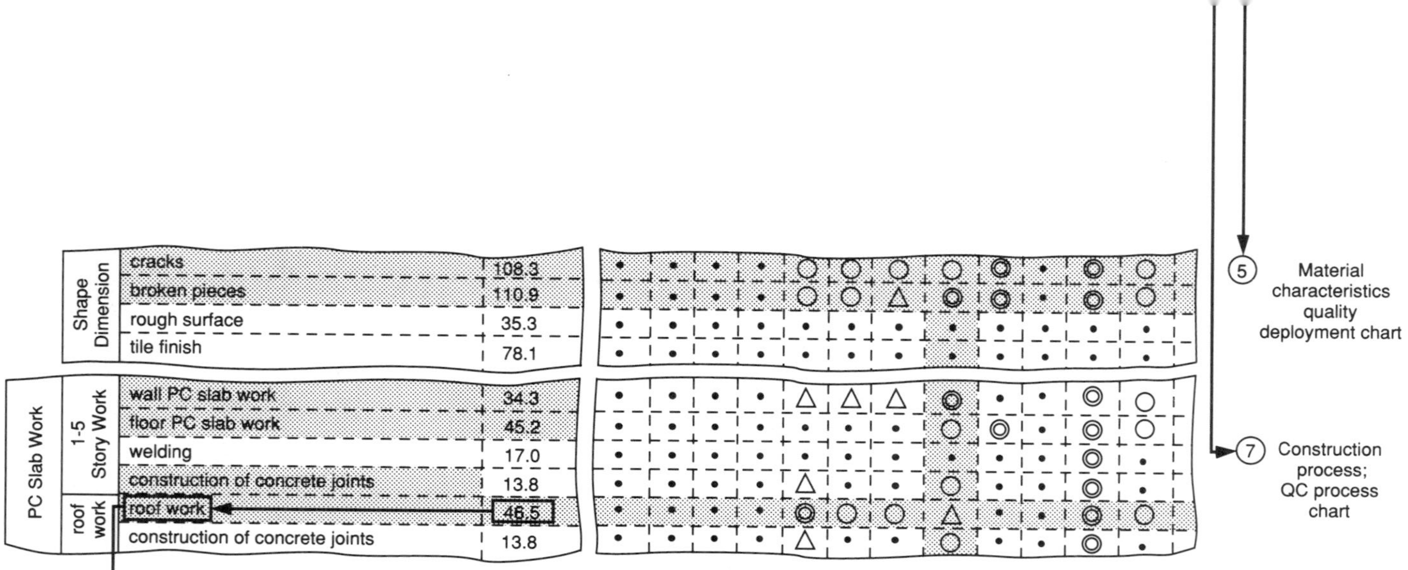

Figure 10-3. Quality Deployment for Pre-fab Multiple Dwellings

Process: Roof work

Process			Control Item		Control Method			Handling of Errors		
Work	material	Checkpoint	Control chart	Control level	Time	Inspection confirmation	Control method	In-charge	In-charge	Method
scribing	PC slab	size error between roof shape & scribing	PC slab work accuracy	±0.0	time of scribing	visual	work drawing	operator	operator	rescribing
PC slab set				Error in filling	time of work (all)	visual		chief	chief	remove cause of defect
adjustment				≤5mm						
Component welding	welding rod electric current	type of welding rods, welding ampere	proper welding rod and current		time of welding	check current by clamp meter as needed	P chart	operator	operator	correct welding rod current

Shape Dimension:
- cracks — 108.3
- broken pieces — 110.9
- rough surface — 35.3
- tile finish — 78.1

PC Slab Work, 1-5 Story Work:
- wall PC slab work — 34.3
- floor PC slab work — 45.2
- welding — 17.0
- construction of concrete joints — 13.8

roof work:
- roof work — 46.5
- construction of concrete joints — 13.8

(5) Material characteristics quality deployment chart

(7) Construction process; QC process chart

Quality Chart

1. Demanded quality dep. chart
2. Component deployment chart
3. Material deployment chart
4. Material deployment chart
5. Material characteristics deployment chart
6. Construction deployment chart
7. Construction deployment chart

	1st level	2nd level	3rd level

Quality Element Deployment Chart

Degree of interest

Degree of importance

Quality element — 1st level / 2nd level / 3rd level

Structure Material			Components		Entrance	Structure	Ease of Living		Pleasant	

Structure Material:
- Roof — roof: cement slab — 21.1
- Wall — wall: cement slab — 35.4
- Floor — floor: cement slab — 19.5

Components / Foundation:
- floor: cement slab
- raw concrete — 9.5
- metal connection — 9.1
- steel wire — 8.9

Entrance:
- inner furnishings — 76.4
- outer furnishings
- canopy (louvers) — 14.1

Structure:
- hand rail — 21.8
- internal staircase — 17.3

Pleasant:
- no outside noise
- privacy from outside — 3.4
- no vibration from outside — 3.4
- no sound leaks to outside — 3.4
- pleasant dining — 3.4
- privacy — 6.9
- place for family — 3.4

Entrance (Ease of Living row): 18.4

Site facility — Internal environment / Livability / Construction

	Importance	
Openess	15.3	
Internal Lighting	7.3	
Ventilation	8.7	
Air circulation	9.8	
Humidity	8.4	
Heat insulation	7.2	
Heat retention	10.3	
Sound insulation	17.8	
Floor impact sound insulation	9.5	
Quietness of facilities	9.5	
Earthquake resistance	13.4	Construction
Wind resistance	12.3	Construction

(4) Material quality deployment chart
(2) Component quality element deployment chart
(1) Quality elements Demanded quality deployment chart

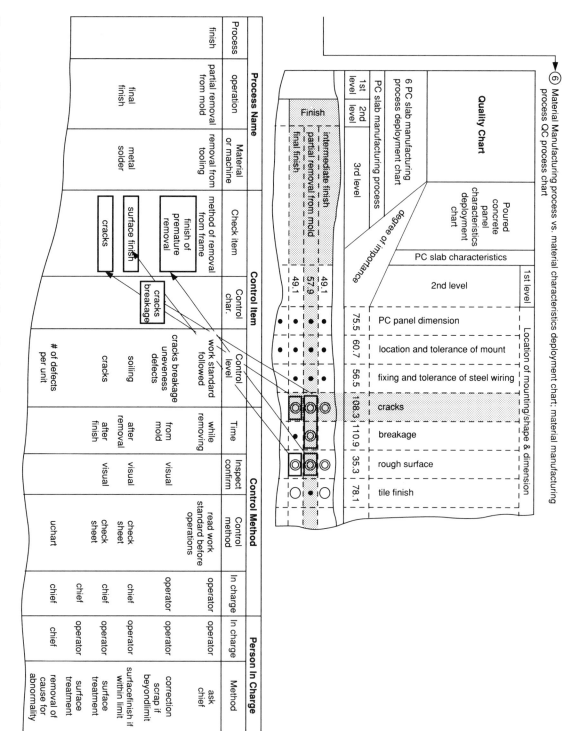

Figure 10-3. Quality Deployment for Pre-fab Multiple Dwellings (Continued)

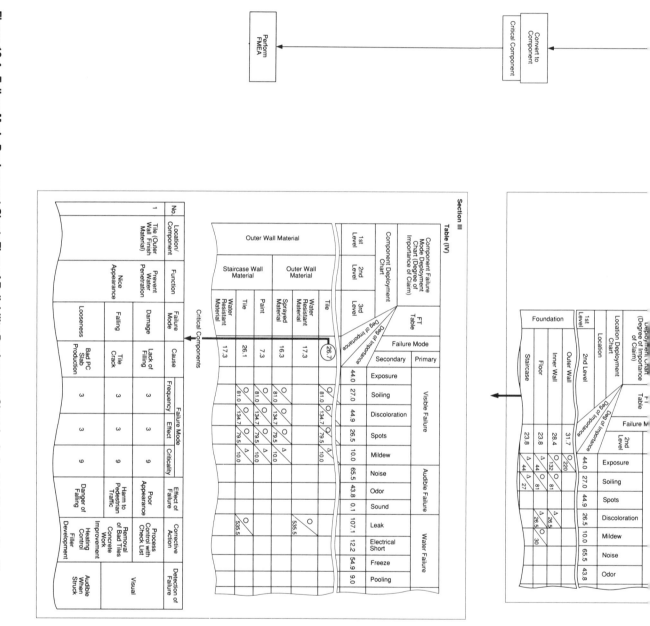

Figure 10-4. Failure Mode Deployment Chart: Flow of Reliability Deployment Chart for Industrial Multiple Dwellings

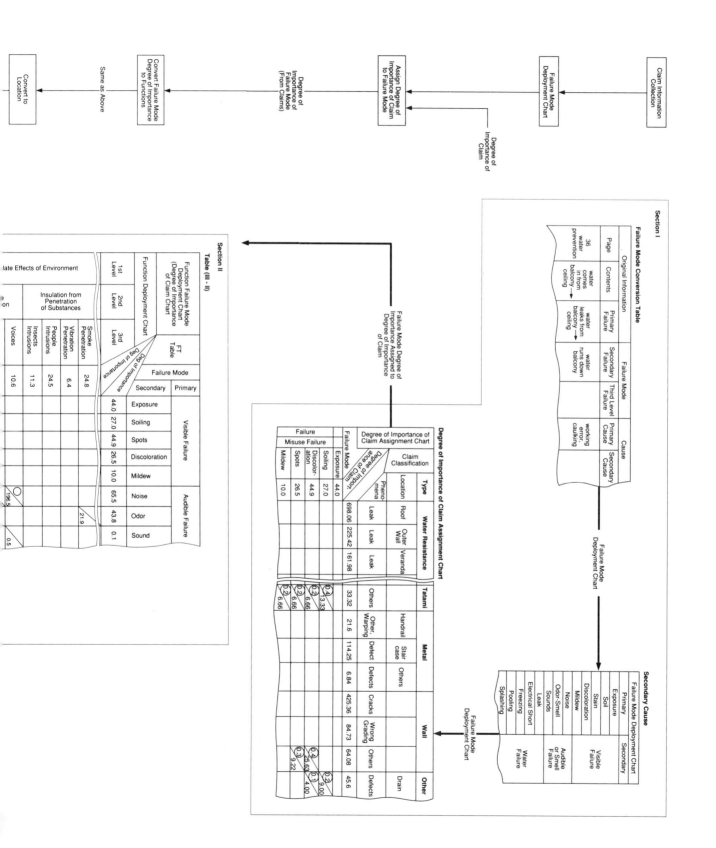

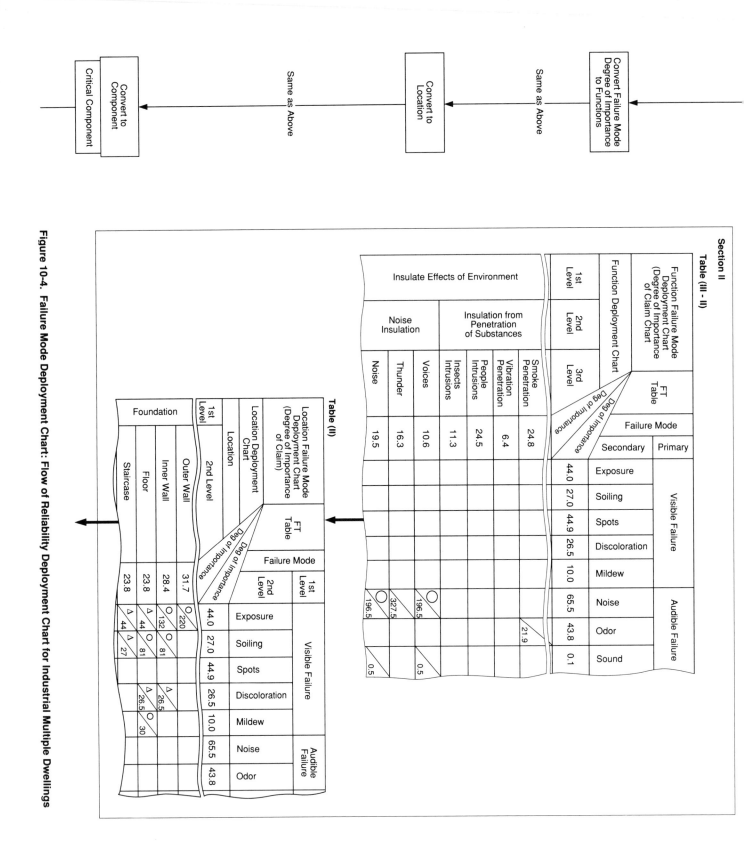

Figure 10-4. Failure Mode Deployment Chart: Flow of Reliability Deployment Chart for Industrial Multiple Dwellings

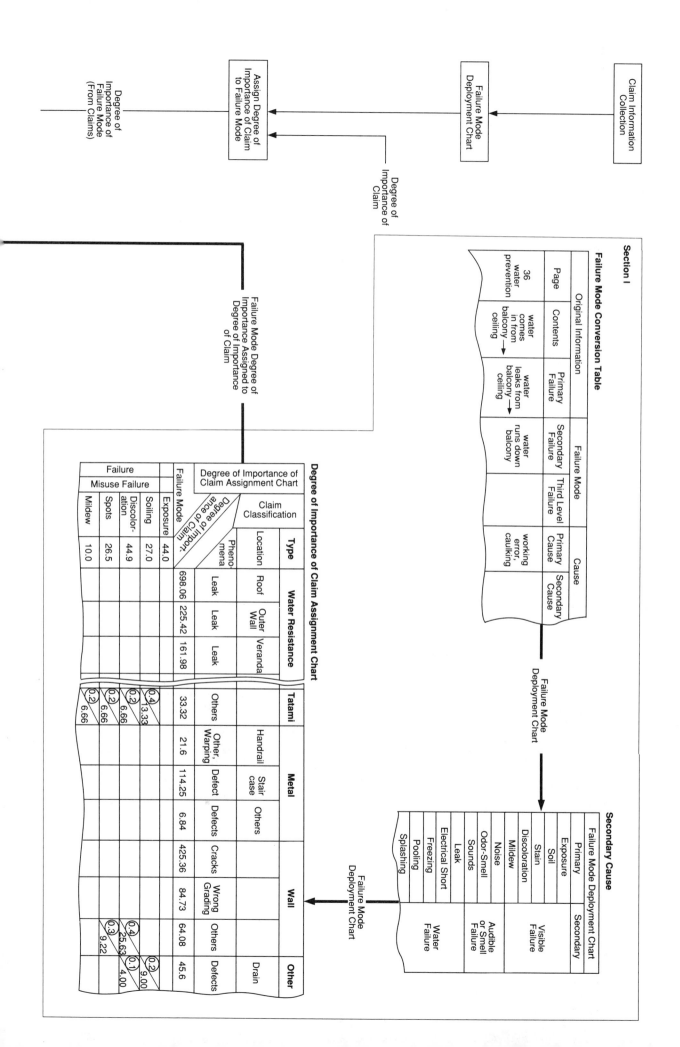

Claim Information Collection

Failure Mode Deployment Chart

Assign Degree of Importance to Failure Mode

Degree of Importance of Failure Mode (From Claims)

Degree of Importance of Claim

Section I

Failure Mode Conversion Table

Original Information		Failure Mode			Cause	
Page	Contents	Primary Failure	Secondary Failure	Third Level Failure	Primary Cause	Secondary Cause
36 water prevention	water comes in from balcony ceiling → water leaks from balcony ceiling	water runs down balcony			working error, caulking	

Failure Mode Deployment Chart

Secondary Cause

Failure Mode Deployment Chart	Primary	Secondary
Exposure		Visible Failure
Soil		
Stain		
Discoloration		
Mildew		
Noise		
Odor-Smell		Audible or Smell Failure
Sounds		
Leak		
Electrical Short		
Freezing		
Pooling		Water Failure
Splashing		

Failure Mode Deployment Chart

Failure Mode Degree of Importance Assigned to Degree of Importance of Claim

Degree of Importance of Claim Assignment Chart

			Type	Water Resistance			Tatami	Metal		Wall			Other
		Phenomena	Claim Classification	Location	Outer Wall	Veranda	Others	Handrail	Stair case	Others			Drain
				Roof				Other, Warping	Defect	Defects	Cracks	Wrong Grading	Others	Defects
Failure Mode		Degree of Importance of Claim		Leak	Leak	Leak				Others			
				698.06	225.42	161.98	33.32	21.6	114.25	6.84	425.36	84.73	64.08	45.6
Failure	Exposure		44.0				0.4 / 13.33							0.2 / 9.00
Misuse Failure	Soiling		27.0				0.2 / 6.66							
	Discoloration		44.9				0.2 / 6.66							0.4 / 25.63
	Spots		26.5				0.2 / 6.66							0.1 / 4.00
	Mildew		10.0				0.2 / 6.66							0.3 / 9.22

Degree of Importance of Claim Assignment Chart

Table (IV)

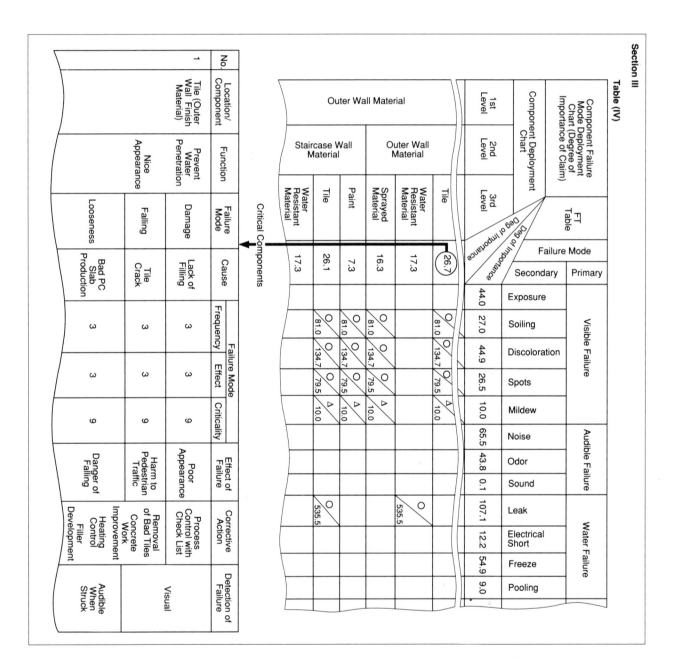

Perform FMEA

Component Failure Mode Deployment Chart (Degree of Importance of Claim)

Component Deployment Chart				Failure Mode													
1st Level	2nd Level	3rd Level	FT Table	Deg of Importance	Secondary / Primary	Exposure	Soiling	Discoloration	Spots	Mildew	Noise	Odor	Sound	Leak	Electrical Short	Freeze	Pooling
						44.0	27.0	44.9	26.5	10.0	65.5	43.8	0.1	107.1	12.2	54.9	9.0
							Visible Failure				Audible Failure			Water Failure			
Outer Wall Material	Outer Wall Material	Tile	(26.7)	17.3			O 81.0	O 134.7	O 79.5	△ 10.0				O 535.5			
		Sprayed Material		16.3			O 81.0	O 134.7	O 79.5	△ 10.0							
		Paint		7.3			O 81.0	O 134.7	O 79.5	△ 10.0							
	Staircase Wall Material	Tile		26.1													
		Water Resistant Material		17.3										O 535.5			

Critical Components

No.	Location/Component	Function	Failure Mode	Cause	Failure Mode			Effect of Failure	Corrective Action	Detection of Failure
					Frequency	Effect	Criticality			
1	Tile (Outer Wall Finish Material)	Prevent Water Penetration	Damage	Lack of Filling	3	3	9	Poor Appearance	Process Control with Check List	Visual
			Falling	Tile Crack	3	3	9	Harm to Pedestrian Traffic	Removal of Bad Tiles Concrete Work Improvement	
		Nice Appearance	Looseness	Bad PC Slab Production	3	3	9	Danger of Falling	Heating Control Filler Development	Audible When Struck

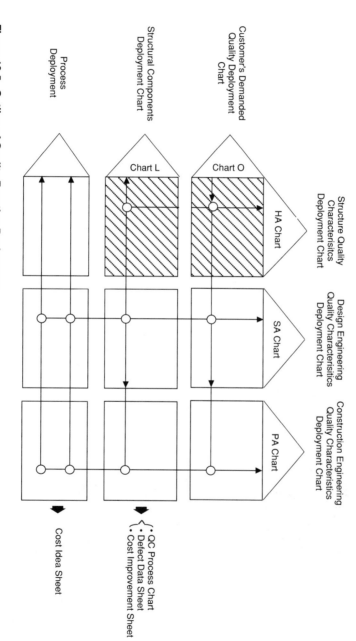

Figure 10-5. Outline of Quality Function Deployment

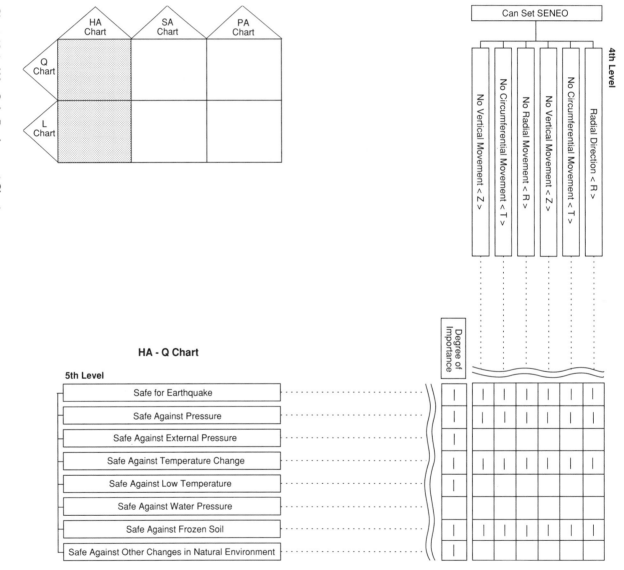

Chart 10-1. HA - Q, L Deployment Chart

Note: Chart Indicates Correspondence of Demanded Quality of Customer (Q) and Structure Functions (HA).

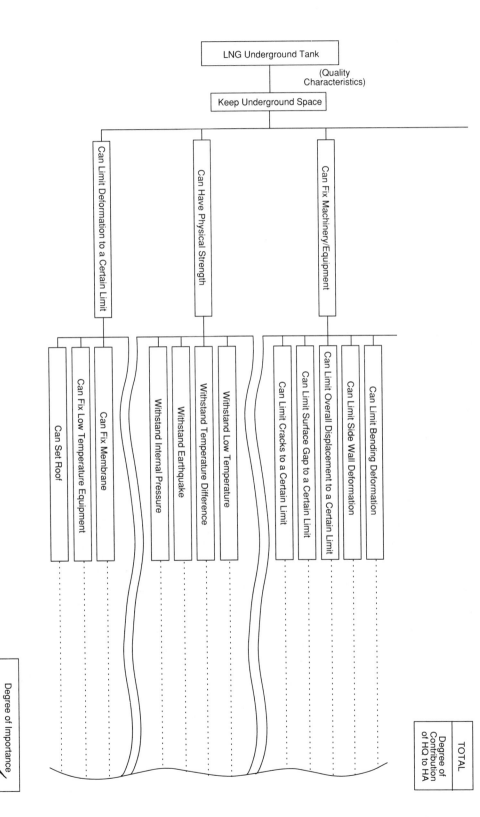

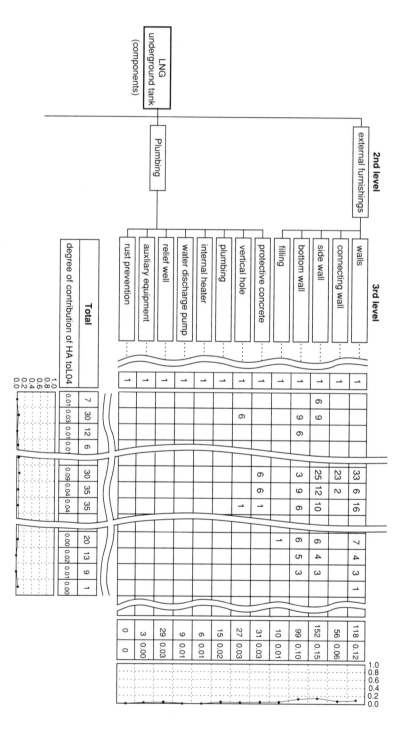

Chart 10-1. HA - Q, L Deployment Chart (Continued)

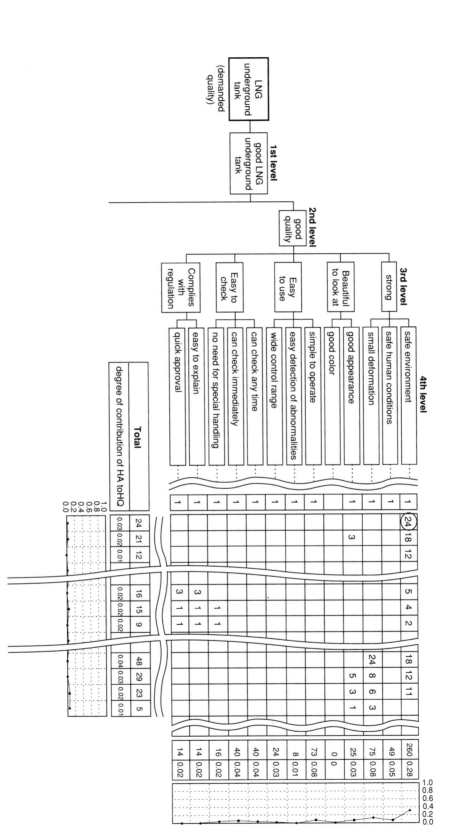

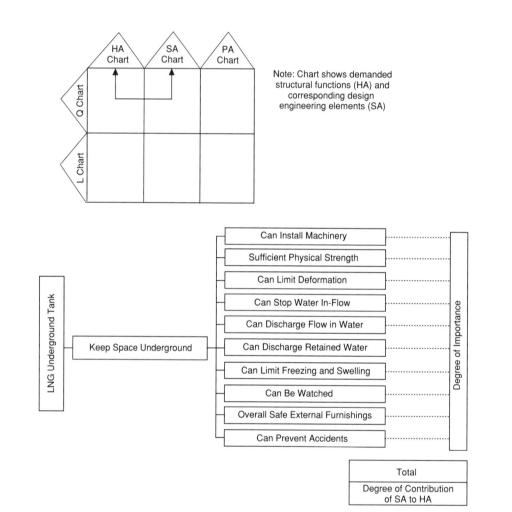

Chart 10-2. HA-SA Deployment Chart

HA-SA — LNG Underground Tank

- Technology to Organize Design Conditions
- Technology to Find Out
- Technology to Decide

	Decide Design Conditions	Decide Design Load	Decide Boundary Conditions	Find Surface Tension	Find Strain	Find Stream	Flow in Water Force	Design for Type of Soil	Crack Conditions	Decide Capacity	Decide Dimensions	Decide Design Strength of Concrete	Decide Plumbing	Decide Water Discharging	Decide Water Usage	Decide on Heaters	Total	Degree of Contribution of HA to SA
				12	24	57						23	33	150			563	0.21
				47	36	16					10	32	22	109			489	0.18
								8			2	36	11	51			259	0.10
							26										26	0.01
							27								36		63	0.02
							27									7	34	0.01
						36											69	0.03
																	1144	0.42
										7		1			2	4	46	0.02
																	20	0.01
Total	0	0	0	59	60	109	80	8	0	7	12	98	66	310	38	11		
	0	0	0	0.02	0.02	0.04	0.03	0.01	0	0.00	0.00	0.04	0.02	0.11	0.01	0.00		

Degree of Contribution of HA to SA scale: 0.6 / 0.4 / 0.2 / 0.0

Bottom contribution scale: 1.0 / 0.8 / 0.6 / 0.4 / 0.2 / 0.0

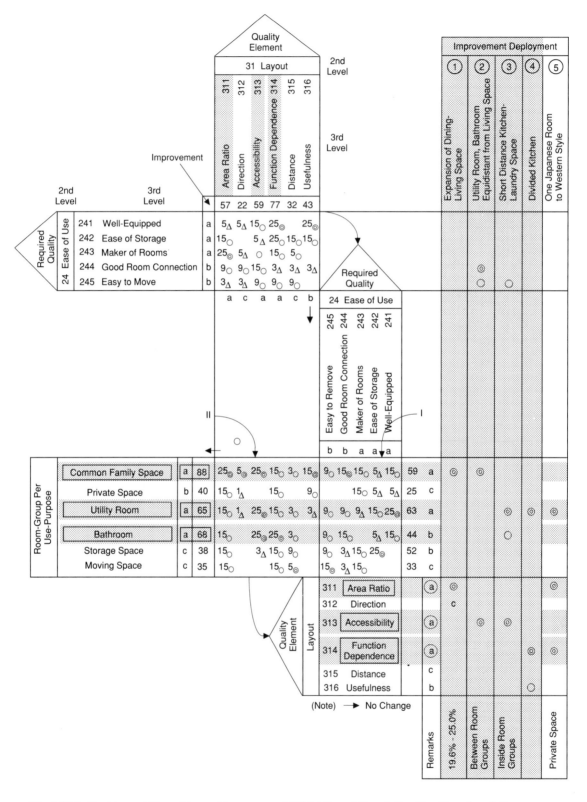

Chart 10-3. Deployment Flow of Layout Improvement (Weighting of Correlation Was Based on 3-step Independent Scoring Method).

Common family space: Living, Dining
Utility Room: Kitchen, Laundry
Bathroom: W.C., Bath

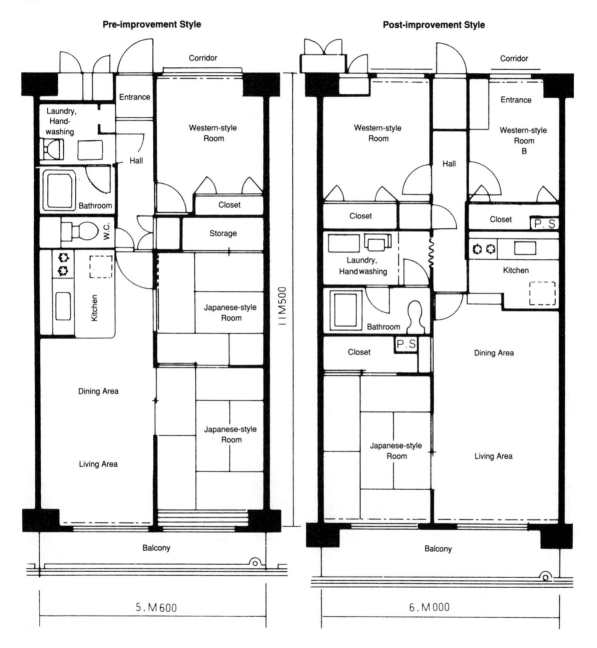

Figure 10-6. Pre- and Post-improvement Layout

CHAPTER 11

Quality Function Deployment for the Service Industry

Tadoshi Ohfuji, Professor of Management Engineering, Tamagawa University;
Teiichiro Noda, Director, Noda Engineering;
and Junji Ogino, Director of Purchasing, Yaesu Book Center

Despite the fact that more and more service industry companies are beginning to use quality control, many people believe that promoting its wider use in this field will not be easy. The reasons for this are that data are difficult to obtain (quantification is difficult) and service is not a measurable material object. Trying to understand the quality of service — which is typically intangible, unstorable, and very immediate — in terms of specific characteristics does indeed seem difficult. Nonetheless, the service industry is finding it necessary to conduct quality assurance activities — such as setting quality targets and establishing a quality design — in order to clarify the quality of its service in relation to customer needs.

Quality function deployment can accomplish this very effectively. It enables us to clarify the quality demanded by the customer and to establish the quality targets by competitive analyses or comparison with competing business situations. These methods define the type of data that is necessary. So even when a company is dealing with such intangibles as service, quality function deployment makes it possible to clarify, plan, and design the services to be offered and to conduct quality control activities.

Outline of Quality Function Deployment for Service Companies

Figure 11.1 illustrates the generalized flow of quality function deployment in the service industry. Because customer demands must be understood, we first make a demanded quality deployment chart followed by a quality element (quality characteristics) deployment chart. In manufacturing industries, we generally make a quality characteristic deployment chart. In the service industry, however, it should be called a quality elements chart. Quality elements are the basic elements that can be measured in evaluating quality; the measurable aspects of those elements are called quality characteristics.

The next step is to make a quality chart (1), which is a matrix made by combining the demanded quality deployment chart and the quality element deployment chart. Once the quality chart is complete, conduct a competitive analysis of the demanded qualities and then establish the quality design by correlating the results of the analysis in the matrix. Then, perform a function deployment for the service operations and make a service operations/quality elements deployment table (2), which will be a two-dimensional chart linked to the quality element deployment chart. Identify the factors in the service process that form the service and extract them to make a matrix like chart 3, which we call the service operations deployment chart. Now, make a QC process chart from matrices 2 and 3. Matrix chart 2 should make the control points for management easy to identify and matrix chart 3 (which is included in the QC process chart) should make the checkpoints for workers clear.

Understanding Demanded Quality

Although we have said that it is difficult to obtain quantitative data in the service industry, numbers are not the only kind of data. Reworded customer "verbatims" can be very good data for learning about demanded quality. Thus, even in the service industry, we can conduct quality function deployment. I have studied examples of quality function deployment in the service industry and found that demanded quality is generally surveyed and studied by one of the following four methods:

1. Conduct a survey by questionnaire.
2. Have company employees put themselves in the customer's place and come up with quality demands.
3. Observe and analyze customer behavior.
4. Analyze past demands and complaints filed by customers.

Methods 1 and 2 are further explained in the Nishizeki-Noda reference at the end of this chapter. Methods 1 and 3 are explained in the Akao-Imaida *et al* reference, and method 4 is explained in the Shindo-Yoshizawa *et al* reference. Other examples use free descriptive detail.

Making the Quality Chart

Once we have gathered information about demanded quality and studied it, we can extract the quality elements, using the procedure outlined in Chart 1.4 in Chapter I. Then we can construct a quality element deployment chart and a quality chart. Although we can use these procedures in the service industry in much the same way that we use them for other industries, quality elements in the service industry tend to include many feelings and subjective impressions. We therefore need to use our ingenuity to come up with characteristics that can be expressed numerically. Charts 11.1 through 11.3 show how these deployments can be applied in service industries. We suggest using quantification method 3 to arrange the quality chart.

Determining Quality Targets and Design Quality

In Chapters 2 and 3 we talked about determining quality targets and design quality. In the service industry we must assess the quality demands very accurately by stratifying the target customer group, because the targeted quality and the quality design will differ according to the customer's age, sex, and intended use of the service. The degree of the customer's interest can be stratified and tabulated by customer attribute and the service plan and design can then be formulated to fit the targeted market. It is also important to make a comparative analysis of competitors' services or business situations. Chart 11.4 is an example of a comparative analysis of potentially competitive business situations. This technique will be discussed in greater detail in the case study "Quality Function Deployment at Okajima" in this chapter. In determining targeted quality and design quality in the service industry, we will analyze and study from the aspect of "must-be quality" and "attractive quality."

Service Operations Deployment

Once the quality targets and quality design have been determined, the methods for realizing them should be clarified and built in'.o the service process. To do this, we determine the points for assuring the quality design in the service QC process chart and describe them clearly. Next, we carry out quality function deployment for the service operations in order to make the quality element deployment chart and the matrix — which will enable us to clarify the control points for workers. The checkpoints for workers will be clarified through the matrix made up of the service process chart factors and the operations function deployment chart. These control points and checkpoints will be used in the QC service process chart. Actual examples of service operations deployment will be discussed in the Yaesu Book Center case study later in this chapter.

Quality Function Deployment at Okajima

Using the Demanded Quality Deployment Chart in a Retail Business

The demanded quality deployment chart, in which the customer's demanded items are systematically arranged, is being used very effectively in new product planning, development, and evaluation. We have also been studying a method for using this demanded quality deployment chart in a retail business. Chart 11.5 shows a representative example of such a deployment. Two situations in which a method could be applied in a retail business are:

1. Developing private labels and original merchandise. The method can be used in essentially the same way as in new product development for the manufacturing sector.
2. The quality of a retailer's work could be clarified by listing the customer's demands for each store (sales area) and product in the demanded quality deployment chart.

Let's examine some of the ways that a demanded quality deployment chart can be used in the second of these two situations.

1. Evaluating the store or the sales area. Determine the degree of importance for each demanded quality item and evaluate each item on a scale of 1 to 5. To calculate the scores, multiply the degree of importance by the evaluation points. The total scores for each item will be the composite score. Regular evaluations can be useful for analyzing changes in the store's or sales area's performance level and for making comparisons with the competition in other types of evaluations. The sequence of steps for using such evaluations is:

1. Evaluate →
2. Organize problems →
3. Determine strategies and countermeasures →
4. Implement countermeasures →
5. Re-evaluate (confirm results)

   2. Planning, designing and building new stores. Once a store is built it is very difficult to do major remodeling. It is therefore important to make every effort at the beginning to plan, design, and construct a store that will satisfy the needs of the customer. With the aid of a matrix, you can arrange demanded qualities in an easy-to-understand order and see which ones should be studied at each step of planning, design, and development. Using this chart, you can identify the items that must be studied and determine when they should be studied. All of this can be recorded in a manual. Furthermore, by combining this chart with PERT (project evaluation and review technique), you can control the construction schedule for the new store.

   3. Layout of the sales area. Consider the modifications that might be made in response to each demanded quality — for example, demanded qualities such as ease of purchase, ease of selection, and enjoyment. Determine which modifications should be made.

   4. Development and deployment of the business environment characteristics (area stores, supermarkets, discount stores, etc.). As Chart 11.4 indicates, this demanded quality deployment chart can be used to study suitable business opportunities when demands for new types of services or new service outlets arise. For example, because of the number of families in which (1) both husbands and wives are working is increasing and (2) young people stay out later at night, we encounter the quality demand "to be able to shop late at night" much more often. As a result, many stores are extending their business hours.

Application I (1981): Planning the FamilyCo Mall

   After receiving a request to help Okajima find some use for the site where the QRS Food Plant was once located, I was able to use quality development to determine what kind of business should be run and how it should be run.

   Correlating the degrees of importance in the demanded quality deployment chart with the characteristics of various types of retail business situations indicated that we should choose a convenience store with extended hours of operation. Using examples from other cities as our guide, we came up with many ideas for various types of convenience stores and then combined the ideas in new ways to create several alternative plans. Finally, using the degree of importance values from the demanded quality deployment chart, we decided on a multipurpose type convenience store that sells "fun" — which we named the FamilyCo Mall. Chart 11.6 shows how we used the chart to make this series of decisions based on classification by business opportunity.

Application II: Planning a Swimming School

Our proposal to include a sports facility in the FamilyCo Mall was accepted. A swimming school, a tennis school, and a golf driving range were considered for inclusion in this project. We finally decided on the swimming school because one of our targets was to maximize the probability that this facility would be used by housewives (See Chart 11.7). We surveyed the political users' quality demands for a swimming school and made a demanded quality deployment chart. Using this chart, we conducted evaluations of our competitors' swimming schools and then designed a product (service) that could be clearly distinguished from those of our competitors.

Application III (1981): Planning the Tome FamilyCo Store

After analyzing the results of door-to-door questionnaire surveys at FamilyCo stores in the towns of Ryuo and Showa and another survey done in Tome City, we modified the degrees of importance of some items in the demanded quality deployment chart. In some cases the changes increased the degree of importance in our planning and designing stages. The following examples show how we used the various types of information.

1. Information obtained from door-to-door surveys in the neighborhoods of existing stores.

   - The customer verbatim "purchasing even one sewing item requires me to go through the general (food section) check-out line" can be translated into "I shouldn't have to wait to make my purchase" which will be included among the demanded quality items. In response to this demand we introduced separate express check-out lanes.
   - The customer verbatim "I can never find a clerk available to answer my questions about products" can be translated into "Store clerks must be available to assist customers in their buying decisions," which should be included among the demanded quality items. In response to this demand, we introduced part-time person-to-person sales clerks in what otherwise would have been a self-service area.
   - The customer verbatim "We want more varieties of Gelica (a diet supplement) as well as better-tasting ones" can be translated into "has a wide variety of related brand-name goods" and "has fine-quality goods" to be included in

the list of demanded quality items. We expanded the display area for Gelica and included better-tasting varieties.

- The customer verbatim "We need a place where we can sit and have a cup of tea" can be translated into the demanded quality item "has a place to rest, such as a plaza." Our response was to create a tea room with nice plants and a skylight that increased the amount of natural light.

2. Information from the Tome City survey.

- Survey results indicated that "shoppers go to Otsuki City and Fujiyoshida City even though most groceries could be purchased locally." We translated this into the demanded quality item "has a large variety of brands." After checking the variety of goods available at the large supermarkets in Otsuki and Fujiyoshida City, we made our variety of products and our sales area larger than theirs.

- In response to information indicating that "many people go to Hachioji and Tachikawa to shop for clothes," we decided to offer some goods in the medium price range in addition to the mass appeal goods.

- Because survey results confirmed that "many boarding houses in that area rent to students from Tome College," we thought about what demands those boarding students might have. We came up with "have food packaged in single-portion units," "sell items individually rather than packaged, so that even one item could be purchased," and "offer food that does not require cooking and is ready to eat." We decided to increase the number of single-portion packages and increase the size of our sales area for Gelica-type items to offer greater variety. We also installed additional microwave ovens for warming up food to sell.

Summary

Using demanded quality deployment charts in the retail business was an attempt to evaluate the demands of the consumer as objectively as possible, and then to make use of this information instead of relying on intuition and experience as in the past. This is only our first attempt, and a great deal of study remains to be done in the future. We would like to see many companies trying this method and discovering many effective ways of doing it. Our Mitsukoshi area store has been using it for competitive comparisons as well as comparisons of store performance before and after renovation.

I would like to express my gratitude to Tetsunosuke Okajima, president of Okajima Company, for allowing me to publish this example of demanded quality deployment.

Using QFD: The Case of Yaesu Book Center

The Yaesu Book Center (YBC) opened in September 1978. When it first opened, the store had few employees experienced in book selling. Most of the business was conducted by employees who had recently graduated from school. In spite of this, YBC attracted a great deal of attention and was highly regarded by book lovers. Since the doors opened, the company has been blessed with a large and loyal following.

As a bookstore, YBC is part of the service industry. It started out as a specialty store with management and staff who recognized their serious lack of business knowledge. To enable them to conduct their business and meet the demands of their customers, we introduced QC circles as a first step. However, we introduced QC with somewhat different goals than those usually pursued in manufacturing industries; we envisioned using it as a way to seek improved efficiency in business operations rather than as a response to poor performance.

In our QC circle, the managers of each area became the group leaders. They brought up problems that were occurring in the daily course of business so that the group could discuss ways to solve them. In promoting QC circle activity, we concentrated on the following three points to achieve the objectives of YBC — to solve problems that have resulted in customer dissatisfaction with the way bookstores have always been operated. To satisfy our clientele, our goals were:

- to have enough books available
- to have enough product information
- to provide enough service

In April 1981 YBC advanced its QC program by setting up its own QA and TQC activities. We first agreed that we should be organized and ready so that the customers could buy their books fast and pleasantly. With this definition of objectives we went about our sales activities, but soon we realized that we had not studied the customers themselves. Thus, we extended our TQC activity to include customer input.

Making the Quality Chart

Our failure to study customer's needs had left us with the following three problems:

1. Specific customer demands were not clear.
2. We had no specific quantitative measurements to use to substantiate the facts of the customers' demands.
3. The relationship between the customers' demands and YBC's service product was not clear.

To solve these problems we made a quality chart and deployed the quality assurance activity. What follows is the procedure we used to make the quality chart and its contents.

1. Determining demanded quality items. In a brainstorming session we gathered together all the customers' demands as they had been expressed in their own words. We translated these verbatims into demanded quality items, using this procedure:

- We changed vague comments into precise expressions.
- We changed comments expressing negative conditions into positive comments.
- We eliminated expressions that were really numerical values of quality characteristics.
- We divided comments into subcategories if they contained two or more subcategories. We grouped comments expressing the same thing together so that each item in that group related to a single idea.

2. Deploying demanded quality. Arrange the demanded quality items that have been translated from verbatim comments in groups of increasing specificity of detail, from first level (most general) corresponding to the fourth level (most specific) using a KJ-like method (described in Chapter 1). Then transfer these grouped items to a chart arranging them according to the rank of the deployment items. We made YBC's QA philosophy, "fast and pleasant service," the first item for deployment in the demanded quality chart (see Figure 11.2).

3. Determining control items (quality characteristics). Control items are extremely important, since they will clearly describe the results of QA operations within the overall QA activity. YBC tried extracting these items, but encountered some difficulty in finding ways to measure the customer demands with data. We tried to make sure we had not missed any demands by referring to measurements used in the QC circle (see Figure 11.3.)

4. Determining operations items. Even before we introduced the quality chart, QA operations had existed at YBC, and we were aware of the customers' demands. So we collected and arranged them as operations items, using the KJ method (see Figure 11.4). In doing this, we paid attention to "the Big Picture" of before sales, at sales, and after sales, so that we could fully understand that a bookstore's main purpose was selling.

5. Assigning degree of importance to the demanded quality items. To assign degree of importance, weight the demanded quality items against each other using data developed from the quantification method. Assigning a degree of importance based on experience, however, is also important. YBC tried both ways. We quantified in the following manner:

- We asked customers to fill out a survey questionnaire (see Figure 11.5).
- We obtained a measure of the degree of importance of various demands by analyzing the questionnaire.

- We constructed a matrix (Figure 11.6) that combined the demanded quality items, control items, and operating items.

Application: Increasing Satisfaction by Improving Book Classification and Displays

1. Why? In the quality chart, "book classification is easy to understand" is an item with a high degree of importance. However, in the survey questionnaires filled out by customers, our "classification and display" received low marks. This meant that classification and display were very important to our customers, and these items were also important to the operation, but the ratings received were not satisfactory.

2. Understanding the current situation. After stratifying the survey questionnaire results, we were able to pinpoint the source of the problem in the second-floor operations by using a Pareto diagram divided by the floor numbers (see Figure 11.8).

3. Analysis. As a result of our experience, we found that our response to customer demands was not satisfactory, particularly in the case of books whose topics could fall between classifications and also books that included multiple topics. We then used a classification checksheet and found that the level of classification in the control items was lowered when books that overlapped several fields were displayed. The following three operations were selected on the basis of the level of classification in the control items (see Figure 11.9).

- Determine how to organize the merchandise.
- Correct wrong classifications.
- Make rounds in the store.

Since "wrong classifications" was not the cause of our problems, we came up with specific strategies to address the other two items.

4. Strategies. In determining the organization of our floor, we decided to display the books that fell into more than one category in more than one area. We posted point-of-purchase (POP) clerks at the boundary areas between book sections to provide POP information.

5. Results. According to the results of the survey questionnaire, customer satisfaction with the classification and display increased, so we considered the results to be good.

6. Standardization. We conducted a multiple-point survey to study the merchandise organization. In response to the survey results, we decided to provide point-of-purchase information in the floor areas near sections of books that fell on classification borderlines.

Conclusion

The quality charts used for this bookstore project differed from previous quality charts in these ways:

Demanded quality. Our customer demands related to the functions of the bookstore as a service, rather than to the functions of the books and their contents. This situation is unlike that in manufacturing industries, where the product that the customer wants to buy (books) does not correspond to the function that controls the quality (in this case the bookstore).

QA operations. The basic functional services for bookstore operations, such as answering questions regarding books, are not the only important services. Services such as responding to customers in a kind and polite manner are also important.

Control items. Since there is no scientific way to measure things in this industry — like length or weight — we needed to create an evaluation system suitable to our experience. We needed to rationalize our measuring method because measuring determines the outcome of the service.

As you can see, in QA activity in a service industry, the attitude toward customer demands is the important point. Using a quality chart enables us to systematize our sales activities in response to customer demands. It can also be very useful in designing management.

In making the quality chart, we realize that assessments of customer needs, as well as those of society, involve some guesswork. They are made relatively quickly — like photographic snapshots — and reflect a particular time. It is necessary then, especially in the service industry, to review them constantly for new developments to determine the organization structure.

References

Akao, Yoji (1985). *Demanded Quality Deployment and QA in Services.* Textbook for the introductory course of TQC seminar in service industry, p. 20.

_____ . (1983). *Demanded Quality Deployment.* Collection of report publication at the Symposium for QC in the Service Industry, p. 14.

Akao, Yoji; Imaida, Shigeru; Omura, Kaji; Yamamura, Nobuhiro; Mitoji, Junichi (1984). "QC Deployment of Passenger Service in the Airline Business." *Quality,* Vol. 14, No. 3, pp. 68-74, JSQC.

Akao, Yoji; Ishii, Masao; Endo, Jun; Takai, Hisashi; Morita, Fujio (1986). "Quality Deployment of Service in the Hotel Industry." Collection of Reports, 2nd Symposium of QC in Service Industry, pp. 115-130.

Honda, Masahisa; Shimada, Kazuaki (1977). *Multivariate Analysis Method for Business.* Sangyo Noritsu Daigaku (Industrial Efficiency College).

Ikezawa, Tatsuo (1981). *The Don'ts of Quality Control.* JUSE.

Kano, Noriaki; Tsuji, Shinichi; Sera, Nobuhiko; Takahashi, Fumio (1984). "Attractive Quality" and "Must-Be Quality." *Quality,* Vol. 14, No. 2, pp. 39-48, JSQC.

Mizuno, Shigeru; Akao, Yoji, eds. (1978). *Quality Function Deployment: Approach to Total Quality Control.* JUSE.

Muroi, Akira (1984). "Understanding and Analysis of Needs by Quality Tables and Application." *Quality Control*, Vol. 35, November special issue, pp. 145-49, JUSE.

Nishizeki, N.; Noda, Teiichiro (1982). "Application of 'Demanded Quality Deployment Table' in Okajima." *Quality Control*, Vol. 33, No. 8, pp. 77-82, JUSE.

Nishizato, Shizuhiko (1975). *Applied Psychology Measuring Structure Method.* Seishin Shobo.

Sakamoto, Masao; Matsuzaki, Katsuro; Yamanobe, Kyoko; Ando, Yukihiro (1984). "Quality Assurance Activity in Joban Hawaiian Center Tourist Hotel. *Quality Control*, Vol. 35, November special issue, pp. 171-175, JUSE.

Shindo, Hisakazu; Yoshizawa, Tadashi; Miyajima, Masaaki (1983). "Application of Quality Table and Quantification Method III Type in Service Industry." Vol. 13, No. 3, pp. 53-60, JSQC.

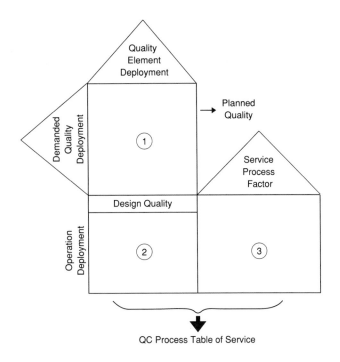

Figure 11-1. Quality Deployment For the Service Industry

Demanded Items			Quality Elements
1st level	2nd level	3rd level	
Good Employees	Good Attitude in Serving Customers	Pleasant atmosphere	Attitude, kindness, etc.
		Liveliness	Service response speed/promptness, attitude, etc.
		Clean	Degree of cleanliness of employees, degree of friendliness, etc.
		Clean clothing	Degree of cleanliness of employees, degree of attentiveness/service, etc.
		Good language, manners	Language, manners, happy impressions, etc.

Chart 11-1. Listing Example of Quality Elements

	Degree of full service					
1st level						
2nd level	Degree of customer service	Degree of information service	Degree of special needs service	Service in unusual circumstances		
3rd level	Attitude / Service response speed / Degree of kindness / Degree of attentiveness/customer service / Degree of friendliness / Language manners / Degree of cleanliness of employees	Display rate / Degree of notability / Degree of clarity / Information collectability / Rate of giving information / Advertisement rate	Discount rate / Rate of treatment / Degree of special privileges	Degree of attentiveness to sudden change / Degree of attention in unusual circumstances		

Chart 11-2. Quality Elements Deployment (Partial)

Quality Table ②		Quality Elements	1st level	Degree of completeness of service								Satisfaction				
			2nd level	Degree of customer service								Easy access to store				
① Demanded Quality			3rd level	Attitudes	Response time	Kindness	Attentiveness	Friendliness	Language manners	Cleanliness of employees		Hominess	Casualness	Atmosphere	Image	High Class
1st level	2nd level	3rd level	Degree of importance	1.69	0.35	1.60	0.96	1.74	1.05	1.07		0.75	3.35	3.16	0.57	0.16
Good employees	Good attitude in serving customers	Good impression	3.6	◎/0.77		◯/0.51		◯/0.51	◯/0.51	◎/0.77				△/0.26		
		Liveliness	0.3	◎/0.08	◯/0.05		◯/0.05		◯/0.05					△/0.03		
		Clean	0.3					◯/0.09		◎/0.13				◯/0.09		
		Clean clothing	0.4				△/0.04	◯/0.09		◎/0.13					◯/0.09	
		Good language manners	1.1				◯/0.28	◯/0.28	◎/0.41							
		Kind	1.1	△/0.18		◎/0.41		◯/0.28								
		Polite	0.7	◎/0.35	◯/0.35			◯/0.23	△/0.12							

Note: ◎ : Strong relation   ◯ : Normal relation   △ : Weak relation

Chart 11-3. Quality Chart (Partial)

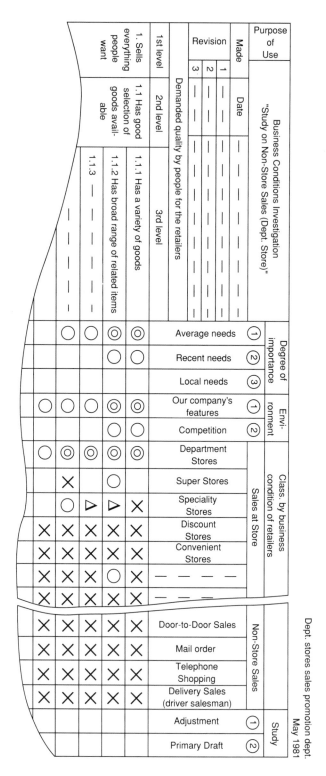

Chart 11-4. Demanded Quality Deployment for Investigating Business Conditions

Purpose of Use: Business Conditions Investigation "Study on Non-Store Sales (Dept. Store)"

Made / Date — Revision 1, 2, 3

Dept. stores sales promotion dept. May 1981

Demanded quality by people for the retailers

			Deg. of importance			Environment		Class. by business condition of retailers — Sales at Store							Non-Store Sales				Study	
1st level	2nd level	3rd level	Average needs ①	Recent needs ②	Local needs ③	Our company's features ①	Competition ②	Department Stores	Super Stores	Speciality Stores	Discount Stores	Convenient Stores			Door-to-Door Sales	Mail order	Telephone Shopping	Delivery Sales (driver salesman)	Adjustment ①	Primary Draft ②
1. Sells everything people want	1.1 Has good selection of goods available	1.1.1 Has a variety of goods	◎	○		◎	○	◎	○	✕	✕	✕	✕	✕	✕	✕	✕	✕		
		1.1.2 Has broad range of related items	◎	○		◎	○	◎	○	▷	✕	✕	○	✕	✕	✕	✕	✕		
		1.1.3	○			○		◎	○	▷	✕	✕	✕	✕	✕	✕	✕	✕		
			○			○		◎	✕	○	✕	✕	✕	✕	✕	✕	✕	✕		
			○			○		○			✕	✕	✕	✕	✕	✕	✕	✕		

Quality Demanded from the Retailer		
1st level	2nd level	3rd level
1. Sells everything customers want	1.1 Has good selection of goods available	1.1.1 Has a wide variety of goods
		1.1.2 Has a broad range of related items
		1.1.3 Has many brands
		1.1.4 Has lower-priced as well as expensive items
		1.1.5 Has many different sizes
	1.2 Has speciality goods	1.2.2 Offers unique, original items
		1.2.3 Has new products
		1.2.4 . . . . .
	1.3 Has good stock of goods	1.3.1 Does not run out of stock
		1.3.2 Does not run out of special sale items
		1.3.3 . . . . .

Chart 11-5. Demanded Quality Deployment Chart in a Retail Business

The Familyco Mall is located in what was once an "S" Food Products Plant.
① It is in the city of Kofu but not in the older section.
② It is an area of population growth.
③ It is close to Yamanashi Cultural Center and the state museum.
④ It is close to several new bars.

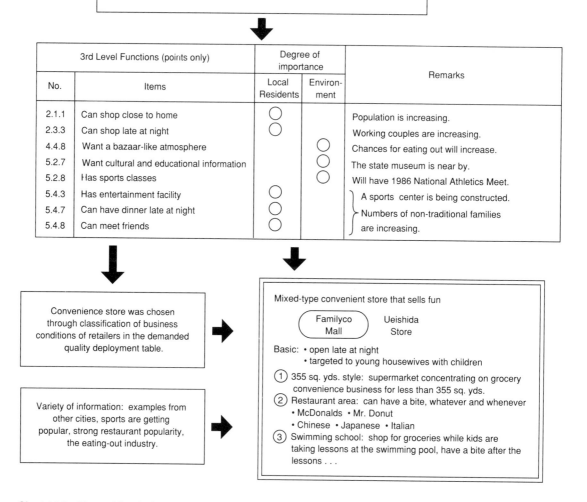

| 3rd Level Functions (points only) | | Degree of importance | | Remarks |
No.	Items	Local Residents	Environ-ment	
2.1.1	Can shop close to home	◯		Population is increasing.
2.3.3	Can shop late at night	◯		Working couples are increasing.
4.4.8	Want a bazaar-like atmosphere		◯	Chances for eating out will increase.
5.2.7	Want cultural and educational information		◯	The state museum is near by.
5.2.8	Has sports classes		◯	Will have 1986 National Athletics Meet.
5.4.3	Has entertainment facility	◯		A sports center is being constructed.
5.4.7	Can have dinner late at night	◯		Numbers of non-traditional families
5.4.8	Can meet friends	◯		are increasing.

Convenience store was chosen through classification of business conditions of retailers in the demanded quality deployment table.

Variety of information: examples from other cities, sports are getting popular, strong restaurant popularity, the eating-out industry.

Mixed-type convenient store that sells fun

Familyco Mall   Ueishida Store

Basic: • open late at night
• targeted to young housewives with children
① 355 sq. yds. style: supermarket concentrating on grocery convenience business for less than 355 sq. yds.
② Restaurant area: can have a bite, whatever and whenever
• McDonalds • Mr. Donut
• Chinese • Japanese • Italian
③ Swimming school: shop for groceries while kids are taking lessons at the swimming pool, have a bite after the lessons . . .

Chart 11-6. Chart of Study Concept of Familyco Mall

Survey of degree of importance by quality function deployment table	Trends of the industry (in big cities)

⬇   ⬇

2nd function (important items)		Chosen criteria	Classification
Healthy		A design with open ceilings to allow sunshine.	Building design
Safe	Non-slip floors	Uses non-slip tiles for all areas, both inside and out of the swimming pool	Building design
	Does not cause cramps	90-minute program including track/gym (30 min.) (other swimming schools have only 30-min. programs.)	Application
Accessible for practice			
Anyone can participate		Toddlers from 1 1/2 years can join (at other schools, 3 years is the limit).	Instruction method
Degree of importance easily seen		Adoption of a computerized member management system	Application
Classes easy to attend		Bus service available up to 30 minutes away (other schools offer 20-minute service).	Application

Note: Classification
    Building design: item that is difficult to change later, unless planned in at the building's design stage.
    Instruction method: items that require a certain degree of know-how.
    Application: item that can be easily met, once noticed.

Chart 11-7. Case Study of Swimming School

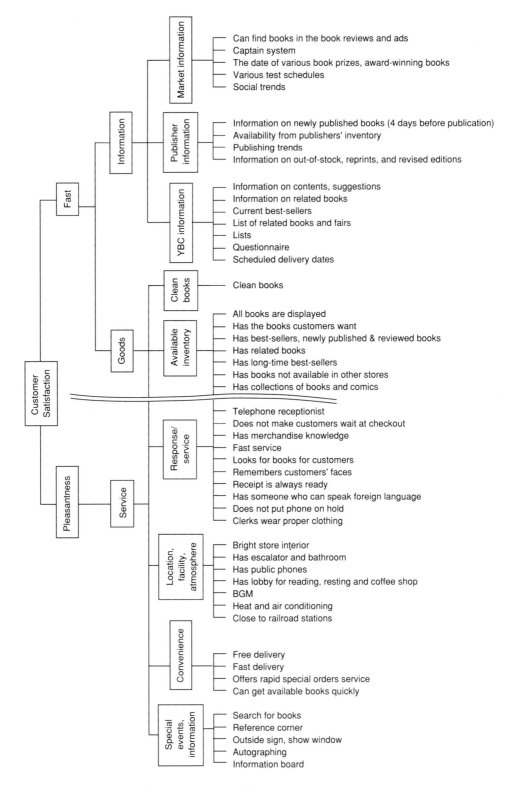

Figure 11-2. Demanded Quality Deployment Chart

Characteristics / Demanded Quality			1st Level Deployment	Fast		Pleasant Atmosphere			
			2nd Level Deployment	Product Arrangement		Service		Product Knowl -edge	Safety
1st Level Deployment	2nd Level Deployment	3rd Level Deployment	3rd Level Deployment / 4th Level Deployment	Compliance rate	Degree of looking for missing books	Time required to deliver books within the store	Number of books that get dirty	Progress in on-the-job training plans	Number of master file drills
				A	B	B	B	A	B

Figure 11-3. Determining Control Items (Quality Characteristics)

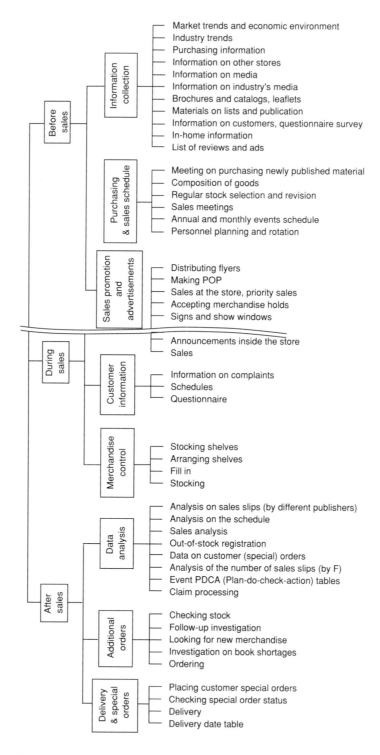

Figure 11-4. Operation Deployment Chart

Thank you very much for coming to this store. Your answers to the following questions will help us make this store more satisfactory to you, the customer.

I. How important are the following items in a book store? Please rank from 1 to 5. (circle number)

(Example) Has a large volume of books.

1	2	3	4	5
not import-ant at all	not important	can't say either	somewhat important	important

1. Has a good variety of bestsellers.

    1   2   3   4   5

2. Scheduled date for availability of out-of-stock books is clear.

    1   2   3   4   5

3. Has a variety of art books (4th floor).

    1   2   3   4   5

4. Has a variety of books on sociology, literature science, and history (2nd floor).

    1   2   3   4   5

13. The store clerks look hard for books for the customers.

    1   2   3   4   5

14. Can easily find books you want.

    1   2   3   4   5

15. Book classifications are easy to understand.

    1   2   3   4   5

16. Attractive, easy to find book displays.

    1   2   3   4   5

17. Books are always clean.

    1   2   3   4   5

II. These questions about yourself. (Please circle)

1. Sex: Male   Female

2. Age: teen's, 20's, 30's, 40's, 50's, 60's, over 70

3. Occupation: office, government, entrepreneur, scholar, high school student, college student, (other)

Figure 11-5. Survey Questionnaire

Figure 11-6. Quality Deployment for TQC in the Yaesu Book Center

Operation Deployment

Phase	Category	Operations
After sales	Special order and delivery	Delivers; Check status of special orders; Places special orders
After sales	Availability/stock	Looks for missing books; Add-on orders; Checks stock
After sales	Data analysis	Analyzes results of special events; Special order slips analysis; Schedule analysis; Sales slip analysis
During sales	Customer service and sales	Gives in-house information; Gets orders; Checks for cause of out-of-stocks; Searches; Answers questions
Before sales	Inspection and display	Rearranges stacks and fills the shelves; Corrects wrong classifications; Checks fixtures; Inspects the facilities; Makes rounds in the store

Demanded quality (with weights):

Demanded quality	Weight	
Properly dressed	0.01	○
Clerks assist customers in looking for books	0.34	◎
Can speak English		

◎ : important   ○ : somewhat important   △ : normal

Demanded Quality Deployment

Hierarchy of demanded quality (1st / 2nd / 3rd / 4th level deployment):

- **Pleasant**
  - **Service**
    - *Reception:* Does not have to wait at checkout; Kind and polite; Has product knowledge
  - **Goods**
    - *Classification and display:* Has clean books; Display is easy to see; Signs are easy to see; Classification is easy to understand; Easy-to-find books
    - *Availability/stock:* Has many specialty books; Has newly published books and books in review; Has books that are not available at other stores; Has large variety & volume of books
- **Fast**
  - **Information**
    - *Search:* Information lists of published books available; Offer information on the contents & give advice; Can find related books; Can tell name of publisher, author, title
    - *Information for getting books:* Can give date of availability; Can tell if the book is available or not; Can tell why not in stock; Can tell if book is in stock or not

Degree of importance

Demanded quality (4th level)	Degree of importance
Does not have to wait at checkout	0.01
Kind and polite	0.38
Has product knowledge	0.34
Has clean books	0.25
Display is easy to see	0.25
Signs are easy to see	0.50
Classification is easy to understand	0.68
Easy-to-find books	0.43
Has many specialty books	
Has newly published books and books in review	0.02
Has books that are not available at other stores	0.13
Has large variety & volume of books	0.4
Information lists of published books available	
Offer information on the contents & give advice	
Can find related books	
Can tell name of publisher, author, title	-0.18
Can give date of availability	
Can tell if the book is available or not	0.01
Can tell why not in stock	0.6
Can tell if book is in stock or not	-0.29

Quality Characteristics (Classification/Division — right side deployment)

- **Quality Characteristics**
  - **Availability of goods (stock) classification**
    - # incidents where availability classification not clear
    - Immediate response rate
    - Rate of missing books
    - Degree of satisfaction in availability
    - Degree of satisfaction in classification
    - Degree of filing books
  - **Service — Reception and response to customers**
    - Degree of satisfaction of service
    - Waiting time at checkout counter
    - Rate of product knowledge
    - Evaluation of reception to customers
  - **Orders**
    - Rate of getting newly published books ordered
  - **Special orders & delivery**
    - Delivery rate
    - Numbers of dates needed for procurement
  - **Environment**
    - Degree of cleanliness
    - Lighting
  - **Goods**
    - Damage rate

Relationship matrix (◎ = strong, ○ = medium)

Quality characteristic ＼ Demanded quality	Does not have to wait at checkout	Kind and polite	Has product knowledge	Has clean books	Display is easy to see	Signs are easy to see	Classification is easy to understand	Easy-to-find books	Has many specialty books	Has newly published books and books in review	Has books not available at other stores	Has large variety & volume of books	Information lists of published books available	Offer information on the contents & give advice	Can find related books	Can tell name of publisher, author, title	Can give date of availability	Can tell if the book is available or not	Can tell why not in stock	Can tell if book is in stock or not
(classification/availability mapping)	○			○	○	○	◎	○		○	○	◎			○			○	◎	○
# incidents where availability classification not clear																	○	○	◎	◎
Immediate response rate									◎	◎	◎	◎								◎
Rate of missing books											○	○							◎	
Degree of satisfaction in availability										○	○	◎								◎
Degree of satisfaction in classification						◎	◎													
Degree of filing books						◎	◎	○												
Degree of satisfaction of service		◎	○												○					
Waiting time at checkout counter	◎																			
Rate of product knowledge			◎										○	◎	◎	◎	○			
Evaluation of reception to customers	○	○	○												○	○	○			
Rate of getting newly published books ordered													◎							
Delivery rate																				
Numbers of dates needed for procurement																				
Degree of cleanliness																				
Lighting																				
Damage rate					◎															

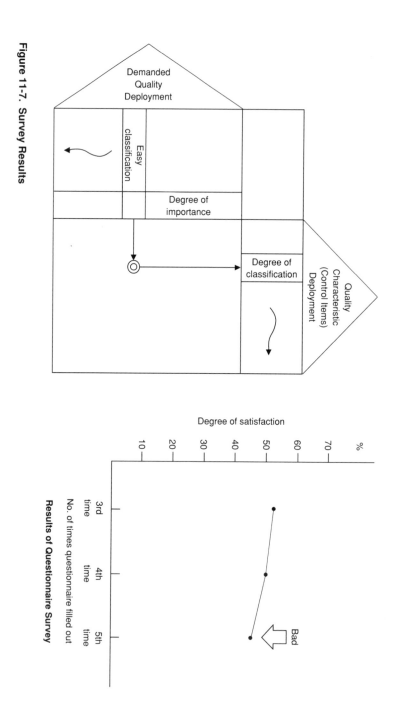

Figure 11-7. Survey Results

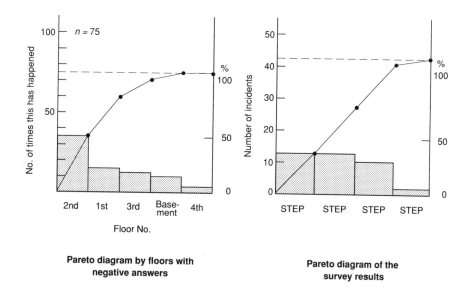

Verification of Classification And
Display on the 2nd Floor

Investigate Customer
Behavior Patterns

STEP 0: Can find the book you want.
STEP 1: Look for immediate signs in the
            entire store. Ask the clerk.
STEP 2: Go to the desired floor.
STEP 3: Look for signs giving broad
            classifications and narrower
            classifications. Ask the clerk.
STEP 4: Look for the book you want.
            Ask the clerk.
STEP 5: The book you want is not there.

**Pareto diagram by floors with
negative answers**

**Pareto diagram of the
survey results**

Figure 11-8. Pinpointing the Problem Using Pareto Diagrams

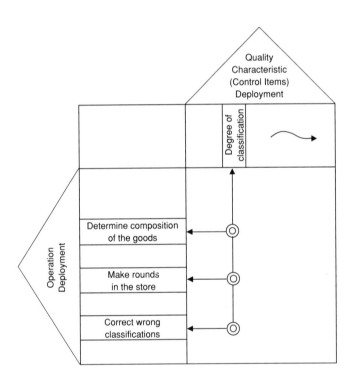

Figure 11-9. Quality Characteristics (Control Items) Deployment

CHAPTER 12

Quality Function Deployment for Software Development

Tadashi Yoshizawa, Professor of Computer Science,
Yamanashi University;
Hisashi Togari, Assistant Section Head, Linear Engineering Department,
and Takemasa Kuribayashi, Reliability QC Department Chief,
Nippon Denki IC Micon System Company;
and the CSK Software Quality Assurance Research Committee

A study group at Yamanashi University has been considering methods of using quality function deployment more effectively for software development. Since 1979 we have been trying to analyze requirements and functions related to the entrance exam systems on a prototype quality chart, using an analysis support system and quality function deployment support system that we have developed by applying the methods of quality function deployment. We have also been working with a computer study group at the Japanese Society for Quality Control (JSQC) and with related groups such as JSQC Software QC Seminars.

We have been seeing reports of actual application of QFD software development since 1982 and recently various applications have been reported by several companies — CSK, IBM, NEC IC Micon, Nippon Systems, Information Service Industry Association, Information Processing Promotion Business Association, and others. This chapter introduces examples from NEC IC Micon that apply to quality charts used for design and from CSK's quality function deployment application manuals.

Outline of Quality Function Deployment for Software

The term software includes many systems, such as basic software operating systems, large-scale on-line systems for the finance industry, application systems like CAD, systems for microcomputers built into home appliances, and others for many complex functions. Thus, demanded quality deployment based on function is not easy; on the other hand, some software has common quality demands such as being "effective" or "easy to use."

While the quality function deployment method for software development is not yet well established, deployment charts for quality requirements common to software and the resulting quality charts are becoming more refined. More comprehensive function deployment is required for individual products, but since suitable examples are not yet available, examples of the use of quality charts for determining the quality plan and quality design are also scarce. Identifying critical functions deployed for individual software is a challenge to be addressed in the future.

Clarifying processes and preparing quality assurance item lists and QC process charts are important steps for software development, just as they are for other types of products. Katayama and IBM Japan offer some examples. The latter company has prepared a system called SQUALAS for applying quality function deployment in support of QA for software developed by customers. The product is being offered by IBM's Information Systems Service Department; the manual and support system for personal computers are being sold by IBM.

Deployment of Demanded Quality

Quality function deployment starts with an understanding of the quality demands for a specific product. After determining what product is to be developed, extracting demanded qualities for specific softwares in a bottom-up fashion tends to produce a list consisting only of the requirements for function and performance. Since software products have many common quality requirements, a top-down deployment approach to required quality items such as the one shown in Chart 12.1 may be more effective.

Quality Characteristics Deployment Chart and Quality Chart

In the field of software engineering, there are many major classifications for quality characteristics, including objectivity, operability, performance, reliability, usability, confidentiality, security, expandability, interchangeability, reusability, and continuity. Measuring these properties is very difficult. The current status of work in this problem is discussed in the Katayama publications cited at the end of this chapter. SQUALAS defines 39 specific quality characteristics.

Quality Assurance Item List and QC Process Chart

In large-scale software development, it is desirable to clarify the divisions of the development process. For the preparation of the QC process charts and the QA item list, specify who will control each assurance item, when, and how. SQUALAS gives examples of standard process divisions.

Problem Points in Using Quality Function Deployment for Software Deployment

As we have mentioned above, one of the problems in applying quality function deployment to software development is a general lack of quantitative measurement methods and ways to test software quality. The product we have developed to meet this need is NEC's software quality measurement/assurance technique (SQMAT): other companies are working on similar types of products. However, the number of products containing built-in microcomputers that require new software is increasing rapidly, along with the interest in software quality control. In response to these trends, we can expect to see quality function deployment used more often.

Surveying user requirements and blindly deploying quality can only result in a huge quality chart with little meaning. Therefore, it is important to narrow down the purpose of quality function deployment and its applications.

The Case of NEC IC Microcomputer Systems

This firm designs large-scale integrated circuits (LSIs) and, as a member of NEC's Electronics Service Group, develops software for microcomputers and personal computers.

While the recent characteristics of LSIs are large-scale complexity and systematization, other characteristics are constantly changing due to the quickening pace of engineering progress. The reason for this is that the LSI has recently undergone a change in function — from being part of a conventional system to being a self-contained system on a chip — a system that includes the software. The LSI is built into a silicon chip that is only a few millimeters square. System design that until recently was conventionally done by system manufacturers is increasingly being done by LSI manufacturers, and methods for interpreting customer requirements and building them into the product are becoming more necessary in LSI and software development.

In the next section, we will introduce two examples:

1. How quality design charts have been used effectively for LSI design.
2. A time sequence quality chart trial, where we examine the cause and effect relationships between design content, design data, and time.

Example I: Application of Quality Design Chart to LSI Design

Action Program

Conventional problems. This department develops analog ICs used in consumer electronics products such as radios, stereos, TVs, VCRs, and CD players. The pace of technological innovation is rapid and customer requirements change drastically in such consumer products resulting in some problems:

- Failure to understand latent user demands can result in a defective prototype.
- Reworded data of the customers' quality demands are difficult to relate to design targets.
- The difficulty of detecting engineering bottlenecks before the design is completed often results in wasted or duplicated studies.

Action emphasis. To solve these problems, we emphasize two things: the need to search for engineering bottlenecks and take corrective through the use of a quality chart before beginning design work, and the need to confirm that quality is being built in at each stage of the design.

Structure of Design Policy Planning (Abstract)

We collected various types of customer information and arranged it so that it could be used for planning our products. Then we planned the design direction, deployed the demanded quality, and established design difficulty ratings, quality targets, and development procedures. We studied the results of these activities at group meetings, where group members made proposals to be submitted to the design direction audit group. Once the audit group had approved the design plan, we could begin the actual design work.

Key Points in the Quality Chart Application
    The key steps in using quality charts are:

1. Focus on critical items among the customers' demanded quality, convert them into quality characteristics, and search for engineering bottlenecks using the quality design chart.
2. Use the design element relationship chart to clarify the correlations among LSI design elements (circuits, process, masks, etc.).
3. Use a control rank-setting sheet to arrange the 4 M's (man, material, machine, method) and study the design difficulty ratings necessary for the LSI design.
4. Use a trouble-prevention sheet and design a trouble-summary T-matrix to analyze quality confirmation results and clarify the processes and methods to be addressed.

    These key points are explained with an example of power ICs for automobiles.
    (1) Quality design chart. As shown in Figure 12.1, the quality design chart organizes demanded quality and the related quality characteristics into a T-format. The shape and small size lend themselves to the search for engineering bottlenecks. The demanded quality items are based on customer information registration cards; these items become an arrangement of market demands. The important thing here is to prevent the demanded quality chart from becoming too large by including only critical items. We limited the list to 30 critical items in this case.
    Quality characteristic items are based on a comparison of the critical quality characteristics of our own past products and those of our competitors. We narrowed the list down to four items. Engineering bottlenecks are predicted on the basis of relationships among quality characteristics, and in the case of LSI designs, causes of bottlenecks generally fall into one of three classifications — circuit, process, or mask patterns. These items are checked during the design process.
    (2) Design element relationship chart. The design element relationship chart is a deployment of design elements, such as quality, cost and delivery, as illustrated by Figure 12.2. In the quality design, function block deployment and circuit deployment will be used to achieve specific circuit characteristics.
    (3) Design deployment with the process decision program chart. The process decision program chart (PDPC) shown in Figure 12.5 is used to deploy a specific design when corrective measures must be developed to resolve engineering bottlenecks. The problems to be solved are identified in the quality design chart, and items to be checked during LSI design are entered on this chart. Portions of the chart dealing with items that require further investigation during design will have information added and will be expanded as the investigation proceeds.
    (4) Trouble prevention sheet. Products being developed are evaluated for quality after the prototypes have been completed, and the results are recorded in quality charts. When problems are discovered during this evaluation, we use a trouble prevention sheet, like the one shown in Figure 12.3, to study the causes of the trouble

— as well as the corrective actions that might be taken to prevent recurrence. The results of these steps are summarized, as shown in Figure 12.4, in the "design trouble-summary T-matrix" so that we can clarify the problem and feed information about the critical processes to be addressed back into the design process.

With the help of quality charts, we can avoid repeating design errors and defective prototypes that result from an inadequate understanding of demanded quality. Currently, we conduct bottleneck engineering detection and take corrective actions for every product we design. To maximize the efficiency of design direction planning, engineering bottlenecks and the corrective measures to be implemented should be recorded in the chart.

Example II: Trial Use of a Time Sequence Quality Chart as a Tool for Software Development

Software Characteristics

When we begin designing a software product, some of the specifications may not be complete. In some cases we start with detailed specifications, including interface characteristics; in other cases, we refine the specifications through a series of meetings. Generally, the newer the product and the longer the scale of development, the less complete specifications will be when design work begins.

Although conventional quality charts were effective for deploying fairly well established specifications and technology, they were hard to apply when specifications and technology were relatively incomplete or when something had been added or changed. We devised the time sequence activity chart as a tool to be used in such cases. The three problems to be addressed were:

1. Broadening customer requirements during the design process.
2. Situations in which the technology could not be selected until the design was complete.
3. Situations in which additions or changes to the work occurred.

In other words, we wanted a quality chart that could be used flexibly to deploy design specifications in various degrees of completion.

Characteristics of a Time-sequence Quality Chart

The configuration features are:

- combination of two L-types;
- expandable to the left, right, and downward; and
- relates understanding of needs and design know-how.

The features during preparation are:

- no rewriting or deletion but only addition, and
- filled in as changes occur, such as the appearance of multiple design targets and selecting them or additional changes of them, etc.

The features of use are:

- In addition to clarifying the cause and effect relationship between design information and design content, which is a feature of the conventional quality chart, the time sequence quality chart enables us to study the process or processes by which cause and effect are related.
- Incompletely specified items are written in as is. This helps us weight selected items that are written in.

Trial Example

Figure 12.6 shows a generalized model of a time sequence quality chart, while Figure 12.7 shows an example of its use. The arrows in the figure indicate the method of entering information during the design stage.

When the complete list of functions is narrowed down to the most critical, the date is entered in the first line of the matrix. In this example, we can read the following information:

1. The dates when demands, targets, and methods were expanded — 10/15/85, 10/21/85, 4/23/86, 6/6/86, 6/10/86, and 9/17/86. The range in "A" in the figure is the pre-10/15/85 portion.
2. Items marked with a ◎ had been adopted but were dropped out and marked with an "X" due to specification changes. The arrow designated a "B" points to a series of such items.
3. Decisions about the details of correcting errors were made during the design stage. The "C" indicates the section where reconversion to demanded quality was made and "D" shows the deployment of this method.

This time sequence quality chart with its information about design processes is useful for analyzing the design and can be used effectively in future designs for similar products.

In these examples, we have shown how NEC uses quality function deployment in both the hardware and software departments of its IC Microcomputer Systems division. In both cases the methods were effective in helping the designers to predict problems at an early stage and to deploy appropriate corrective actions. The individual departments in this company have been using quality charts to improve their design work.

Case Study: CSK

The software quality assurance (SQA) study group at CSK has been working on quality function deployment for software since June 1983. The group has been applying quality function deployment to existing systems as a model for teaching the concept of quality function deployment in this company. The group has prepared a quality function deployment manual for the purpose of educating CSK engineers in software quality development. The manual contains actual examples of quality function deployment making it useful on the job. CSK is currently promoting quality function deployment as an effective tool for developing the company's software.

Quality Function Deployment Activities at CSK

Figure 12.8 shows steps in CSK's QFD activities. The current manual gives examples of each step, with the details of specific measures. Among the examples is a "histogram" preparation software product, which is familiar to most of us. An outline of the software development process using QFD follows.

1. Collecting the demands. Four or five members engage in a brainstorming session to regenerate original data for the subject system from the point of view of the user. The original data is analyzed to clarify latent demands and is then converted to language data.

2. Classification of demands into quality requirements and function requirements. The reworded language is classified into quality and function deployment requirements as follows:

CUSTOMER VERBATIM
(e.g., "Easy to see output")

REWORDED DATA
- Can be reviewed at appropriate size.
- Can be expanded or reduced.
- Graphics can be moved.

DEMANDS (REWORDED DATA)
"Can be reviewed at appropriate size"

QUALITY DEMANDS
Can be reviewed at
appropriate size

FUNCTION DEMANDS
Can be expanded or reduced

3. Making a demanded quality deployment chart. The KJ method is used to group the classified quality demands so that we can make the demanded quality deployment chart.

4. Establishing the quality plan. After customer demands have been surveyed using questionnaires and interviews, "attractive" and "must-be" qualities are made third-level quality demands. The results of competitive comparisons are used to establish selling points, including strategic policy considerations. Based on this, the quality plan is determined and the rate of improvement (level-up) is calculated. Absolute weights and demanded quality weights are then calculated.

5. *Making a function system chart.* The KJ method is used to arrange the classified function demands described above so we can prepare the function system chart.

6. *Extracting and arranging quality characteristics.* With software, extracting measurable quality characteristics is difficult, so we extract abstract quality elements first. Next, we extract quality characteristics for each quality element and quality demand to define them more clearly. Then we construct the process control plan chart, which spells out the measuring methods for the quality characteristics based on the CSK process code list.

7. *Making the quality chart.* The quality chart is made by arranging demanded quality and quality characteristics in a matrix and a reviewing their correlations by applying Quantification Method III.

8. *Making the quality deployment chart.* To make a quality deployment chart like the one shown in Figure 12.9, determine the specification values and deploy them to the processes.

9. *Application to future development work.* We evaluated our performance in achieving the demands established as sales points during the quality planning stage. Then we evaluated our achievement of the most critical processes — the ones that build in the quality characteristics. Finally, we reviewed the entire development process to analyze its applicability to future development work.

Future Activities

Currently, we are still trying to apply quality function deployment to new system development using the methods described in our manual and introduced here. However, these methods are very time-consuming. We think that artificial intelligence (AI) techniques can be adapted to quality function deployment and that they could reduce the time required by constructing a quality function deployment support system.

As modulization of software advances, quality function deployment should become even more important. The early completion of a quality function deployment support expert system using AI is highly desirable for application to CSK's own QA system.

References

Aizawa, Hitoshi, et al (1982). "General Form Analysis Program Development." *Quality Control*, Vol. 33, November special issue, pp. 360-366, JUSE.

Akao, Yoji, et al (1983). "Quality Deployment including Cost, Reliability, and Technology." *Quality*, Vol. 13, No. 3, pp. 61-70, JSQC.

Fujiwara, Kenji (1984). "Application of Quality Deployment to In-House Computer System." 4th SPC Symposium Abstracts A-7.

IBM Japan, ed. (1986). *SQUALAS Basic Structure Toward the QA of Software Developed by our Customers*. NGC 18-1527-1.

_____ . (1986). *SQUALAS Application Guide: Toward the QA of Software Developed by our Customers*. NGB 18-1533-0.

Information Service Industry Association (1985). *Report of Study on Software Quality Assurance*.

Joho-shori Shinko Jisyo Kyokai, ed. (1986). *Study of Software Quality Evaluation Models (Software Quality Function Deployment)*.

Kanno, Fumitomo (1986). *Software QC*. JUSE.

Kano, Noriaki et al (1982). "Applying the T-Type Matrix to Trouble Reduction in Designing (1)(2)." *Quality Control*, Vol. 33, November special issue, pp. 424-427, JUSE.

Katayama, Sadaaki (1985). "Trial of Quality Deployment for Software Development Planning." JSQC 27th Conference Abstracts.

_____ . (1986). "Quality Deployment/Quality Function Deployment for Development Planning of System including Software (CAD System)." 6th SPC Symposium Abstracts, B-9.

Kokusho, Hidemi (1984). "Application of Quality Deployment to In-House Computer System." *Quality Control*, Vol. 35, November special issue, pp. 1-7, JUSE.

Kuribayashi, Takemasa, et al (1986). "Using Time Sequence Quality Charts as a Tool for Software Development." *Quality Control*, Vol. 35, November special issue, pp. 424-427, JUSE.

Mineo, Akiyoshi et al (1986). "Applying the Design Quality Chart to LSI Design." *Quality Control*, Vol. 37, May special issue, pp. 188-193, JUSE.

Miura, Shin et al (1986). *Dictionary of TQC Terminology*. Japan Standards Association.

Mizuno, Shigeru; Akao, Yoji (1978). *Quality Function Deployment*. JUSE.

Nakamura, Kenji (1984). "QC for Software Introduction at DP Center." *Quality Control*, Vol. 35, November special issue, pp. 73-77, JUSE.

Nishihara, Masataka, et al (1986). "Preparation of Quality Deployment Manual for In-House Software." *Quality Control*, Vol. 37, November special issue, pp. 419-423, JUSE.

Nishimoto, Yasuhiro, et al (1985). "Quality Deployment for Software." *Quality Control*, Vol. 36, No. 5, pp. 47-55, JUSE.

Nomura, Kazuhiko, et al (1986). "Approach of Quality Chart Application to Software Design." *Quality Control*, Vol. 35, May special issue, pp. 169-173, JUSE.

Sekigawa, Hachiro (1985). "Required Quality Realization in Mechatronics Products." JSQC 20th Symposium Abstracts, pp. 7-13.

Shindo, Hisakazu (1985). "Applying the Quality Deployment Chart." *Quality Control*, Vol. 36, No. 5, pp. 6-11, JUSE.

Shindo, Hisakazu et al (1986). "Applying the Required Quality Deployment Chart, Standardization, and Quality Control." Vol. 39, No. 5, pp. 72-84, Japan Standards Association.

Shindo, Hisakazu; Yoshizawa, Tadashi; Miyajima, Masaaki (1983). "Applying the Quality Chart and Quantification Theory III to the Service Industry." *Quality*, Vol. 13, No. 3, pp. 52-60, JSQC.

Tagami, Yuji, et al (1985). "Application of Quality Deployment to Software." 5th SPC Symposium Abstracts, pp. 71-78.

Uchida, Minoru (1984). "Process Control Implementation for System Development." *Quality Control*, Vol. 35, November special issue, pp. 73-78, JUSE.

Yokoi, Takashi; Shindo, Hisakazu (1983). "Trial of Quality Deployment for Data Processing Service Industry." 3rd SPC Symposium Abstracts A-2.

Yoshizawa, Tadashi, et al (1982). "General Purpose Wave Form Analysis Program Development." *Quality Control*, Vol. 33, November special issue, pp. 360-366, JUSE.

_____ . (1984). "Quality Chart Preparation Analysis Support System." JSQC 25th Conference Abstracts, pp. 85-88.

Yoshizawa, Tadashi, et al (1982). "General Purpose Wave Form Analysis Program Development." *Quality Control*, Vol. 33, November special issue, pp. 360-366, JUSE.

_____ . (1984). "Quality Chart Preparation Analysis Support System." 25th Conference Abstracts, pp. 85-88, JSQC.

Yoshizawa, Tadashi; Arizuma, Hitoshi; Shindo, Hisakazu (1979). "Requirement and Function Analysis for System or Mechanization of Entrance Exam." Engineering Department Reports, Vol. 30, pp. 39-64, Yamanashi University.

1st Level Items	2nd Level Items
Usable	With necessary functions Economically effective With necessary performance
Worry-free use	Correct results Few problems Quick recovery from problems No damage Secure
Easy to use	Easy to operate Requires little work Can use whenever needed
Long time use	Does not become quickly obsolete Expandable functions Adaptable to environmental changes

Chart 12-1. Common Quality Requirements

easy to assemble	few components	mechanical strength	no sudden breakage	resists economical change		small offset	no interchannel effect	wide linearity	low power consumption	quality	item	required value	existing value	circuit	process elements	mask pattern	( ) others	Ideas for NE
30	29	28	27			5	4	3	2	1			required value	existing value	1	2	3	4	
				○				Δ		◎	attractive quality	1. circuit current (Icc)	~ 5 ~ 10 mA	~10 ~ 20 mA					improve KC ΔΔΔ date output (D chain &T$_r$ chain area ratio capability)
							◎	○				2. distortion (T.H.D)	~ 0.01 ~ 0.05 %	~ 0.1 ~ 0.5 %					handle with new circuit 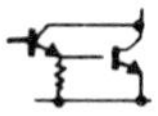
			◎									3. output noise (V$_n$)	~ 0.5 ~ 1.0 mV	~ 1.0 ~ 3.0 mV					use of KC ΔΔΔ date output (2. NB)
			◎									4. surge pressure resistance	> 60V (200ms)	> 50V (200ms)					handle with new circuit (ref.○○×× circuit)

Demanded quality — Defects, BNE remarks — Quality Characteristics — Probable Bottlenecks

Figure 12-1. Design Quality Chart

1. Circuit	2. Process element capacity		3. Mask pattern	
what to consider	ideas for NE	what to do	ideas for NE	what to do
1. adequacy of area ratio 2. match with distribution 3. check stability				
1. check effects of early results 2. check distortion at opening			1. designation of A1 wiring impedence 2. designation of arrangement without effect of thermal reg	1. B/B impedence 2. check effect with empirical formula 3. check past claims
1. check current V_s V_n 2. remove external noise	use NB 4 times (reduce r_{bb} by crossing)	1. check i_n to e_n TEG difference 2. check NF vs. I_e		
1. check patents	P_o T_r $\alpha \Delta \Delta \Delta \Delta$	1. confirm difference in element capacity of other makes	1. designation of power step pad location 2. check insertion of base resistance	1. check other companies' pattern (watch C)

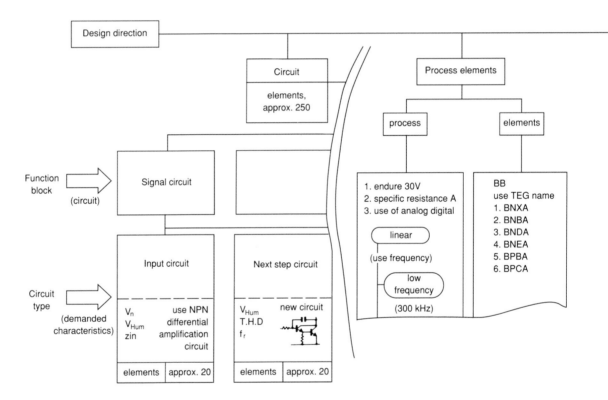

Figure 12-2. Design Element Relationship Chart

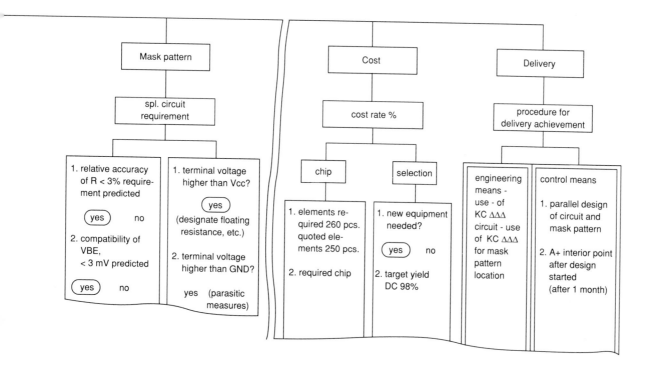

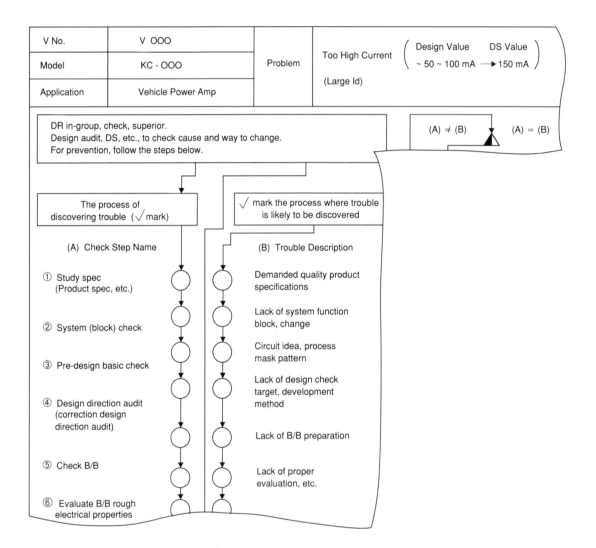

Figure 12-3. Trouble Prevention Sheet

Proto-type	Mask Pattern Design				Circuit Design								Pre-Study				Discovered Step / Build-In Step		Pre-Study				Circuit Design							
expansion/assembly	color key check	mask pattern design audit	mask pattern study	mask pattern design direction audit	circuit explanation meeting	circuit design audit	overall study	temperature property study	dispersion study	trouble study	B/B rough electrical properties evaluation	B/B move study	design direction audit	review of pre-design basics	system (block) study	spec. study	Step To Be Discovered		spec. study	system (block) study	study of pre-design basics	design direction audit	B/B move check	B/B rough electrical properties evaluation	trouble study	dispersion study	temperature property check	overall study	circuit design audit	circuit explanation meeting
17	16	15	14	13	12	11	10	9	8	7	6	5	4	3	2	1			1	2	3	4	5	6	7	8	9	10	11	12
						//							~~////~~ (13)				spec. study	1	/											
						//							~~////~~ //				system (block) study	2												
													~~////~~ (16)				study of pre-design basics	3			////									
																	design direction audit	4			/									
																	B/B move check	5					/							
																	B/B rough electrical properties evaluation	6			//			~~////~~						
																									///					

Figure 12-4. Design Trouble Summary T-Type Matrix

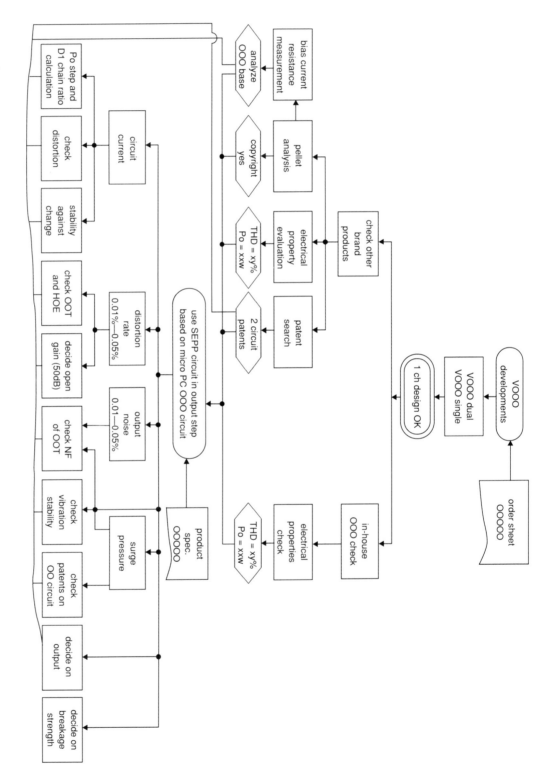

Figure 12-5. Deployment Using the PDPC Development Method

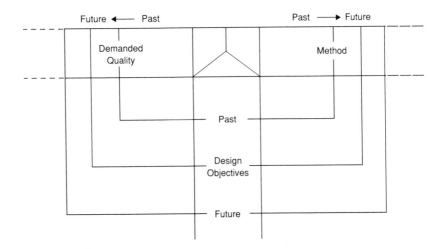

Figure 12-6. Model of a Sequential Quality Chart

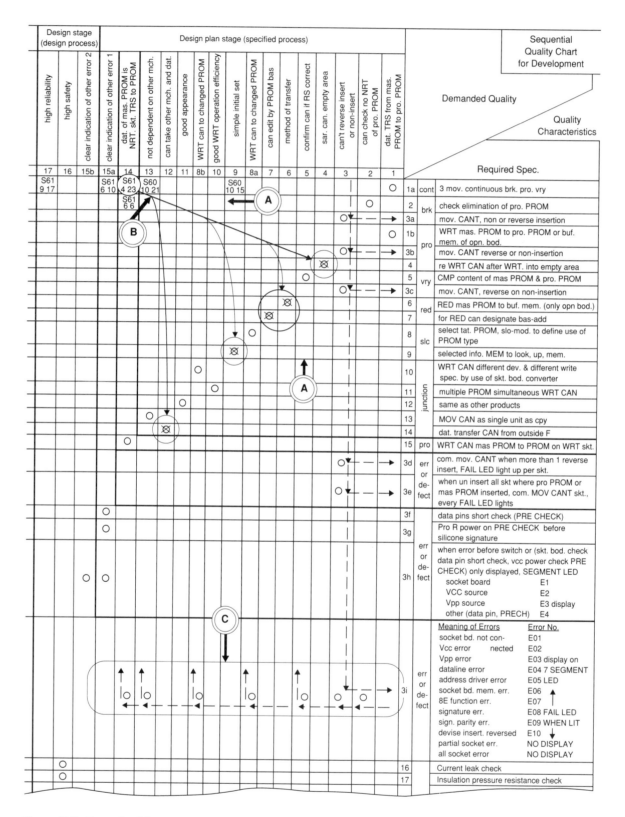

Figure 12-7. Example of Sequential Quality Chart

	Sequential Quality Chart for Development		Design plan stage (specified process)																						
		Method	continue of sub-routine, CAL	dat. of pro. PROM each byte check	15 v charge to MVP Vcc (32 pins)	mas. PROM non-bod. TRS to Pro PROM	set can of wrt-add	CAN & CMP dat of Prom PROM & mas. PROM to Red	mov. mas PROM to buf. mem.	user-select type (user-select and recognize)	mov. for MEM selected dat. (COM.) to mem.	use adp. bod.	multiple wrt-skt	ref. drawing of other related co. & carry each com req.	each com. key	use RS-232C CBIB	dat. of mas. PROM	direct CMP dat. to Pro PROM and Mas. PROM	all skt. normal finish, pass lamp lights up. LED below buzzer, skt. lights up (mas. wrt. both green)	partial skt. error LED below buzzer, skt. lights up (mas. green, wrt. green, red)	8 wrt. skt	according to NEC appearance design standard	E-01: Signal check	E-02: Source Vcc check	E-01: Signal check
Other Makers Level	Design Target		1	2	3a	4	5	6a	7	8	9	10	11a	12a	13	14	15	6b	3b	3c	11b	12b			
Non	RSE		O								S60 10 15					S60 10 21	S61 4 23	S61 6 7					S61 6 10			
"	"			O													S61 6 6									
"	"				O																					
"	"					O																				
"	during high-speed write/ no-write operation is performed on a complete PROM. (B/C WRT)						O	⊗																		
"	RSE							O									O									
"	"				O																					
"	"							⊗																		
"	"						⊗																			
"	"									O																
"	"										⊗															
"	"											O														
"	"												O													
same as mdl.	"													O								O				
Non	"															O	⊗						O			
"	"																O									
"	"																		O	O						
"	"				O														O	O						
"	"				O														O	O						
"	"																		O	O						
"	"																		O	O						
at same level	less than 1.0 mΔ (internal resistance 1 ml in leakage meter																									
	no error operation after change of AC 1000V for one minute																									

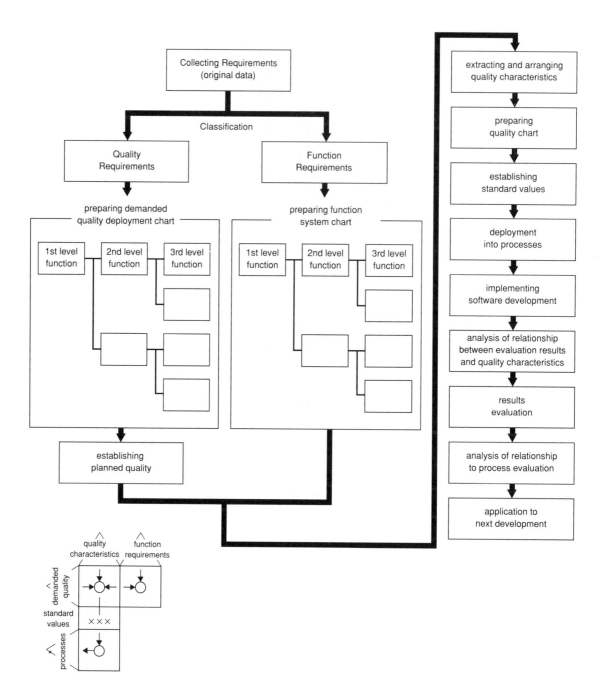

Figure 12-8. Steps in CSK's QFD Activities

			Quality Characteristics				Function Requirement		Quality Planning								
			2nd Level — Degree of Freedom				3rd Level — Output Function (Expands or Shrinks)		Comparison				Planning			Weighting	
		3rd level	Rate of expansion	Rate of shrinkage	AA compatibility		Can transfer graphics	Can designate rates of expansion or shrinkage	Degree of importance	Degree of satisfaction	Own firm	B company	Planned quality	Rate of level-up	Sales point	Absolute weight	Demanded quality weight
Good Output	Easy to See Output	can see in proper size	O	O			O	O	5	5	2	3	5	2.5	◎	18.6	16.2
		hard copy is good size			O			O	4	4	3	3	4	1.3	O	6.2	5.4
Major Process / Medium Process		Minor Process															
Investigation Analysis / Prepare New System Plan		pre-design of new system	O	O	O												

Figure 12-9. Quality Deployment Chart (Partial)

About the Author/Editor-in-Chief

Born in Japan in 1928, *Yoji Akao* graduated in 1940 and received his Ph.D. in 1964 from the Tokyo Institute of Technology's Department of Ceramics. He is presently chairman and professor at Tamagawa University's Department of Industrial Engineering. His fields of study include quality control and statistical engineering.

He serves as vice president of the Japanese Society for Quality Control, a member of the Deming Prize Committee (1964-), vice director of the JUSE editorial committee for the *Journal of Statistical Quality Control*, and vice councillor in the head office of QC Circles (1973-).

Dr. Akao's outstanding achievements in his chosen field have been recognized many times, including the Deming Prize in 1978 and the Quality Control Literature Prizes in 1960 for his work in testing defectives and in 1978 for quality function deployment.

Among his published books are:

Quality Function Deployment: An Approach to Total Quality Control (JUSE, 1978) with co-author Shigeru Mizuno.

Practical Applications of Quality Deployment in New Product Development (JUSE, 1988).

Practical Applications of Policy Management (Japan Standards Association, 1988).

His published articles include: "New Product Development and Quality Assurance: A System of Quality Deployment, Standardization and Quality Control," Vol. 25, No. 4, JSA, 1972.

"Quality Deployment System and Case Study" with Yoshiharu Yamada, *Quality*, Vol. 7, No. 3, JSQC, 1977.

"Quality Evolution (Deployment) System and FMEA" with N. Kamizawa et al, ICQC-Tokyo Proceedings, 1978.

"Quality Function Deployment CWQC in Japan: A Strategy for Assuring that Quality Is Built into New Products" with M. Kogure, *Quality Progress*, Vol. 16, No. 10, 1983.

"Survey and Review of Quality Function Deployment in Japan," with T. Ohfuji, ISQC, pp. 171-176, 1987.

Correspondence to Yoji Akao can be sent in care of: 6-1-1, Tamagawagakuen, Machida-shi, Tokyo 194, Japan. Telephone 0427-28-3472.

A Glossary of Quality Deployment Terminology

*by Glenn Mazur with the help of Bob King of G.O.A.L./QPC
and Bill Slabey of the American Supplier Institute*

Quality Function Deployment (QFD)
Quality Deployment

The title of Dr. Akao's book in Japanese is actually *Quality Deployment* — not *Quality Function Deployment*. Quality deployment refers to the charts, tables, and descriptive matrices used to design the quality or "goodness" needed in the product or service. In North America and Europe we call these charts and so forth "QFD".

Quality function deployment is defined twice by Yoji Akao, first narrowly and then broadly:

- *QFD narrowly defined:* The business or task functions responsible for quality (design, manufacturing, production, etc.).
- *QFD broadly defined:* A combination of these business or task functions responsible for quality (design, manufacturing, production, etc.) *and* the quality deployment charts.

Function Deployment

Function deployment is often a later step in QFD where the basic functions of the product or service are identified by experienced people at the producing company. Certain products or services start with these basic functions because their product or service is transparent to the consumer.

Function deployment has been likened to the "voice of the engineer" identifying the "must be" attributes of the product or service. These basic or "must be" functions are unspoken by the consumer unless the consumer has experienced the absence of the quality. For example, in the hotel, motel, or bed and breakfast industry, the basic ("must be") functions are to provide a place to sleep, shower, and go to the bathroom. If a hotel does not provide the basics of a working bath or shower, the consumer is dissatisfied. Having them does not guarantee customer satisfaction, it just ensures no strong customer dissatisfaction. Another example is an auto maker that produces a low, sleek, mid-size car that doesn't fit a standard drive-through car wash. The consumer expects the experienced producer to provide these basics without asking.

When a customer's spoken quality demands oppose these functions, however, the producer must balance the spoken demands with the practical functional requirements of the product or service. An example would be a rapid oil change service. The consumer wants the oil changed quickly. The experts in the oil change service must balance this spoken demand with the basic function of an oil change — that is, to remove the harmful byproducts of fossil fuel being burned in an internal combustion engine. These contaminants are heavy, thick, and slow to drain from the crankcase. While the gravity method takes time, a faster but more expensive method is to suction it out of the crankcase. This, however, might damage the gaskets that seal the engine. By allowing enough time to remove the harmful contaminants from the engine, the experienced oil change service people will not violate the basic function of an oil change.

The functions of a product or service are best determined by using a function tree (FT) diagram. Target values typically are identified and included to describe these basic qualities thoroughly. Once determined, they can be related against mechanisms, components, or parts to determine function costs among the various design alternatives. The manufacturing terms *mechanisms*, *components*, and *parts* should be taken as specifically relevant to discrete manufacturing, and also as a means of describing a systems approach that works equally well with services and nondurable goods.

Quality Chart
Quality Table

In QFD, quality charts and quality tables are matrices that relate different ways of describing the product or service against one another; for example, customer demands versus mechanisms, mechanisms versus tests, tests versus failure modes, failure modes versus customer demands, parts versus process parameters, and so on. While the purpose varies from chart to chart, they all have the common goal of looking for unique insight into the nature of the product or service and what is necessary to improve it. Charts are a means to — not an end in themselves. While handwritten in Japan, these charts or tables are computer-generated in North America.

Customer Verbatims
Source Data
Raw Data
Voice of the Customer (User)

Customer verbatims, or raw data and so forth, are the *actual words* customers use when commenting on the product or service. Many QFD specialists prefer that, until analyzed by the QFD team, this source data not be reworded or paraphrased for fear of losing any of their meaning.

Reworded Data
Data Expressed in Words

The QFD team interprets and rewords the customer verbatims into information that has singular, specific implications to the product or service being studied. It is especially important to reword customer verbatims that include two or more items.

Demanded Quality
Required Quality
What's
Customer/User: Wants, Needs, Requirements, Careabouts

The reworded data grouped together under a definitive heading subsequently can be broken into various subheadings or levels of customer demanded quality.

Quality Plan
Planned Quality
Quality Planning

After analyzing the demanded quality items, certain ones are selected for improvement based on the customer's rate of importance, opportunity for a sales point, or an opportunity to copy the competition. This is called the quality plan.

Quality Characteristics
Substitute Quality Characteristics (SQCs)
Counterpart Characteristics
How's
Design Requirements
Product Features
Design Characteristics
System Design Requirements
Product Acceptance Standards
Specifications for Product Acceptance
Performance Characteristics
Design Parameters

For each demanded quality item, a technical characteristic is identified that is measurable, controllable, and evaluative of the whole product or service. It must be testable and unconstraining to designers or process people. These items when properly targeted and deployed will make certain the customer's demanded quality is achieved.

Quality Elements

Quality elements are used commonly in service industry QFD where there are no measurable characteristics for things such as "pleasantness." They are used also to name the higher levels of measurable quality characteristics such as "shape." The lower level measurable quality characteristic under "shape" might be "heighth" or "width."

Relationship Matrix

The strength of the relationship between the two sides of the matrix are determined and graphically depicted using the following symbols:

> Relationships
> ◎ = Strong
> ○ = Moderate
> Δ = Weak

Correlation Matrix

The positive and negative qualitative correlations among the various quality characteristics are identified and depicted graphically with the following symbols:

> Correlations
> ◎ = Strong Positive
> ○ = Positive
> ✕ = Negative
> ✖ = Strong Negative

> **Quality Design**
> **Design Quality**
> **How Much**
> **Target Values**

Once the quality characteristics are identified, they must be assigned a specific target value. For example, a restaurant customer wants a hot cup of coffee. The quality characteristic the restaurant measures, controls, and specifies is the "serve temperature" in degrees Fahrenheit. The target value for the "serve temperature" must be identified so it can be deployed into the next phase of "coffee design."

> **Primary or 1st Level**
> **Secondary or 2nd Level**
> **Tertiary or 3rd Level**
> **Quartern or 4th Level**

The KJ-type method or the affinity diagram is used initially to organize and group the items into various levels of detail. Often as a second step, a more logical tree diagram is used to define the final hierarchy.

Bottleneck Engineering (BNE)
Breakthrough Engineering

Called "neck" engineering (NE) in Japan, these terms refer to the technological breakthroughs necessary to solve a design bottleneck and result in a competitive position. In the United States, this has been broadened to include any process or knowledge shortcoming that needs to be overcome to improve the product or service.

Index

Other Books on Quality

Productivity Press publishes and distributes materials on continuous improvement in productivity, quality, customer service, and the creative involvement of all employees. Many of our products are direct source materials from Japan that have been translated into English for the first time and are available exclusively from Productivity. Supplemental products and services include newsletters, conferences, seminars, in-house training and consulting, audio-visual training programs, and industrial study missions. Call 1-800-274-9911 for our free book catalog.

Variety Reduction Program (VRP)
A Production Strategy for Product Diversification
by Toshio Suzue and Akira Kohdate

Here's the first book in English on a powerful way to increase manufacturing flexibility without increasing costs. How? By reducing the number of parts within each product type and by simplifying and standardizing parts between models. VRP is an integral feature of advanced manufacturing systems. This book is both an introduction to and a handbook for VRP implementation, featuring over 100 illustrations, for top manufacturing executives, middle managers, and R&D personnel.
ISBN 0-915299-32-1 / 164 pages / $59.95 / Order code VRP-BK

Handbook of Quality Tools
The Japanese Approach
edited by Tetsuichi Asaka and Kazuo Ozeki

The Japanese have stunned the world by their ability to produce top quality products at competitive prices. This comprehensive teaching manual, which includes the 7 traditional and 5 newer QC tools, explains each tool, why it's useful, and how to construct and use it. Information is presented in easy-to-grasp language, with step-by-step instructions, illustrations, and examples of each tool. A perfect training aid, as well as a hands-on reference book, for supervisors, foremen, and/or team leaders. Here's the best resource on the myriad Japanese quality tools changing the face of world manufacturing today. Accessible to everyone in your organization, dealing with both management and shop floor how-to's, you'll find it an indispensable tool in your quest for quality.
ISBN 0-915299-45-3 / 320 pages / $59.95 / Order code HQT-BK

Management for Quality Improvement
The 7 New QC Tools
edited by Shigeru Mizuno

Building on the traditional seven QC tools, these new tools were developed specifically for managers. They help in planning, troubleshooting, and communicating with maximum effectiveness at every stage of a quality improvement program. Just recently made available in the U.S., they are certain to advance quality improvement efforts for anyone involved in project managaement, quality assurance, MIS, or TQC.
ISBN 0-915299-29-1 / 318 pages / $59.95 / Order code 7QC-BK

Productivity Press, Inc., Dept. BK, P.O. Box 3007, Cambridge, MA 02140 1-800-274-9911

Poka-Yoke
Improving Product Quality by Preventing Defects

compiled by Nikkan Kogyo Shimbun, Ltd./Factory Magazine (ed.)
preface by Shigeo Shingo

If your goal is 100% zero defects, here is the book for you — a completely illustrated guide to poka-yoke (mistake-proofing) for supervisors and shop-floor workers. Many poka-yoke devices come from line workers and are implemented with the help of engineering staff. The result is better product quality — and greater participation by workers in efforts to improve your processes, your products, and your company as a whole.
ISBN 0-915299-31-3 / 288 pages / $59.95 / Order code IPOKA-BK

Zero Quality Control
Source Inspection and the Poka-yoke System

by Shigeo Shingo, translated by Andrew P. Dillon

A remarkable combination of source inspection (to detect errors before they become defects) and mistake-proofing devices (to weed out defects before they can be passed down the production line) eliminates the need for statistical quality control. Shingo shows how this proven system for reducing defects to zero turns out the highest quality products in the shortest period of time. With over 100 specific examples illustrated. (Audio-visual training program also available.)
ISBN 0-915299-07-0 / 328 pages / $70.00 / Order code ZQC-BK

The Poka-Yoke System (AV)

by Shigeo Shingo, translated by Andrew P. Dillon

Shingo shows how to implement Zero Quality Control (ZQC) on the production line with a combination of source inspection and mistake-proofing devices in this two-part program. Part I explains the theory and concepts and Part II shows practical applications. Package includes facilitator's guides with worksheets and is available in either slide or video format (please specify when ordering). Each part is approximately 25 minutes long.
235 Slides / ISBN 0-915299-13-5 / $749.00 / Order code S6-BK
2 Videos / ISBN 0-915299-28-3 / $749.00 / Order code V6-BK

Achieving Total Quality Management
A Program for Action

by Michel Perigord

This is an outstanding book on total quality management (TQM) — a compact guide to the concepts, methods, and techniques involved in achieving total quality. Written in an accessible, instructive style by a top European quality expert, it is methodical, logical and thorough. Part I, a historical outline and discussion of the quality-price relationship, is followed by an investigation of the five quality imperatives (conformity, prevention, excellence, measurement, and responsibility). Major methods and tools for total quality are spelled out in Part III, and Part IV reviews implementation strategies. Practical and comprehensive in scope, it shows you how to make TQM a company-wide strategy, not just in technical areas, but in marketing and administration as well.
ISBN 0-915299-60-7 / [350] pages / $39.95 / Order code ACHTQM-BK

Productivity Press, Inc., Dept. BK, P.O. Box 3007, Cambridge, MA 02140 1-800-274-9911

The Improvement Book
Creating the Problem-Free Workplace
by Tomo Sugiyama

A practical guide to setting up a participatory problem-solving system in the workplace. Focusing on ways to eliminate the "Big 3" problems — irrationality, inconsistency, and waste — this book provides clear direction for starting a "problem-free engineering" program. It also gives you a full introduction to basic concepts of industrial housekeeping (known in Japan as 5S), two chapters of examples that can be used in small group training activities, and a workbook for individual use (extra copies are available separately). Written in an informal style, and using many anecdotes and examples, this book provides a proven approach to problem solving for any industrial setting.
ISBN 0-915299-47-X / 236 pages / $49.95 / Order code IB-BK

The Quality and Productivity Equation
American Corporate Strategies for the 1990s
by Ross E. Robson (ed.)

How well will your business succeed in the next decade? What challenges are in store, and how are you plannning to meet them? Here's what over thirty of America's most forward-thinking business and academic leaders (including John Diebold, Malcolm Forbes, Donald Ephlin, Alan Magazine, and Wickham Skinner) are already thinking about and doing. Based on presentations made at Utah State University's College of Business "Partners in Business" seminars for 1989. Take advantage of their expertise to shape your own strategy.
ISBN 0-915299-71-2 / 500 pages / $29.95 / Order code QPE-BK

TQC Wisdom of Japan
Managing for Total Quality Control
by Hajime Karatsu, translated by David J. Lu

As productivity goes up, the cost of quality comes down. And as quality improves, the cost to produce comes down. Karatsu, winner of a Deming Prize who has been involved with the quality movement in Japan since its inception, discusses the purpose and techniques of Total Quality Control (TQC), how it differs from QC, and why it is so effective. There is no better introduction to TQC than this book; essential reading for all American managers.
ISBN 0-915299-18-6 / 136 pages / $34.95 / Order code WISD-BK

Productivity Press, Inc., Dept. BK, P.O. Box 3007, Cambridge, MA 02140 1-800-274-9911

Also Available

Productivity Newsletter

Productivity Newsletter has been helping America's most effective companies improve quality, lower costs, and increase their competitive power since 1979.

Productivity has direct, immediate access to a unique network of international information you can't find anywhere else. Every month, you'll read about dozens of specific strategies and techniques that can make a dramatic difference in your career and in your company's future.

· Learn exactly which productivity strategies work and which do not from detailed case studies
· Discover the latest international developments and future trends
· Read about important innovations, new books, and the people and companies responsible for them
· Save money on Productivity conferences and seminars with special subscriber discounts.
To subscribe, or for more information, call 1-800-888-6485. Please state order code "BA" when ordering.

TO ORDER: Write, phone, or fax Productivity Press, Dept. BK, P.O. Box 3007, Cambridge, MA 02140, phone 1-800-274-9911, fax 617-868-3524. Send check or charge to your credit card (American Express, Visa, MasterCard accepted).

U.S. ORDERS: Add $4 shipping for first book, $2 each additional. Add $10 for each AV program you order. CT residents add 8% and MA residents 5% sales tax.

INTERNATIONAL ORDERS: Pre-payment in U.S. dollars must accompany your order (checks must be drawn on U.S. banks). For international orders write, phone, or fax for quote and indicate shipping method desired. When quote is returned with payment, your order will be shipped promptly by the method requested.

NOTE: Prices are subject to change without notice.

COMPLETE LIST OF TITLES FROM PRODUCTIVITY PRESS

Asaka, Tetsuichi and Kazuo Ozeki (eds.). **Handbook of Quality Tools: The Japanese Approach**
ISBN 0-915299-45-3 / 1990 / 325 pages / $59.95 / order code HQT

Buehler, Vernon M. and Y.K. Shetty (eds.). **Competing Through Productivity and Quality**
ISBN 0-915299-43-7 / 1989 / 576 pages / $39.95 / order code COMP

Christopher, William F. **Productivity Measurement Handbook**
ISBN 0-915299-05-4 / 1985 / 680 pages / $137.95 / order code PMH

Ford, Henry. **Today and Tomorrow**
ISBN 0-915299-36-4 / 1988 / 286 pages / $24.95 / order code FORD

Fukuda, Ryuji. **CEDAC: A Tool for Continuous Systematic Improvement**
ISBN 0-915299-26-7 / 1990 / 144 pages / $49.95 / order code CEDAC

Fukuda, Ryuji. **Managerial Engineering: Techniques for Improving Quality and Productivity in the Workplace**
ISBN 0-915299-09-7 / 1984 / 206 pages / $34.95 / order code ME

Hatakeyama, Yoshio. **Manager Revolution! A Guide to Survival in Today's Changing Workplace**
ISBN 0-915299-10-0 / 1985 / 208 pages / $24.95 / order code MREV

Hirano, Hiroyuki. **JIT Factory Revolution: A Pictorial Guide to Factory Design of the Future**
ISBN 0-915299-44-5 / 1989 / 227 pages / $49.95 / order code JITFAC

Japan Human Relations Association (ed.). **The Idea Book: Improvement Through TEI (Total Employee Involvement)**
ISBN 0-915299-22-4 / 1988 / 232 pages / $49.95 / order code IDEA

Japan Management Association (ed.). **Kanban and Just-In-Time at Toyota: Management Begins at the Workplace** (Revised Ed.), Translated by David J. Lu
ISBN 0-915299-48-8 / 1989 / 224 pages / $36.50 / order code KAN

Japan Management Association and Constance E. Dyer. **The Canon Production System: Creative Involvement of the Total Workforce**
ISBN 0-915299-06-2 / 1987 / 251 pages / $36.95 / order code CAN

Jones, Karen (ed.). **The Best of TEI: Current Perspectives on Total Employee Involvement**
ISBN 0-915299-63-1 / 1989 / 502 pages / $175.00 / order code TEI

Karatsu, Hajime. **Tough Words For American Industry**
ISBN 0-915299-25-9 / 1988 / 178 pages / $24.95 / order code TOUGH

Karatsu, Hajime. **TQC Wisdom of Japan: Managing for Total Quality Control**, Translated by David J. Lu
ISBN 0-915299-18-6 / 1988 / 136 pages / $34.95 / order code WISD

Lu, David J. **Inside Corporate Japan: The Art of Fumble-Free Management**
ISBN 0-915299-16-X / 1987 / 278 pages / $24.95 / order code ICJ

Mizuno, Shigeru (ed.). **Management for Quality Improvement: The 7 New QC Tools**
ISBN 0-915299-29-1 / 1988 / 324 pages / $59.95 / order code 7QC

Monden, Yashuhiro and Michiharu Sakurai (eds.). **Japanese Management Accounting: A World Class Approach to Profit Management**
ISBN 0-915299-50-X / 1989 / 584 pages / $59.95 / order code JMACT

Productivity Press, Inc., Dept. BK, P.O. Box 3007, Cambridge, MA 02140 1-800-274-9911

Nakajima, Seiichi. **Introduction to TPM: Total Productive Maintenance**
ISBN 0-915299-23-2 / 1988 / 149 pages / $39.95 / order code ITPM

Nakajima, Seiichi. **TPM Development Program: Implementing Total Productive Maintenance**
ISBN 0-915299-37-2 / 1989 / 428 pages / $85.00 / order code DTPM

Nikkan Kogyo Shimbun, Ltd./Factory Magazine (ed.). **Poka-yoke: Improving Product Quality by Preventing Defects**
ISBN 0-915299-31-3 / 1989 / 288 pages / $59.95 / order code IPOKA

Ohno, Taiichi. **Toyota Production System: Beyond Large-Scale Production**
ISBN 0-915299-14-3 / 1988 / 162 pages / $39.95 / order code OTPS

Ohno, Taiichi. **Workplace Management**
ISBN 0-915299-19-4 / 1988 / 165 pages / $34.95 / order code WPM

Ohno, Taiichi and Setsuo Mito. **Just-In-Time for Today and Tomorrow**
ISBN 0-915299-20-8 / 1988 / 165 pages / $34.95 / order code OMJIT

Psarouthakis, John. **Better Makes Us Best**
ISBN 0-915299-56-9 / 1989 / 112 pages / $16.95 / order code BMUB

Robson, Ross (ed.). **The Quality and Productivity Equation: American Corporate Strategies for the 1990s**
ISBN 0-915299-71-2 / 1990 / 558 pages / $29.95 / order code QPE

Shingo, Shigeo. **Non-Stock Production: The Shingo System for Continuous Improvement**
ISBN 0-915299-30-5 / 1988 / 480 pages / $75.00 / order code NON

Shingo, Shigeo. **A Revolution In Manufacturing: The SMED System,** Translated by Andrew P. Dillon
ISBN 0-915299-03-8 / 1985 / 383 pages / $70.00 / order code SMED

Shingo, Shigeo. **The Sayings of Shigeo Shingo: Key Strategies for Plant Improvement,** Translated by Andrew P. Dillon
ISBN 0-915299-15-1 / 1987 / 208 pages / $39.95 / order code SAY

Shingo, Shigeo. **A Study of the Toyota Production System from an Industrial Engineering Viewpoint** (Revised Ed.),
ISBN 0-915299-17-8 / 1989 / 293 pages / $39.95 / order code STREV

Shingo, Shigeo. **Zero Quality Control: Source Inspection and the Poka-yoke System,** Translated by Andrew P. Dillon
ISBN 0-915299-07-0 / 1986 / 328 pages / $70.00 / order code ZQC

Shinohara, Isao (ed.). **New Production System: JIT Crossing Industry Boundaries**
ISBN 0-915299-21-6 / 1988 / 224 pages / $34.95 / order code NPS

Sugiyama, Tomo. **The Improvement Book: Creating the Problem-free Workplace**
ISBN 0-915299-47-X / 1989 / 236 pages / $49.95 / order code IB

Suzue, Toshio and Akira Kohdate. **Variety Reduction Program (VRP): A Production Strategy for Product Diversification**
ISBN 0-915299-32-1 / 1990 / 164 pages / $59.95 / order code VRP

Tateisi, Kazuma. **The Eternal Venture Spirit: An Executive's Practical Philosophy**
ISBN 0-915299-55-0 / 1989 / 208 pages / $19.95 / order code EVS

Productivity Press, Inc., Dept. BK, P.O. Box 3007, Cambridge, MA 02140 1-800-274-9911

AUDIO-VISUAL PROGRAMS

Japan Management Association. **Total Productive Maintenance: Maximizing Productivity and Quality**
ISBN 0-915299-46-1 / 167 slides / 1989 / $749.00 / order code STPM
ISBN 0-915299-49-6 / 2 videos / 1989 / $749.00 / order code VTPM

Shingo, Shigeo. **The SMED System**, Translated by Andrew P. Dillon
ISBN 0-915299-11-9 / 181 slides / 1986 / $749.00 / order code S5
ISBN 0-915299-27-5 / 2 videos / 1987 / $749.00 / order code V5

Shingo, Shigeo. **The Poka-yoke System**, Translated by Andrew P. Dillon
ISBN 0-915299-13-5 / 235 slides / 1987 / $749.00 / order code S6
ISBN 0-915299-28-3 / 2 videos / 1987 / $749.00 / order code V6

TO ORDER: Write, phone, or fax Productivity Press, Dept. BK, P.O. Box 3007, Cambridge, MA 02140, phone 1-800-274-9911, fax 617-868-3524. Send check or charge to your credit card (American Express, Visa, MasterCard accepted).

U.S. ORDERS: Add $4 shipping for first book, $2 each additional. CT residents add 8% and MA residents 5% sales tax.

FOREIGN ORDERS: Payment must be made in U.S. dollars (checks must be drawn on U.S. banks). For Canadian orders, add $10 shipping for first book, $2 each additional. For orders to other countries write, phone, or fax for quote and indicate shipping method desired.

NOTE: Prices subject to change without notice.